Scribbles, Sorrows, and Russet Leather Boots

The Life of
Louisa
May Alcott

illustrated by
Liz Rosenberg   Diana Sudyka

CANDLEWICK PRESS

First edition 2021

Library of Congress Catalog Card Number pending
ISBN 978-0-7636-9435-7

21 22 23 24 25 26 LBM 10 9 8 7 6 5 4 3 2 1

Printed in Melrose Park, IL, USA

This book was typeset in Garamond.
The illustrations were done in ink.

Candlewick Press
99 Dover Street
Somerville, Massachusetts 02144

www.candlewick.com

This book is dedicated to the greatest
little woman I know, my daughter, Lily

LR

For my daughter, Isabel

DS

I hope I shall yet do my great book, for that seems
to be my work, and I am growing up to it.

—Louisa May Alcott,
NOVEMBER 1858 JOURNAL

CONTENTS

CHAPTER ONE

Ðuty's Child Arrives

"On a dismal November day, I found myself, & began my long fight," Louisa May Alcott wrote about her entrance into the world on November 29, 1832. She called her birth day "dismal," though records show a mild autumn all across the United States. Louisa must have been thinking of the family's mood, the inner rather than the outer weather. Her parents had reason to worry. Bronson Alcott had recently lost his patron, and his new school near Philadelphia seemed doomed to become another failure. Newborn Louisa, black-eyed and squalling, tumbled into the world like her heroine, Jo March, the "blunderbuss," making a poorly timed appearance.

Louisa both loved and hated her late-November birthday, "the most disagreeable month in the whole year," as she wrote in her best-known novel, *Little Women*. Jo adds wryly, "That's the reason I was born in it." Many of Louisa's birthdays came and went "without any presents," to quote *Little Women*'s famous opening.

November 29 belonged to her father first. Louisa, a lifelong night owl, was born just past midnight on Bronson's birthday, and only twenty months after her big sister, Anna. Louisa spent her growing-up years hemmed in by other family members—especially her charismatic father. They were inextricably linked to the very end, dying within two days of each other. Her obituary in the *New York Times* included a long description of *his* funeral and a list of *his* distinguished mourners. Bronson Alcott, they wrote, was "venerable," Louisa praised as "the daughter who had solaced his decline."

Tall, fair-haired, optimistic Bronson Alcott was the sun around which the Alcott family revolved. Louisa moved more than twenty times during her childhood, to allow "the Hoper" scope for hoping. No one questioned Bronson's right to pull up stakes, towing wife and children behind. Yet there is no question that Louisa greatly loved and admired her father.

For Louisa, self-sacrifice started young. Here is a story every biographer loves to tell: Louisa was little more than a toddler. The Alcott family organized a birthday party for the three-year-old and her father, set at Bronson's popular Temple School. Bronson wore a laurel crown woven by his students. He gave speeches and told long, stirring stories about the past. When the Alcotts finally handed around the party cakes to all the children, it was discovered they were short one "plummy cake." Louisa and a last little guest stood waiting. Louisa's mother leaned down and murmured, "It is always better to give away than to keep the nice things."

The three-year-old birthday girl gave away her own birthday cake—and never forgot the lesson. It became her role in the Alcott family, her lifelong burden, her way of being in the world—and the driving force for everything she achieved.

In 1832, the year Louisa was born, the young Alcott family had settled in Germantown, near Philadelphia. It was a peaceful time; they had two baby daughters. Husband and wife were happily in love. Thirty-year-old Abby Alcott called their modest home a "little paradise." Thirty-one-year-old Bronson agreed. "Love is the key . . . nor is there a heaven to any who love not. We enter Paradise through its gates only."

Germantown, the place, reflected their beliefs about social equality and freedom. It had been settled by two bands of outsiders, Quakers and Mennonites, and was said to be the birthplace of American abolitionism. The once-thriving colonial town had settled into a sleepy hamlet. By

Louisa's day, the unpaved main street was so muddy that residents joked you needed to ride a horse to get from one side to the other.

The Alcotts lived in a square white farmhouse near the town center. This farmhouse doubled as Bronson Alcott's new place of business, his experimental school. Rather than lecture at his students, Bronson asked questions, using Socrates as his model. At a time when corporal punishment was common, Bronson believed in exercising gentleness and affection. This school was to be a place where young minds could freely develop and grow—but the man who had sponsored and paid for it all, a generous Quaker named Reuben Haines, passed away just before Louisa was born.

Into this scene Louisa made her awkward entrance.

The Alcotts' firstborn, Anna, was a sweet, docile child. Bronson recorded her every move in his journals. Once Louisa was born, he began detailing her progress as well. There never were two sisters more unalike. Anna was fair and mild; Louisa dark-haired and willful. She showed extraordinary energy, even as an infant. "A fine fat creature," Abby wrote, and one neighbor described her as "a beauty." Bronson observed that baby Louisa was already stronger and more active than her sister, with "unusual vivacity, and force of spirit." While fair-haired Anna resembled him, Louisa took after her mother, with long dark hair and dark sparkling eyes. Fairness outside, Bronson believed, reflected fairness and sweetness within. Louisa and Abby, he wrote, were demons of willfulness he could "not quite vanquish."

Louisa had large, expressive eyes that appeared dark blue, gray, or black, depending on the day and mood. A neighbor took notice of supposed early signs of intellect, "a high forehead, and altogether a countenance of more than usual intelligence." Her mother called Louisa "a sprightly, merry little puss," but Louisa was less placid than Anna, harder to soothe. Even as a baby she was given to "moods." Bronson observed the sisters' interactions, taking notes, conducting experiments, even allowing the toddler Anna to stick her hand into the fire—twice!

Battles between Anna and Louisa broke out daily. Over time, they would become devoted companions. But they saw the world differently. Louisa once wrote about their stark contrast in "tastes, temperaments & lives. If we did not love one another so well we never could get on at all." In her earliest literary novel, *Moods*, she created two ill-matched sisters: "Neither . . . understood the other, and each tormented the other through her very love. Prue unconsciously exasperated Sylvia, Sylvia unconsciously shocked Prue, and they hitched along together, each trying to do well." Sylvia filled the house with wildflowers; Prue followed behind, dogging her "with a dustpan."

Abby Alcott clung to their life in the big white cottage.

They had a housekeeper, a cook, and elegant furnishings. Abby proudly described their Pembroke table and chairs upholstered in a "very beautiful French fabric," bought with wedding-gift money. In a rare innovation, the Alcotts created a separate dining room, "exclusively for eating," and opened their double parlor into one large, sunny space. Bronze busts of scientists and philosophers topped the mantelpiece, but all of this buying emptied their funds. It horrified Abby's thrifty father, Colonel May. Abby begged a further $300—this from the man who had once sold everything, including his own rings, to rid himself of debt.

The new loan only went to more purchases, much to the Colonel's dismay. He never again lent money to his daughter or son-in-law. An Alcott "loan" would never be repaid. Abby thought it proved her father's lack of affection. She turned to her gentle minister brother Samuel Joseph May for financial and emotional support.

Bronson and Abby kept the struggling school open. The pupils' parents were at first delighted by Bronson's experiments, then doubtful, and finally horrified. He was "always asked to leave," writes biographer Susan Cheever.

Life in Germantown went from bad to worse. The Alcotts had to give up one of their servants. They took on boarders, and the added domestic work fell to Abby. Bronson's school lost students and money with each passing month. The Alcotts struggled on for another year and a half. "We hardly earn the bread," Abby wrote to brother Sam. "The butter we have to think about." After a failed attempt at a second school closer to Philadelphia— where one bewildered parent described Bronson as "the most eccentric man who ever took on himself to train and form the youthful mind"—the Alcotts gave up and headed to Boston, Abby's birthplace.

Abby generally became energized by every move they made—but not this time. If Bronson was the eternal Hoper—his childhood nickname—he'd met his match in Abby. She could not bear what she called "stupidity"—sitting still and doing nothing. Each change raised her to a new pitch of excitement and hope. She wrote in her diary, "I rise with necessity and am stronger . . . at every blow."

Bronson was less forceful. "God will provide," he would say. His friend Henry Thoreau, author of *Walden*, described Bronson as "the sanest man" he'd ever known. "I do not see how he can ever die; Nature cannot spare him." "He is the best natured man I ever met. The rats and mice make their nests in him."

As for Louisa, her stubborn nature asserted itself more each day. Abby called Louisa "a beauty," but the toddler learned the knack of escaping her watchful eye and dashing away at every opportunity. She was charming but difficult, and Bronson worried that Louisa held a bad influence over her older sister. Anna went through a period of fighting back, but she soon came under Louisa's sway. Bronson called it the "power of might" over the weak. He described his olive-skinned daughter as "active, vivid, energetic," and "luxuriant," but he also kept a distance from household troubles during Louisa's toddler years.

In fact, after the failure of his Philadelphia schools, Bronson moved into his own separate apartment for a time, leaving wife and babies to fend for themselves during the week. He insisted on his need for personal contemplation and "reflection." In her private writings, Abby accused her husband of being "unkind, indifferent," and "improvident." Was it worthwhile staying married? He no longer called Abby his beloved "Mrs. A." but addressed her as his "friend" and "companion." Bronson left his wife and the babies alone so often that Abby nearly died of a miscarriage in the house. If a neighbor hadn't dropped by, she would likely have bled to death.

Bronson preferred a move to Boston—the intellectual and artistic hub of America, he declared—over Germantown. But Abby fretted. Boston was her childhood home. There, she had always felt like an outsider in her wealthy but closed-minded family. To return home in failure would put her before the judgment of her May relatives.

By the time Louisa was eighteen months old, her family had already moved four times. It was only the beginning of an unending search for home. In New England, Bronson quickly found another patron. A vibrant young woman named Elizabeth Peabody offered to help him start his new school in Boston.

Elizabeth had been raised in Boston's highest intellectual circles. She'd been planning to start her own school when she and Bronson Alcott crossed paths. He spoke about his ideas for a new educational system based on joy and play, and the "affection and love between child and teacher." His theories enchanted Elizabeth. In her journal she wrote about Alcott's magnetic "embodiment of intellectual light." She determined at once to join forces with him.

Elizabeth Peabody had been educated by her mother at home, in theology, philosophy, history, and literature. She'd learned ten languages, including Sanskrit and Chinese. Among her mentors were the intellectual giants of her times, including the famed Ralph Waldo Emerson, who would become essential to the Alcott family's future. Elizabeth's connections and introductions proved to be of lifelong value. Author Megan Marshall writes, "Anybody who was anybody in Boston knew Elizabeth." She cut a striking figure around town with her dark hair, sharp, flashing eyes, and colorful style. Her cherry-red cloak made her instantly recognizable on the street. She was "a woman who talked easily and could coax a shy man to speak freely."

Within hours of meeting Bronson, Elizabeth Peabody had secured the school's first pupil, a son of a wealthy friend. In less than a week, she'd enlisted six more.

Peabody swept away all obstacles, including Bronson's and Abby's initial reservations, and the proposed Elizabeth Peabody School instead became the Temple School, named for its location: two lofty rooms in the Masonic temple facing Boston Common. When Abby explained that Bronson couldn't teach foreign languages or mathematics, Elizabeth offered her services. The only possible choice was to say yes—but first they must move the Alcott family from Philadelphia to Boston.

Louisa, the terrible two-year-old, made the seemingly simple boat ride a parental nightmare. Minutes after the family boarded the steamer, Louisa disappeared. Had she run off again? No one knew. The Alcotts raced all over the ship, asking if anyone had seen a lost little girl in her best dress. After an anxious search through the steamer, Louisa was found playing in the noisiest, most dangerous place aboard ship: the engine room. Even as a toddler, Louisa longed "to see everything, do everything and go everywhere; she feared nothing." She had already made friends with the engine man, to learn how "the wheels go round." She was busy poking into the corners of the engine room when her frantic parents finally found her, beaming like a candle, "all nice and dirty" in her once-white traveling dress.

CHAPTER TWO

The Cast of Characters

The Alcotts' lives were tightly bound up with the lives of others. Louisa lived through the Civil War, the bloodiest of all American conflicts. But hers was also an era of new hopes and ideas. Bronson Alcott helped form the movement known as transcendentalism. Transcendentalists looked for change in every "part and particle" of life: in religion, politics, the roles of men and women, education, literature, and art—even in the clothes they wore and the food they ate.

The Alcotts' closest friends were philosophers, writers, clergymen, and public speakers arguing about equal rights for women, the abolition of slavery, the casting off of old rules. The Alcotts lived for their ideals—often at the sacrifice of daily comfort and even, at times, at risk to daily survival.

Neither Bronson Alcott nor Abby May was raised to become a dreamer. Abby was an outsider among her well-connected and generally conservative relations. The May family descended from American presidents and founding fathers. Great-aunt Hancock was famous for her hot temper, proving the saying "The Mays are peppery."

Her father, Colonel Joseph May, had made and lost a fortune before Abby was born. He'd been too young to fight in the American Revolutionary War, but he dressed the part anyway—in old-style military breeches, boots, and a three-cornered hat. Everyone called him the Colonel.

A year before Abby's birth, the Colonel made a disastrous shipping investment. To settle his debts, he sold everything—down to the gold rings on his fingers. The family moved from their mansion to a modest house in Boston, and the Colonel went to work as a shipping clerk.

Abby's mother was an invalid during much of Abby's childhood and youth. Abby described herself as the youngest of twelve, "born sickly, nursed by a sickly mother." In appearance she took after her father, with her dark, deep-set eyes, sloping nose, and rich, ruddy complexion. There the resemblance ended. She was stormy, willful, and given to "moods"—a description that also fit her daughter Louisa.

Abby struggled to make and keep friends. She felt

chronically misunderstood and easily took offense. Like Louisa, she was sharp-tongued, bright, and impatient. As a teenager she wrote in her journal, "I have felt a loneliness in this world . . . making a misanthrope of me."

Early on, Abby declared her determination to "earn her own bread," a shocking proposal for her time. She and her older sister Louisa planned to open a school together, but Louisa's marriage dashed those hopes. Abby cast about for new ideas. She had been engaged to a cousin—a marriage of convenience, not love—and when he died, she informed her family that from then on she would "refuse callers." She was twenty-five years old—considered too old to marry—when her mother died, leaving her even more lost and at sea. Her father soon remarried a younger woman. Abby moved in for a time with her minister brother Samuel Joseph May and his wife, still aching for a sense of purpose. She met Bronson when she was at her most vulnerable. Yet she had prepared herself for an independent existence, and might never have married at all if Bronson Alcott had not come striding into her life.

Bronson's childhood of rural poverty taught him to expect little and hope for less. He was originally named Amos Bronson Alcox, born in a ramshackle farmhouse in Wolcott, Connecticut, in 1799, at the edge of the new century. Bronson Alcott changed his first and last name—and his destiny.

His farmer father prepared his sons for lives of hard

physical labor. His mother, the more eccentric of the two, smoked a corncob pipe and taught Bronson how to write by tracing letters in sand spilled on the kitchen floor. It was she who dubbed her son "the Hoper." She was determined that he get a good education—Bronson's father equally determined that he would not. He believed only in "hard work with feet and hands and back."

Bronson attended a cramped one-room schoolhouse with a bored, irritable schoolmaster. This brief taste of formal education left him and his bright cousin William with a distrust of school. Yet they went on to become lifelong educational reformers. Both believed "there was something deeply wrong with primary education" and it was up to them to change it.

At eighteen Bronson left home on foot to become a teacher in the American South, where he had heard New England tutors were in demand. When that rumor proved false, he threaded his way back and forth, north and south, working as a peddler in remote rural communities. He sold everything from needles and thread to scissors and cooking utensils. Bronson was good at it. He enjoyed conversation. Shy at first, he learned to be at ease with people from all walks of life. Sometimes he stayed in mansions; other times he slept with the field slaves. When he could, he borrowed books from his customers, devoured the ideas, and thought them over as he walked from place to place.

After five years of peddling, Bronson walked the five hundred miles back home, $600 in debt. His farm family was dismayed when Bronson relaxed at home, unemployed, rather than working to repay his father. Only his pipe-smoking mother remained unperturbed.

Bronson would not think of his experience as a loss. He'd had an education in humanity, had time to learn, and had been made welcome wherever he went. In the long walking stretches between customers, he'd thought over all he'd seen and heard. He began to develop theories on everything under the sun. Now he just needed to put his ideas into action.

By the time she met Bronson, Abby had given up on romance. An intense young woman, she pledged to focus her "attention and reflection" on serious matters "which philosophy dictates and religion sanctions." Then suddenly, at the age of twenty-six, she opened her brother's door to find a fair, bright-blue-eyed stranger waiting there. Bronson stood over six feet tall, considered a giant in his day. He was as mild as Abby was fiery, as reserved as she was bold. Her minister brother Sam had invited Bronson to visit to discuss educational reform. Both he and Abby were dazzled by the brilliant young speaker.

Bronson had an electrifying effect on his listeners as his ideas and words poured out. But strangers often mistook his shyness for indifference. He was attracted to Abby immediately but could not bring himself to make the first move. It took him "two years from their first meeting," writes Susan Cheever, "to get up the nerve for a kiss." It was up to Abby to put things in motion. After their initial meeting, they began communicating by letter. But when they met in person after a lengthy correspondence, Bronson bowed stiffly and kept his distance. Abby was hurt and angry. She came expecting "to see a friend," she fumed, and found "merely an acquaintance." She vowed not to think of Bronson again—then immediately followed him to Boston.

There Abby and Bronson reconnected and began talking about opening a school—though the cautious Bronson asked Abby to wait till he'd found a place worthy of her. For every two steps they took forward, fate or Bronson's timidity shoved them back. The long courtship took a greater toll on Abby than on Bronson. The day she accepted his proposal, he wrote in his journal: "I love her because she is good. I love her because she loves me." Abby declared more passionately, "I have something to live for."

The Alcotts married in May 1830 at a Boston chapel in a modest ceremony. Cheever notes that their honeymoon consisted of the short "walk from the chapel back to Newall's boardinghouse on Franklin Street." Bride and groom were close to the unheard-of marrying age of thirty. Their honeymoon and new living quarters were modest, but their wedding attire must have dazzled onlookers. Bronson sported a blue swallowtail coat and white trousers tucked into high boots. He carried a carved ivory-topped cane and wore a bell-shaped beaver hat that added several inches to his already impressive height.

Abby wore a hooped plaid silk dress with enormous sleeves. She had her own beaver hat, topped by a foot-high plaid silk bow. Her white-stockinged feet, clad in black sandals, peeked boldly from below her dress.

The newlyweds set off for their new life together in a boardinghouse. Abby didn't care. She was madly in love. "I hope we may go through life affected by this lunacy," she declared.

Bronson still owed his father hundreds of dollars. His financial prospects were dim. But husband and wife shared opinions, passions, and ideals. Both were dedicated to Bronson's vision of a democratic, perfected, and communal world. Abby wrote with exuberance, "I am not only his lover, his mistress, but his pupil, his companion. I live to promote the happiness of him with whom all my interests are blended, temporal & eternal for not even death can separate us."

Fortune smiled on the newlyweds—in the form of a welcome anonymous wedding gift of $2,000. It must have come from Colonel May, who muffled every hint of extravagance. Bronson deducted $700 from the sum to repay his father. The payment seemed to the young couple a promise that they could begin life anew. That optimism carried them safely through a few false starts, not to mention the birth of their lively second child, Louisa. The question was whether their optimism could sustain them through all the ups and downs ahead.

CHAPTER THREE

The Temple School

The early success of the Temple School changed the Alcotts' fortunes. Thanks to Elizabeth Peabody and her gift for publicity and promotion, visitors came from all over to watch Bronson in his famous and exciting school on Boston Common. For a time, Bronson became famous and exciting, too.

The school opened at ten in the morning on September 22, 1834. Temple School's first students—eighteen of them—ranged from five to ten years old, the offspring of Boston's elite. One boy's father was chief justice of the Massachusetts Supreme Judicial Court. Five-year-old prodigy Josiah Phillips Quincy was grandson of Harvard University's president, who also served as the mayor of Boston.

Elizabeth Peabody donated her own green velvet sofa and other possessions to furnish the school's two rooms, but Bronson spared no expense further beautifying the space. Busts of Jesus, Plato, Shakespeare, and Socrates gazed over the students' heads. Fresh flowers brightened the rooms. Alcott believed every part of a school should contribute to the students' happiness and elevate their spirits. He borrowed more money for books, art, and well-made furniture. His rent for two "fine rooms" upstairs came to the vast sum of $300 a month. All of this spending was piled on top of the $1,000 Bronson still owed from Germantown.

Bronson's educational ideas were radical for the time. Children were given freedom of thought, expression, and movement. Each student's desk held its own storage shelves. Hinged blackboards swung forward and back. Recess came twice a day. There were alarm clocks, maps, cubes, paper tablets, blocks to play with, books of poetry and fairy tales to read, a large hourglass to mark the time. Students were encouraged to speak out, sing, clap their hands, and march about the room.

First, Bronson Alcott asked his new students about the purpose of school. One pupil answered, "To learn." "To learn what?" probed Alcott, and so it went, with Elizabeth Peabody taking notes. She wrote, "Every face was eager and interested."

Among the Temple School's earliest visitors was Ralph

Waldo Emerson, one of the most influential thinkers in New England. Emerson was enchanted by Alcott and his experiment. Here at last was the real-life embodiment of Emerson's ideas. He dedicated himself to the Alcott family early and remained steadfast long after other supporters had fallen away. His support, both financial and emotional, was so essential that the family dubbed him their "Great Friend." Louisa had her first teenage crush on him; Anna let him kiss her on her wedding day. Even the hard-to-please Abby declared her lifelong gratitude.

Ralph Waldo Emerson—his friends called him Waldo—understood the Alcotts' struggles. He had been raised in poverty by a single mother. He'd attended Harvard only with the help of scholarships and a generous aunt. He became a minister, and at age twenty-five married the beautiful seventeen-year-old Ellen Tucker, a sensitive poet. The levelheaded Emerson adored his young wife. He was devastated when she died two years later from consumption. Emerson haunted her grave day and night, and fourteen months after her death, he opened her coffin. He was so shocked by the sight of her corpse that he quit the ministry and headed off to Europe.

He came home months later and became a lecturer and essayist. Emerson remarried, choosing a wealthy woman named Lydia Jackson, whom he dubbed Lidian. Together they created a community of great minds in sleepy Concord, Massachusetts. Over time, a host of intellectual stars flocked to Concord, including the core group of the transcendentalists. Emerson supported and encouraged every friend. The younger Louisa looked up to him as a father, and later she rebelled against his idealism like a daughter. But Emerson saved the Alcott family from the brink of starvation time and again, and she never forgot her gratitude. She noted that he had "a sweet way of bestowing gifts under a book, or behind a candlestick, when he thinks Father wants a little money."

But for now, they needed no charity. Bronson was busy teaching, speaking, meeting with influential people. And then, just at the height of his career, he made a surprising about-face. Abby Alcott had been raising their two young daughters alone—with Louisa becoming more of a handful every day. Abby had only an hour free from childcare each day to go for a walk, or escape to the parlor to read while the children slept. Bronson saw that his wife was at the end of her rope. He jumped in and took charge of the girls' upbringing.

Abby had written to brother Sam in despair, "Boston seems more like a sepulcher than a home to me." Her old feelings of isolation returned. Being alone with two small children every day did not help matters. "There are few here that I care anything about and fewer that care anything about me." Even Bronson admitted, "My wife and children suffer from this neglect." When he looked at his family more closely, he was distressed by what he saw. Two-year-old Louisa had grown wild and aggressive. Her father worried about her "deep-seated obstinacy of temper." She bullied Anna and won her own way in every contest. Bronson noted, "She seems practicing on the law of might—the stronger and colder . . . over the weaker and more timid."

Bronson tested his children's skills at self-restraint, just as he tested his pupils'. One afternoon he showed Anna and Louisa a big juicy apple before dinner and asked if children should ever take things without asking. No, they answered, of course not. But Louisa snuck back into the room, snatched the apple, and ate it. Her justification was blunt: "I wanted it." She added penitently, "I was naughty."

Bronson tried to subdue her. When she pinched her sister Anna, Bronson gave her a pinch. Louisa fought back. He removed meat from Louisa's diet, believing that the meat had made Louisa more savage. As always, he kept careful notes in his journal. "Hers is the wild exuberance of a powerful nature," he wrote—half admiringly, half in despair.

Bronson tested the limits of that "powerful nature" in hopes of taming it. He left another apple in a room with Louisa while he and Abby listened at the door. Louisa picked up the apple and stroked it longingly. "No—no—father's—me not take father's apple—naughty—naughty." Then she ate it. Afterward the toddler explained, "Me could not help it. Me must have it." Poor Louisa!

Bronson supervised everything from the girls' diet to their first school lessons. He taught them how to read by shaping their bodies in the letters of the alphabet, assigning each letter a different posture and personality. *S* curved like a goose, while *O* moaned aloud. The letter *I* was a show-off, calling attention to himself "as he strutted across the room, [repeating] his own name with great self-importance." Bronson allowed his daughters rare freedoms—plenty of time to play, choices about their daily activities, even the liberty of running naked through the house. Such ideas seem commonplace now, but in his day they looked near lunacy.

If Bronson fretted over Louisa's faults, he also encouraged her gits and took proud note of her progress. "She adds new words to her vocabulary daily," he reported. "I believe she appreciates all the relations of expression."

Words were Louisa's first playthings. Her father gave her his precious books to play with; she used them as her first building blocks—literally. She built towers and bridges from his dictionaries and encyclopedias. She pretended to read his journals and was permitted to scribble over the pages of the books. She left her mark—her actual mark—on her father's work at an early age. As if foretelling the author's future, the trace of her toddler handprint covers his words in his journal.

Louisa was bright and ferociously determined, her thoughts "so fast and evanescent," Bronson wrote that he struggled to keep up. She longed to attend his Temple

School, like her big sister Anna, but she was too unruly. And when Abby learned that she was pregnant again—for the fifth time in three years—Louisa alone was parceled out to Boston relatives. There she would remain till the new baby arrived. She was warned to be well-behaved, obedient, and quiet—and she was none of them.

That spring, Elizabeth Peabody moved into the Alcotts' lodgings, accepting room and board instead of a salary. Abby was grateful for Elizabeth's female company— at least at first. Abby gave birth that summer to her third daughter and named the baby Elizabeth Peabody Alcott in honor of their helpful guest.

Louisa, brought back home after the baby's birth, was unmoved by her new sibling, though later she'd adore this third sister, Lizzie. "I don't love little sister, I wish she was dead, I will throw her out the window," she declared. Banished to her room for this outburst, the toddler Louisa sobbed to her father, "Father don't love me, mother don't love me, little sister don't love me, God won't love me."

After a long talking-to, Louisa finally kissed her baby sister and declared her loyalty. She told her father, "And I love you and I love God, and everybody." She was learning the rules of the Alcott household. Often they meant swallowing or disguising emotions. Bronson turned the scene with Louisa and baby Lizzie into a public lesson at his school about the meaning of contrition.

Louisa had ample opportunities to be contrite. She

continued to shout, stomp, squabble, make mischief, and run away from home with alarming frequency. Their new neighborhood, Beacon Hill, sat in a busy area of Boston, overflowing with peddlers, market carts, strangers passing by. The town crier would stride past the Alcott house, ringing his bell with the latest bit of news or local crime.

Boston offered tempting adventures. Louisa played with the bedraggled street urchins around Boston. No one knew exactly where she went. "Many a social lunch have I shared with hospitable Irish beggar children, as we ate our crusts, cold potatoes, and salt fish on voyages of discovery among the ash heaps," she wrote later. In exasperation, Abby tied Louisa to the sofa to keep her from running away.

One afternoon Louisa wandered even farther than usual, rolling hoops with some poor children in a neighborhood far from home. She couldn't find her way back, and after wandering around, she finally fell asleep with her head resting on the back of a large, friendly dog. She woke at twilight to hear herself described by the town crier—"Lost! A little girl in a pink dress and green morocco shoes!" "That's me," she answered, calmly rising to meet him.

An "abolitionist at the age of three," according to Abby, Louisa chased her hoop into the Frog Pond at the heart of Boston Common and almost drowned there. She was rescued by a brave young Black boy, "becoming a friend to the colored race then and there." She also lived with two passionate abolitionist parents and had grown up knowing about the horrors of slavery. Her closest uncle was Abby's brother, Samuel May, who left the ministry for a time to become a full-time abolitionist. Sam risked everything—career, reputation, and his life—to defend the integration of a nearby school. In the face of ugly opposition he wrote, "I am ashamed of my country and my race."

Elizabeth Peabody took exhaustive notes on the Temple School and on Bronson Alcott's innovative teaching methods and published them in a book titled *Record of a School*. It became "the instruction manual for a new era," earning glowing reviews and attention. Elizabeth was dubbed "a woman of genius." The Temple School became a national sensation. Success went to Bronson's head. Now he began thinking of writing his own book. Even the anxious Abby Alcott, always "woefully disappointed in [her] expectations," believed that this era of success would be "enduring as well as brilliant. Everybody has 'there' [sic] ups and downs. This I believe is to be our *up*, turn."

In reaction to his good fortune, Bronson, true to form, kept expanding the Temple School instead of paying off debts. The school soon held forty students, more than twice the original number. Bronson moved wife and daughters—and Elizabeth Peabody—into a grander house in a new neighborhood. He exhibited symptoms bordering on mania. His energy knew no limits. He began referring to his "mission" at the school and calling the pupils his "disciples." In his journal he noted "a delightful feeling of self-gratification" and declared that he was on "the verge of some important discovery regarding human nature." Abby fell right in step with his delusions: "My husband is to be the Messiah to announce to the world a new revelation."

The Temple School added a drawing teacher and a new lecturer. But Bronson still didn't pay Elizabeth Peabody a salary. She labored to exhaustion, writing for hours after her teaching, often ending her workday with a sick headache. The Temple School was underheated, and the winter of 1834–1835 proved brutally cold. "I will kindle a fire for the mind," announced Bronson. Elizabeth and the pupils shivered despite this "fire." Differences began to emerge between Bronson and Elizabeth, slowly at first, and then with increasing distrust on both sides.

Elizabeth not only disagreed with some of Bronson's theories; she was troubled by his teaching tactics. Bronson had once written, "The true teacher defends his pupils against his own personal influence. . . . He will have no disciples." He did not always follow his own good advice.

His teaching methods could be bizarre. He'd tempt his students into bad behavior, then scold them for it. He suggested that the pupils might rather go sledding than finish their lessons, but when a few students agreed, he banished them from the classroom. When they returned, he refused to look at them. Bronson never used physical discipline, but he employed disgrace, disappointment, and exile from his affections. He even resorted to martyrdom, forcing two misbehaving boys to strike him with a ruler. The bewildered boys wept bitterly.

Louisa and her family bore the brunt of his theories at home. Bronson was a zealot when it came to health and hygiene, especially nutrition. He kept to a diet of water, crumbly brown graham flour, fruit, and vegetables. Sometimes Abby snuck a little chicken or meat to her daughters. Elizabeth Peabody made the mistake of joking that Bronson's belief that people could live to age two hundred on his strict diet made longevity seem "uninviting." Bronson accused her of being suicidal. Offended, Elizabeth left the table. Abby declared that anyone who disagreed with her husband was a devil.

Elizabeth confided her growing unease in letters home. She wrote about Bronson's arrogance and Abby's fits of rage. Her sister Mary urged her to distance herself from the Alcotts. One night, Abby raged all evening against a friend of Elizabeth's. By the time she was done, Elizabeth was trembling. She wrote, "I think it . . . more comfortable to live on the top of a whirlwind than to live with her."

Bronson pressed her to begin a new, more radical book based on his students' understanding of the Gospels. He

proposed to interview children about religion, capitalism—
and procreation. Elizabeth balked, sure that readers would
be appalled. Bronson also planned to quote the children by
name, another idea she opposed. Young people, she felt,
deserved their privacy.

Lack of privacy caused their final break. One day
Bronson scolded Elizabeth in words that sounded eerily
familiar. She realized that Bronson had been reading her
private mail. Yes, he coolly admitted. Why not? The Alcotts
read their own daughters' journals and annotated them.
They equated secrecy with deception and guilt.

Elizabeth was furious. Abby promptly flew into a rage,
informing Elizabeth that she was damned. Mary Peabody
begged her sister to leave the Alcotts' at once or let Mary
take her place, but to stop "sacrificing your own comfort."
Elizabeth moved out in August 1836, fleeing all the way to
Salem. The friendship between Elizabeth and the Alcotts
abruptly ended. Abby went so far as to change the name
of her third daughter from Elizabeth Peabody to Elizabeth
Sewall. The youngest Peabody sister, Sophia, came to serve
the school in Elizabeth's place. She promptly fell in love
with Bronson's high ideals.

Sophia took dictation for the new book, *Conversations
with Children on the Gospels*, without reservations. Unlike
Elizabeth, whom Bronson privately denounced as "offen-
sively assertive," Sophia was gentle and pliant. She waxed

enthusiastic to her fiancé, writer Nathaniel Hawthorne, calling Bronson one of "the oracles of God," and praising "the eternal azure of Mr. Alcott's spirit."

On Louisa's third birthday came the grand celebration at the Temple School, with her famous sacrifice of the "dear plummy cake." The birthday girl was given instead a kiss and her "first lesson in the sweetness of self-denial." Her first, perhaps—but certainly not her last. She wryly commented about herself, "L. began early, it seems, to wrestle with her conscience."

Marmee (Abby's name among her girls) kissed the three-year-old who would "not let the little friend go without" a birthday treat. Bronson took a stricter stand. He wrote disapprovingly about Louisa's "impetuous" and self-centered nature. "She looks only toward the objects of her desires and steers proudly, adventurously, and yet without compass or chart save the gale and gleaming stars of her own will." Bronson lectured her on the virtues of patience, using gingerbread as a call for self-control. "Do you know what patience is?" the philosopher asked. "Yes," said Louisa. "It means wait for gingerbread."

That year the long-wished-for son was born at last to the Alcotts. A joyful Bronson at once proclaimed him a "young Hoper" and wrote to his mother to celebrate the stroke of great fortune. Joy did not linger long. The infant boy died soon after his birth. Bronson was devastated.

Abby mourned the son all her life, commemorating his birthday every year. That annual ritual must have been a painful reminder to Louisa that she could never be "the man of the family," the son they had wanted.

For Louisa, not being the longed-for son was hard enough, but it was worse to be treated like a girl. Jo March cries aloud in *Little Women*, "It's bad enough to be a girl, anyway, when I like boys' games and work and manners! I can't get over my disappointment in not being a boy." Her creator, Louisa, could outrun the neighborhood boys, but they wouldn't let her play football on Boston Common. "I revenged myself by driving my hoop all around the mall without stopping, which the boys could *not* do," she wrote triumphantly.

By the mid-1830s, the tide of fortune began to turn against the Alcotts. The city of Boston was suffering a financial depression after its recent boom. Parents began doubting Alcott's unconventional teaching methods. The old pattern began again. One by one families withdrew their children from the Temple School.

Bronson's *Conversations with Children on the Gospels*, published in December 1836, was the final blow. Critics called the book "indecent and obscene," its author "half-witted or insane." Elizabeth Peabody, who'd asked for her name

36

to be removed from the book, rushed forward to defend him. Ralph Waldo Emerson wrote, "I hate to have all the little dogs barking at you, for you have something better to do than to attend to them." But the "little dogs" had teeth. Enrollment at the Temple School plunged from forty down to ten.

The Alcotts sank further into debt. Soon after the book's release, Bronson had to auction off the many wonders that had graced his school—three hundred of his beloved books, the fine desks and chairs, even the busts of Plato and Socrates went up for auction. (Socrates didn't sell.) Seven-year-old Louisa shouted at the sheriff who came for their belongings, "Go away, bad man, you are making my father unhappy." Young as she was, she already acted as the family's defender.

The school shrank down to a single room in the Masonic temple's windowless basement. "Despair snuffs the sun from the firmament," Bronson mourned. The Alcotts themselves moved to smaller and dingier lodgings. Abby took out her fury on the world. "You have seen how roughly they have handled my husband," she fumed to her brother Sam. Bronson remained calm while she raged against fate. "I rail, and he reasons and consoles me as if I was the injured one."

In the end, the Temple School lasted almost five years—the longest run of public success that Bronson

Alcott would ever see. Its last pupil was a little African American girl named Susan Robinson. Bronson acted according to his deepest beliefs in taking on his new pupil. But integration of the school was the last straw for many. By winter, the only other students left were his own daughters. "It never was so dark with us," Abby confessed.

"We are as poor as rats," she told brother Sam. In fact, they were worse than poor—the family was $6,000 in debt. It was a fortune. Under its crushing weight, they barely scraped by, accepting hand-me-down clothing, sacks of potatoes, and an occasional gift of cash from pitying relatives. When donations arrived, Abby accepted them not as charity but as "testimonies of their regard" for her "dear husband and children." She never distinguished between money and love. Lack of one meant lack of the other.

As for Louisa, she observed all this and quietly determined never to go into debt. She learned early to avoid extravagance, to distrust good fortune. She hated being dependent on others. If her father refused to work for a living, very well then: she would work hard enough for all of them.

CHAPTER FOUR

Concord and Dove Cottage, the Peaceful Days

After the Temple School collapsed, the Alcotts moved to Concord with Ralph Waldo Emerson's encouragement and help. His belief in Bronson was unshaken. Emerson called him "the most extraordinary man and the highest genius of his time." No wonder Bronson was glad to move closer. The Alcotts could not have come to a more healing place.

In the spring of 1840, Emerson found the Alcotts a small cottage near the Concord River. He arranged for the low rent of fifty-two dollars a month. Louisa described the place in *Good Wives* (part two of *Little Women*): "a tiny house, with a little garden behind, and a lawn about as big as a pocket handkerchief." She recast it as the fictional home of newlyweds John Brooke and Meg March, eldest of the four March sisters.

Louisa memorialized the family's cramped living space with humorous affection. "The shrubbery consisted of several young larches, who looked undecided whether to live or die. . . . The dining-room was so small, that six people were a tight fit, and the kitchen stairs seemed built for the express purpose of precipitating both servants and china pell-mell into the coal-bin."

From the safety of their cottage, Bronson wrote to his mother that he was busy at his "old trade *hoping*, which thus far has given food, shelter, raiment, and a few warm friends." It might have been more accurate to say that a few warm friends had given him food, shelter, raiment, and hope. After some false starts writing a novel, Bronson rightly concluded, "I had music in my soul but no voice." He turned to giving public talks, which paid little but fed his sense of purpose: "to work in Soul, and to mould substance into forms of human Beauty."

The cottage—fondly renamed Dove Cottage—perched on two acres of land overlooking rolling fields that led to the Concord River. It was a child's paradise, especially after crowded and chaotic Boston. Life at Dove Cottage was full of family togetherness, gentle adventures, and new friends. Abby's spirits rose as they settled in, and the girls—now aged nine (Anna), seven (Louisa), and five (Lizzie)—woke to the sound of their mother singing and went to bed hearing the same joyful sound.

Louisa wrote in her novel *Under the Lilacs,* "It takes so

little to make a child happy, it is a pity grown people do not oftener remember it and scatter little bits of pleasure before the small people, as they throw crumbs to the hungry sparrows." The Alcott parents worked hard to nourish their "hungry sparrows." Bronson labored twelve hours a day fixing Dove Cottage inside and out. He excelled at home repair, using skills he'd learned at his father's side: "hard work with feet and hands and back." He planted gardens, transplanted trees, repaired steps, whitewashed fences and sheds. A gifted landscaper, Bronson set trellises all around the house, which bloomed with climbing vines and flowers. "My garden shall be my poem," he proclaimed. "My spade and hoe the instruments of my wit."

For the first time ever, the Alcott girls attended someone else's school. This ushered in a whole new collection of friends. Louisa, at age seven, was the rambunctious, noisy cutup. Anna lovingly described her later as "a dreadful girl, full of wild pranks." For her seventh birthday, her mother gave her a doll along with the sardonic wish that "she will be a quiet playmate for my active Louisa."

Anna attended an academy in town, while Louisa and Lizzie set off to Ralph Waldo Emerson's house, which held a school for younger children. Emerson provided the girls with encouragement, introductions to his friends, and access to his reading materials. Louisa was thrilled to have the use of Emerson's library. He suggested books for her, and these became the backbone of her future reading.

These early days in Concord were carefree. Louisa called them "the happiest of my life." Abby declared that the children were "in raptures" over their cottage. Here in peaceful Concord, Louisa began taking writing more seriously. That spring she composed her first poem, "To the First Robin." "Welcome, welcome, little stranger, / Fear no harm, and fear no danger." It heralds both the springtime bird and the Alcotts' arrival in Concord.

One of Louisa's new friends was the easygoing, straw-hatted naturalist and writer Henry David Thoreau. Henry was a close young friend of Emerson's. He would build his famous cottage on Emerson's land at the edge of Walden Pond, borrowing Bronson Alcott's ax to cut the timber. Henry and his brother, John, ran a small school in town. John taught writing and math, Henry classics, Greek, and higher math—but he also led the local children on nature walks, taught them Native American history, and escorted them on fishing and bird-watching expeditions. The playful, rugged twenty-three-year-old was one of the likely models for *Little Women*'s Laurie, and more obviously a model for Louisa's first literary romantic hero—the rugged, masculine Adam of her novel *Moods*.

Thoreau was fun-loving, broad-shouldered, full of energy. He played the flute well and brought it along whenever he escorted the Alcott children on walks, or on rows in his boat. Thoreau was unlike any adult Louisa knew.

That summer in Dove Cottage, Abby gave birth to

her fourth and final daughter—her eighth pregnancy in less than ten years. The newborn was called Baby, but later she was christened Abigail May, known ever after simply as May. Untamable Louisa was sent into exile one more time for the birth of this youngest sister. She stayed in town cooped up with stiffly formal relatives. Her family informed her that she was missing out on all their summer fun, which they described in detail. They enjoyed picnics, adventures, and visits with the baby while Louisa stayed inside her grandfather's stuffy house.

Baby May became at once "the flower of the family," as Louisa later observed with much love and a touch of envy. May was golden haired and graceful, "spoiled and petted," much like her fictional alter ego in *Little Women*, Amy March. In many ways, the two unalike artistic sisters were most alike—both gifted, both fiercely ambitious. But May was "universally adored" and Louisa was not. Things came easily into May's possession. Louisa struggled for everything she got.

The sisters would become close as adults. But when Louisa first returned from her grandfather's house, she snubbed the newborn and hid in the kitchen. She was not the only disappointed one. Bronson had been desperately hoping for a son. Now, he wrote, he must be "content to rear women for the future world." One hears the glum resignation in his words. Louisa, who so longed to be that son, surely heard it, too. Bronson steeled himself to father only four "little women." Louisa would turn that belittling upside down and inside out, creating the most true-to-life (Meg), most touching (Beth), most comical (Amy), and most audacious (Jo) young heroines America had ever seen.

Bronson chased a new interest now—a magazine launched by the transcendentalists, named by Bronson himself: *The Dial*. Bronson composed for one of its first issues his fifty philosophical epigrams titled "Orphic Sayings." After he'd read them, Emerson was at a loss for words. "Not very good," he confided in his journal. "I fear he will never write as well as he talks." He passed them along to the magazine's editor, Margaret Fuller, for publication. She liked them even less than Emerson did.

Alcott's "Orphic Sayings" float around the reader's head like soap bubbles. He wrote, "Intact, aspirant, she [the soul] feels the appulses of both spiritual and material things; she would appropriate the realm she inherits by virtue of her incarnation; infinite appetencies direct all her members on finite things; her vague strivings and Cyclopean motions confess an aim beyond the confines of transitory natures . . ." The sentence seems to hang there forever.

Louisa may have learned how *not* to write by studying her father's prose. She was succinct even in her earliest journal entries and stories. Jo March says, "I like good strong words that mean something." Compare Bronson's rambling above to the opening of *Little Women*: " 'Christmas won't be Christmas without any presents,' grumbled Jo, lying on the rug."

The Alcott girls, a friend recalled, were "always very busy about the house, but never too busy to romp and play." Louisa relished the sociability of Concord with her "charming playmates in the little Emersons, Channings, Hawthornes and Goodwins." It was a happy era for the family still reeling from the loss of the Temple School. Bronson found like-minded friends in Concord. Dove Cottage was within easy walking distance to town. Abby relished the new peace and quiet; Bronson set to work in the garden. "I place myself in peaceful relations to the soil," he declared.

Louisa later wrote about her family, "They all wear rose-colored spectacles, and are lineal descendants of the inventor of aerial architecture." She nicknamed the Alcotts "the Pathetic Family" and claimed they were "a hopeful race." They bounced back quickly from discouragement, at least in the early days. Louisa was certainly thinking of her father when she described the philosopher as "a man up in a balloon, with his family and friends holding the ropes which confine him to earth and trying to haul him down."

Bronson simply could not be hauled down. Daily, grinding poverty began to hound the family—with shortages of everything from food to linens to clothing. Bronson's spirits sank when he saw that his farming labors could not support the family. He began to head into a deep depression. Abby wrote anxiously to her brother Sam, "If his body don't fail his mind will."

The marriage showed the strain of all these difficulties. Abby considered a separation from her husband. But she did her best to hide her doubts from herself and from others. Emerson's son Edward observed that even with "beliefs, tastes and aims differing so widely as to make domestic harmony seem impossible, courage, respect for each other and love won the day, and kept father, mother and children a united family."

In February 1841 Abby's august father, Colonel Joseph May, passed away. The Colonel left an inheritance to be divided equally among his many children and stepchildren. For Abby the death came as a double blow. "My father did not love me!" she exclaimed. As the neediest of his children, she believed she deserved the lion's share of his fortune.

One provision in the Colonel's will stung especially— Abigail's share of the inheritance could not be spent to benefit "her husband or liability of his debts." Since Bronson now owed more than $6,000, the Colonel was doubtless trying to protect his daughter's inheritance from creditors. But Abby reacted with injured dignity: "I am despised and rejected by my kindred," she fumed.

* * *

At public school, Louisa simply "got by," with no hint of the brilliant young woman she would become. She enjoyed the social side of school, but not the "dull hours" of study. She "never liked arithmetic or grammar, and dodged these branches on all occasions." The rest she just tolerated. She actively enjoyed only composition, history, geography, and, most of all, reading.

Activities after school earned more enthusiasm. The children set forth on long hikes, with and without Henry Thoreau as their guide. They held athletic contests, told stories, and bathed in a local stream—shocking their proper New England neighbors. They got into every kind of mischief, with a rambunctious Louisa leading the way.

Abby made sure that all her daughters acquired practical skills to ensure their survival. They would have, she insisted, the financial independence she lacked. The girls grew adept at sewing, cleaning, and cooking. Even Louisa, who hated housekeeping duties except as a vigorous form of exercise, showed skills as a needleworker. She was in demand among friends and schoolmates as a maker of fanciful doll hats. Later, Abby would even suggest that the teenage Louisa become a milliner.

Louisa was famous—or notorious—in Concord for her bravery, foolhardiness, and strength. She was a self-declared tomboy, fearless, popular with boys and girls alike. Her friend Lydia Hosmer recalled, "Louisa was always the leader in the fun. It seems to me that she was always romping and racing down the street, usually with a hoople higher than her head . . . continually shocking people . . . by her tomboyish, natural and independent ways." She could roll her hoop a mile from home and back again without stopping. Louisa never refused a dare, no matter how dangerous—she rubbed red pepper in her eyes, jumped off a high beam in a barn, and once had to be carried home on a board with two sprained ankles.

Among the Alcott sisters, Louisa was by far the strongest and fiercest. A natural athlete, she craved movement and activity, just as her mother hated the "stupidity" of keeping still. "I must have been a deer or a horse in some former state," Louisa mused, "because it was such a joy to run. No boy could be my friend till I had beaten him in a race, and no girl if she refused to climb trees, leap fences, and be a tomboy."

In *Little Women*, her alter ego, Jo, declares, "It's bad enough to be a girl, anyway, when I like boys' games and work and manners!" Childhood friend Frederick Llewellyn Hovey Willis remembered Louisa as bold and athletic. "She could run like a gazelle. She was the most beautiful girl runner I ever saw. She could leap a fence or climb a tree as well as any boy and dearly loved a good romp."

Of course, Louisa's adventures were not always easy and happy. Sometimes she acted out in frustration or anger. Like her mother, she was subject to "moods" at an early age. "Her violence is at times alarming," Bronson wrote in dismay. As a child growing up in a family that valued self-discipline and harmony, Louisa made repeated efforts to control her temper—and repeatedly failed.

The famous feminist/writer Margret Fuller once came to Dove Cottage to observe the exemplary Alcott children. It took a long time for the girls to appear, and they finally emerged bedraggled, wet, and filthy from their latest adventure, barking and neighing like farm animals. "Here," said Abby, with her usual humor, "are the model children!"

Even with the family in dire straits, Bronson refused to hire himself out for pay. He called such work "slavery." His ideas and idealism ruled the everyday. The family drank only spring water, as Bronson refused to be "partners in human slavery," observed a neighbor, by the use of sugar, spice, or cotton. Most of the daily household work fell on Abby. She struggled against depression and exhaustion, swallowed by an "ocean of difficulties." In her diary she sounds close to the edge. "I am tired and weary," she wrote, "and would gladly lay me down."

No one was more like Abby in personality and temperament than her "difficult" daughter, Louisa. No one sympathized more with her struggles. "You are the best of women," Louisa once told her mother. Local friends also took Abby's part. "I do not believe Mr. A will succeed anywhere," a neighbor predicted tartly. Another reported, "Their housekeeping was not easy for the wife to manage, and alarmingly frugal for a cold zone. The conditions of family life were hard." Anna recalled these conditions as "the troubles that have made Louy & I old so young."

Still, Abby was determined to make life in Concord as joyful as possible for her girls. She rushed through her morning chores so she could devote her afternoons to them. Their "jolly times" included outings in woods and fields, wild chases, poetry recitations, songs, and games. Compared with other parents, Abby was unthinkably lenient. She allowed card games, and coed social gatherings, convinced that the two sexes could and should be friends. She never fussed about the girls' appearance. They were permitted one great pillow fight each week before bedtime.

When Bronson was despondent, he appeared remote, but Abby even at her most despairing involved herself in her daughters' daily activities and cares. Edward Emerson wrote admiringly that she was "loving" and "sympathetic," and "had a well-stored, fertile mind."

Bronson scraped by with his public "Conversations" in New England and New York. These Conversations were halfway between a public lecture and a salon, and now and again Bronson employed his old Socratic method of questioning his audience—sometimes to unintended effect. A well-dressed young lady in blue fled under his interrogation. But his efforts brought in little or no money.

At times, his public behavior was outright eccentric. At a New England convention, while the men bickered over what role women might be allowed in the abolitionist movement, Bronson suddenly jumped to his feet. "You are all wrong, blind, and carnal," he announced. "I am as pure and as wise as was Jesus Christ. . . . I eat nothing but pure vegetables. The rest of the world eats animal flesh, and that is just what you are: cattle, sheep, fowl and swine."

The audience was shocked into silence. Then one man called out, "The speaker just told us that we are just what we eat. . . . Does it not follow . . . that he is a potato, a turnip, a pumpkin, or a squash?"

Conversations at Emerson's house in Concord triggered lively debates. Emerson's friends, including the famed minister Theodore Parker, put Bronson through his paces. Emerson noted, "Parker wound himself around Alcott like an anaconda. You could hear poor Alcott's bones crunch."

As the great composer Charles Ives wrote, "If the dictagraph had been perfected in Bronson Alcott's time, he might now be a great writer. As it is, he goes down as Concord's greatest talker." Thoreau called him a "great expecter." Concord constable Sam Staples named him a "great feller for talkin' big . . . but his daughters is the gals though—always *doin'* something."

The gals didn't have a choice. Abby was too nervous and anxious to carry on alone. The four sisters learned to help her and each other. In Bronson's "Order of In-door Duties," posted in the house, he exhorted them to do all their chores with "prompt, cheerful, unquestioning obedience." If we think of Bronson as an old version of a new-age radical parent—and he was—we must remember that nineteenth-century expectations were very different from our own. Even the progressive Alcotts expected from their children "unquestioning obedience."

The family slipped close to destitution, unable to pay even the small rent on Dove Cottage. Yet they continued to give away their few possessions. Three scant meals a day shrank to two when, encouraged by Abby, the family shared their food with others less fortunate. The scene in *Little Women* where the girls sacrifice their grand Christmas breakfast and return home to a simple but ample meal tells a half truth—that simple breakfast would have seemed a feast to the four Alcott girls. The Dove Cottage rooms were bare; lacking a stove, the family cooked in the fireplace. Bronson would accept donations for his Conversations, but with quiet stubbornness he refused any reliable income.

Abby wrote to her brother Sam in despair, "I believe he will starve and freeze before he will sacrifice principle to comfort. . . . I and my children . . . have less to sustain us in the spirit, and therefore, are more liable to be overcome of the flesh." She added loyally, "No one could in truth reproach him."

For once, her sympathetic brother disagreed. He himself had left the ministry because of his principles, after his failed efforts to integrate a local school. He worked briefly for Elizabeth Peabody's brother-in-law, but disagreements drove him from that job as well. Now he was struggling, too.

Seeing the Alcotts' predicament, Emerson offered to move the family to his house—without first consulting his wife, Lidian—but there Abby drew the line. She was too independent and could not live, she declared, "in another person's yoke." Her pie would burn another woman's fingers, she admitted, simply "because it is mine."

During this dreary time, Emerson hid much-needed gifts of money "under a book, or behind a candlestick" when he visited the Alcotts at Dove Cottage. Still they were at the edge of ruin. Abby wrote, "Mr. A[lcott] can earn nothing here but food." Even food was not abundant. Anything beyond bare subsistence was out of reach. With unusual clarity, Abby wrote, "Fuel must be paid for, water must be paid for, the land out of which we would dig our bread must be paid for—what is to be done?"

The children were always hungry. At nine years old, Louisa was shooting up like a weed, skinny and coltish. In desperation Abby sent her to Providence, Rhode Island, to stay with well-to-do relatives. At least there she would be well fed. Louisa noticed some poor and unwashed children living nearby, poorer even than the Alcotts. She raided her hosts' pantry and brought figs and cakes out to the hungry children. She made several trips before she was caught, scolded, and sent to her room to repent. Louisa could not think what she had done wrong—feeding the poor was a *good* thing. Despite her relatives' early efforts to reform her, she would always exhibit the same generosity, especially toward the young. She never forgot her own hungry days.

Bronson took to roaming the countryside, visiting some of the many cooperative societies springing up around New England in the mid-1800s. Each group had its own ideas about how to build a new utopian society. None of them suited Bronson. He briefly considered joining nearby Brook Farm, the communal society mocked in Nathaniel Hawthorne's novel *The Blithedale Romance*. In the book, Emerson comes in for special ridicule. But Bronson lacked even the meager funds required for admittance.

The Alcotts lived on a starvation diet of bread, potatoes, apples, squash, and now sugar—which they'd added to their diet, despite Bronson's principled opposition. When Abby's aunt Hannah Robie visited in December 1841, she was appalled by their living conditions. The night she arrived, the family dined on bread and water. The children were thin, hungry, and ragged. Aunt Hannah had brought bundles of used clothing, which Abby would refashion for the girls. Abby asked for her help selling a treasured silver heirloom, along with a few old family spoons. Hannah Robie not only brought the silver back to Boston; she carried news of the Alcotts' struggles. But family help would not come for years.

Bronson had one much-needed boost during this grim time. He was courted long-distance by two English educators, James Greaves and a young headmaster, Henry Gardner Wright. They had read *Record of a School*, Elizabeth Peabody's book about Bronson's Temple School, and they'd put Alcott's ideas to work. They urged him to come visit their school in England—renamed Alcott House.

Greaves wrote in a flowery letter, "I am induced, without apology, to address you as a friend and companion in the hidden path of Love's most powerful revelations." Greaves hoped "to obtain a more intimate acquaintance with one, in our Sister Land, who is so divinely and universally developed."

The praise from abroad helped bolster Bronson's battered self-worth. Greaves hoped to visit Concord, adding this alarming bit of autobiography: "In the year 1817 some strong interior visitations came over me, which withdrew me from the world in a considerable degree, and I was enabled to yield myself up to Love's own manner of acting, regardless of all consequences." Bronson might have overlooked the hint of lunacy, but Abby did not. Greaves's words set off alarms: "I met with an account of the Spirit's work in and by the late venerable Pestalozzi, which so interested me, that I proceeded at once to visit him in Switzerland; and remained with him, in holy fellowship, for four years." Four years! One can imagine the struggling Alcotts faced with an uninvited houseguest "in holy fellowship, for four years." In any event, the unfortunate Mr. Greaves died not long after. If funds could be found, Alcott would travel to England to meet his new admirers.

Bronson was too flattered to evaluate his new English fans. Headmaster Henry Wright had impregnated, married, and abandoned a parlor maid. The scandal nearly closed Alcott House. Meanwhile, a new character named Charles Lane stepped into the scene. He would soon become a central and sinister figure in the life of the Alcotts.

Charles Lane had been embroiled in a bitter divorce case for three years when he met Bronson. He never disclosed the details to anyone, but he'd won full custody of his nine-year-old son, William. Lane now promoted celibacy as the only alternative to the plagues of marriage. His beliefs were narrow-minded, fixed, and fanatical. But Bronson saw only a new disciple.

Bronson turned to Emerson for funds to make the overseas trip. For once, his old friend declined. According to Cheever, "Alcott, he had come to think, was only truly interested in Alcott." Emerson wrote of Bronson in his private journal, "His disease makes him the worst of bores."

But in January 1842, tragedy struck the town. First Henry Thoreau's brother John died of tetanus, having cut his finger while shaving with a rusty blade. He died a slow, terrible death in Henry's arms. It threw Henry into a complete nervous collapse. Then Emerson's five-year-old son Waldo contracted a fever. He died a few days later.

"All his wonderful beauty could not save him," Emerson wrote. "My boy, my boy is gone. Fled out of my arms like a dream."

Louisa stopped by to inquire after the sick child and found a devastated Emerson sunk in mourning, barely able to speak. He had turned into an old man overnight. The brokenhearted Emerson paid for Bronson's passage to England and covered all the extra expenses, including luggage and a fine new suit.

The Alcotts held out great hope for this trip abroad. For Abby, especially, it was a time of mingled optimism and terror. Sea travel was slow and dangerous. Bronson would be out of reach for weeks at a time, and he would be gone for months.

Bronson arranged for his younger brother, Junius, to stay at Dove Cottage in his absence. In the end it wasn't clear who was the caregiver and who the cared-for. Junius was a gentle soul, and the Alcott children liked him. But he was a companion rather than a protector, as Abby must have known. She summoned her reserves of courage again and braced for whatever might come next.

CHAPTER FIVE

Bronson Across the Sea and Back

Left with four hungry children to feed, Abby cast about to eke out a living any way she could. "I have no accomplishments for I never was educated for a fine lady, but I have handicraft, wit and will enough to feed the body and save the souls of myself and children." It would take years of legal battles before the money she had inherited from her father could be freed for her own use.

She put out word that she would welcome work as a seamstress and declared firmly, "My girls shall have trades." Anna showed skill at housekeeping and taking care of the younger children. She went to Aunt Hannah Robie in Boston, but soon fled back home, too homesick to stay on.

Louisa demonstrated her flair for designing doll clothes. Her turbans were especially popular, adorned with feathers stolen from local chickens. Lizzie was still at school, and May only a baby, but when Louisa wasn't busy plying her needle and flying here and there, she still managed to get into scrapes. On one occasion she "slipped into the brook, and was half drowned." She broke a window, buried her doll, and cracked a tooth turning somersaults on a haystack.

Abby summed up the year 1841–1842 in one word: "Heroic." "It was a period in my life," she wrote, "more full of hardships, doubts, fears, adversities; struggles for my children; efforts to maintain cheerfulness and good discipline." The girls were ages one, six, nine, and eleven when Bronson sailed away. Between 1838 and 1879 more than half the transatlantic steamer voyages between America and Europe ended in sea wrecks. Twenty-four vessels never reached port, ten were burned, eight sank in collisions, and three were downed by ice. Abby tried to ignore these grisly statistics.

She wrote in her journal, "I dread and yet desire this separation." She worried about her ability to maintain a cheerful home in Bronson's absence. Louisa was particularly sensitive to her mother's dark moods, and subject to her own. But Bronson's six months' absence proved some of the gayest and freest of Louisa's youth. She fought less with her sisters and seemed calmer. Abby was delighted by the change. Louisa's gentle uncle Junius neither judged nor lectured the girls. He took them for daily walks and joined in their activities. Abby made time in her workday to read to them aloud. They spent the evenings "talking and singing." Discipline was no longer a daily struggle.

Nine-year-old Louisa and her sisters went for walks into nature with Henry Thoreau, who told them gravely that the cobwebs shining on the grass were handkerchiefs dropped by fairies. He taught the girls how to identify plants and flowers and the habitats of woodland creatures. Thoreau was handsome in a homely way—or homely in a handsome way, dressed in his baggy gray pants and straw hat. Wherever he went he brought along a notebook, pen, and his flute. He took the sisters for long trips in his hand-built canoe and pointed out the local birds: the scarlet tanager, the great horned owl, a heron standing on one leg.

Lizzie's seventh birthday that June was honored with a simple party. Anna wrote, "We had the cornbarn fixed up with green boughs and curtains and at 8 oclock we marched in there, & eat supper, and mother wrote a toast." Abby's toast, in the form of a gay, rhyming poem, reported that the family feasted on "nuts, figs and cake" in honor of Lizzie's day. No one asked Lizzie to sacrifice her "plummy cake."

Abby and the girls waited for Bronson to return from England in a cloud of glory. Time and distance had convinced Abby that the separation was a blessed necessity, "the one thing needful to sustain the just balance of his mind. Dearest! best of men," she added.

Instead of the hoped-for fortune, Bronson came home that fall of 1842 with a new pipe dream and three unannounced houseguests—Charles Lane and his ten-year-old son, William, and Henry Wright, Alcott House's disgraced headmaster. Their goal: to build a new utopia. As usual, Abby and the girls at first viewed the change hopefully. A giddy Louisa asked her mother, "What makes me so happy?"

Abby welcomed the English guests as "the good and the true." As usual, any brand-new plan filled her with optimism. Bronson and his English guests planned out own their communal society and began to scout around for locations. None of the three men had jobs or prospects. Lane had some money of his own, but no plans to part with it. Now the Alcotts had to accommodate and feed nine in the tiny Dove Cottage.

Emerson offered hospitality for the English visitors, but Lane shrewdly refused. He could control the Alcotts at Dove Cottage, where he held the purse strings. Emerson distrusted Lane and Wright from the start, calling them the "two cockerels." He refused any part in Bronson's utopia. "I would as soon exert myself to collect money for a madman," he exclaimed.

The Alcotts quickly fell into a new, unhappy era. The honeymoon with their English guests didn't last the month. The tiny, overcrowded cottage left no space for Louisa and her sisters to play. The girls sacrificed their own room to Charles Lane, along with their recent freedoms and pleasures.

No one knew anything about Charles Lane's past; he kept closemouthed on the subject. Under Lane's rule, the Alcotts lived strictly on fruit, vegetables, and porridge. Milk, butter, and molasses vanished from their diet. He was an idealist only in the most rigid sense. They awoke at six each morning to take cold baths and listen to his lectures. He watched and criticized every move—with Abby and her daughters coming in for special scrutiny.

"I am almost suffocated in this atmosphere of restriction and gloom," Abby lamented. "I am so weary," she had earlier written, of "new propositions, communities, experiences, hopes, fears, heavens, hells, improved methods of living. . . . I take my baby, turn my back to the window and annihilate for the time being, everything." Strong words from the wife of Bronson Alcott! She added, "My children are very real to me." Her husband, apparently, had become somewhat less so. The Alcotts even experimented with living in separate bedrooms for a time.

Abby copied into her journal a quote declaring that married couples should "feel that there is a certainty in the world, in spite of all the power of Hell . . . that they love each other, that they belong to each other, that nothing, nothing in the world shall separate them." This is exactly what Charles Lane sought to destroy. Lane saw Abby as a dangerous foe. "Her pride is not yet eradicated. . . . Her peculiar maternal love blinds her to all else." A mortal struggle between them slowly but surely began.

Friends of the family watched Lane's influence over the Alcotts with growing concern. Abby's friend Lydia Maria Child painted a sharp portrait of Lane: "His countenance . . . looks as if the washwoman . . . scrubbed it on a washboard." She added, "There is an expression which would make me slow to put myself in his power."

Lane and his son William took over Bronson's study, while Wright moved into one of the upstairs bedrooms. The four girls were relegated to a cramped alcove outside their parents' room. Privacy for Bronson and Abby was minimal. Lane and his rules, theories, and regulations intruded everywhere.

Louisa responded by acting her worst—running, shouting, stomping, slamming doors. The sisters tried to escape by playing outdoors, away from his strict supervision, but the blustery weather trapped them inside. After long hours of school with Lane as schoolmaster—covering everything from geography and geometry to French and Latin—the girls were expected to do hours of household chores and watch over baby May.

Louisa was sent out to chop wood, a hard and dangerous chore for a ten-year-old. She lost a chunk of her finger in the process. In Louisa's earliest surviving journal, she wrote that she hated "the school part, or Mr. L[ane]." She was learning early on that she could write out the thoughts she dare not speak aloud.

Lane and Alcott continued their search for a spot for their new utopian community. Alcott's messianic complex reared its head. He proposed to create "the Generation of a new race of persons . . . who shall project institutions . . . altogether original, and commensurate with the being and wants of humanity." The first defector from the cause was the light-footed headmaster, Henry Wright. Though married and the father of an infant back in England, he now met and fell in love with a young American reformer named Mary Gove. Wright moved into Gove's parlor, where they scandalized the neighbors by pulling down the shades.

Life at Dove Cottage grew more difficult. The inmates did away with plates as an unnecessary luxury, eating off napkins. Alcott refused to pay his taxes and was arrested, then released on bail. Abby labored like a servant all day, but in the evenings she had to listen to lectures on the ills of the family, the evil nature of women, and the deadly perils of maternal love.

The popular *Godey's Lady's Book* published a poem urging married men: "Be to her virtues very kind. . . . Let all her ways be unconfined, and place a padlock on her mind." Louisa watched her mother being "frowned down into stiff quiet and peace-less order," as Abby wrote. The ten-year-old responded with outbursts and bad behavior.

Mother and girls took to using a family letter box, where they could pass notes privately back and forth. Later that letter box made its famous appearance in *Little Women*. The Alcott family could pay each other compliments, voice complaints, and make suggestions through the family post office. As Anna would write, "All the Alcotts have a passion for letters, and I think there are but few families who have so many."

Louisa yearned for a corner in which to write, but the family could not afford even a separate room for all four sisters, much less a space of her own. As freedom in the household tightened, Abby turned to ten-year-old Louisa for companionship and comfort, sharing with her a picture of a sick mother watched over by her daughter: "For I imagined that you might be just such an industrious daughter and I such a feeble but loving mother, looking to your labor for my daily bread."

This image only reinforced Louisa's vision of herself as the guardian, "head of the household"—a job she took to heart. Underneath the sick mother / supporting child image, Louisa pasted a poem she had written for Abby, one that echoed her mother's dream of rescue.

TO MOTHER.

I hope that soon, dear mother,
You and I may be
In the quiet room my fancy
Has so often made for thee, —

The pleasant, sunny chamber,
The cushioned easy-chair,
The book laid for your reading,
The vase of flowers fair;

The desk beside the window
Where the sun shines warm and bright:
And there in ease and quiet
The promised book you write;

While I sit close beside you,
Content at last to see
That you can rest, dear mother,
And I can cherish thee.

With the family under increasing pressure from all sides, Louisa turned to scribbling her early poems, letters, and journal entries. She received little encouragement from her father. Bronson was not only distracted; he was unusually harsh. Each Alcott child's tenth birthday was typically treated as a momentous event, introducing a new decade and a new phase of life. Anna had received lovely writing instruments made of silver and gold. Bronson gave Louisa nothing for her tenth birthday, not even the usual handmade bookmark.

Instead he wrote her a birthday letter warning against "anger, discontent, impatience, evil appetites, greedy wants, complainings, ill-speakings, idlenesses, heedlessness," and last but not least, "rude behavior." It was a long list to level against a child. He added a touch of fire and brimstone at the end: "It leaves the poor misguided soul to live in its own obstinate, perverse, proud, discomfort; which is the very Pain of Sin and is in the Bible called the worm that never dies, the gnawing worm, the sting of Conscience."

As the Alcotts prepared to leave the Concord community that had made them happy, they began detaching even from each other. Lane's method was divide and conquer. He urged Bronson to distance himself as far as possible from wife and children.

Louisa later published a fictionalized memoir about this era in the family's life, called "Transcendental Wild Oats." In it, Bronson is "Lamb," while Lane is "Dictator Lion"— with the grisly results you might expect from such a match. One of Louisa's sharpest, most autobiographical pieces of writing, "Transcendental Wild Oats" is set with jewel-like, often comical portraits. But the experience was anything but funny as they were living it.

That dismal Christmas, Abby fled to relatives in Boston, taking with her both Louisa and, oddly enough, Lane's son, William. She left the men at home to fend for themselves. It was a calculated move as well as an escape from housekeeping duties she was finding increasingly "arduous and involved."

Abby and the two children revived themselves in Boston with all sorts of forbidden delights: Christmas caroling, parties, sleigh rides, and concerts. It was Charles Lane himself, of all people, who followed them to Boston. He made friends with Abby's relations and sent Abby notes pleading for her trust. On their return home, Lane used the family letter box to win Abby over, singing her praises: "Your destiny, your heart binds you to a circle in which you may become a radiation of beneficence." Abby was pleased and pacified—for the time being.

CHAPTER SIX

Wild Oats

By spring of 1843, Lane had given up on the idea of finding an outside patron to fund the new utopia. "I do not see anyone to act the money part but myself," he wrote at last. He prepared to support the project alone.

Emerson, the Alcotts' stalwart supporter, refused any part in the commune. He begged Bronson to at least relocate in Concord, near his friends. Instead, Bronson and Lane found a remote ninety-acre farm in the town of Harvard, more than ten miles away. It might as well have been two hundred. The farm was accessible only by cart track—a far cry from sociable Dove Cottage. But Bronson called it "the bowl of Heaven."

As Cheever has observed, "The Fruitlands farmhouse is only twelve miles due west of [Dove] Cottage, but it feels as if it is on another planet." The two-story house, set atop a steep slope in the town of Harvard, Massachusetts, was dilapidated, both barns collapsing. Thanks to a few old fruit trees on the property, Bronson named the place Fruitlands. Witty onlookers called its residents "fruitcakes."

Abby, who had now been suffering under Lane's rule for months, charged him back rent to pay off their debts, leaving Lane short of cash. Abby's brother Sam, along with Emerson, signed on as guarantors of the purchase. Bronson left Concord debt-free, but Lane owed $500 for the property.

Lane and Alcott looked to form a utopian community of "Consociates." The Fruitlands residents would live off the land. They would harm neither man nor beast. The diet was to be strictly vegetarian. Every endeavor would aim for the sublime. Self-perfection and the perfection of the human race were the goals of the enterprise.

These ideas drew to Fruitlands both idealists and out-right cranks. One man claimed he had lived for a year on nothing but crackers. Another was a nudist. The assembled dreamers and lunatics provided quite a life lesson for Louisa and her sisters. Not much escaped Louisa's sharp eye. One new member had just been released from a mental asylum. Louisa wrote, "When his spirit soared, he climbed trees and shouted; when doubt assailed him, he lay upon the floor and groaned lamentably. At joyful periods, he raced, leaped, and sang; when sad, he wept aloud; and when a great thought burst upon him in the watches of the night, he crowed like a jocund cockerel, to the great delight of the children and the great annoyance of the elders."

The day of the move, Louisa tells us in her "Transcendental Wild Oats," was unseasonably chilly for June. In hindsight, it felt like an omen of worse misery to come. A damp wind cut at the eight travelers carting their possessions by horse-driven wagon. Abby and the three youngest girls rode atop the wagon, huddled under an old shawl and an umbrella. Young William Lane sat beside Bronson, who was driving the cart. The bust of Socrates rode safely inside the crowded wagon, while Charles Lane and twelve-year-old Anna Alcott trudged along in the mud beside it.

Abby approached the Fruitlands venture with enthusiasm. But the higher Abby's expectations rose, the harder they came crashing down. "The soul expands in such a region of sights and sounds," she wrote that first week of their home amid "woodland, vale, meadow, and pasture." She boasted, "We owe *nobody nothing*. . . . It is a comfortable feeling after a perturbation of 10 years." In fact, they still owed their Boston creditors $6,000 from the Temple School. From that era, only two treasures remained: a collection of nearly a thousand rare books and the unsold bust of Socrates.

The family arrived at Fruitlands past twilight, Louisa

taking in the "barren-looking valley." The homestead was sparsely furnished at best. Aside from books, and the "few busts and paintings," the house was dilapidated and bare. Abby saw a kitchen that was large but ill-equipped for food preparation and cooking. She was expected to feed eleven fellow Consociates on "cakes of maple sugar, dried peas and beans, barley and hominy, meal . . . potatoes, and dried fruit." Coffee and tea were forbidden; salt spurned as an unnecessary luxury.

But the Alcotts kept up their spirits during those very early days. They camped out on the floor that night, which seemed delightful to the girls. Abby wrote in a hopeful letter to her brother, "If we can attract toward us a few of the right caliber I do feel as if a great work may be effected here. The true life ought to be lived here if any where on earth, away from the false and degrading customs of society."

Abby initially declared, "Our children are very happy." Once the family settled in, the girls' education would begin again. The first few days at Fruitlands that June of 1843 were "pleasant," according to the journals Louisa and Anna kept. They missed their Concord friends, but Louisa felt relieved to run free after their cramped living quarters that winter and spring. "I ran in the wind and played be a horse, and had a lovely time in the woods with Anna and Lizzie." They played at being woodland fairies, too. Louisa bragged, "I 'flied' the highest."

Even the deprivations seemed like adventures. The children treated it all as a lark, making picnics of their Spartan meals and a camping trip of the haphazard sleeping arrangements. With so many Consociates crowded into one area, the three older Alcott girls were exiled to a crawl space in the attic for their living quarters—hot in summer, freezing in winter. Abby and Bronson shared their small bedroom with three-year-old May.

Instead of using oil lamps, the Consociates planned to make their own candles. It soon grew clear, in typical Fruitlands fashion, that no one had any idea how to make them, so they burned pine knots instead. When the knots burned out, they made every possible use of the daylight or simply went to bed early. Only Abby stayed awake, using her precious minutes alone for sewing, reading, and thinking.

As usual, she was first to weary of the hardships—and as usual, she was also expected to make the best of them. Exhausted, underfed, and anxious, she confided to her journal, "I hope the experiment will not bereave me of my mind."

By age ten, Louisa had become her own worst critic. Her parents no longer had to tell her she was unruly—she told herself. Under the pressure of the new living situation at the commune, she and Anna began quarreling again. Louisa's journal is riddled with regrets. "I felt sad," she wrote, "because I have been cross today and did not mind Mother." "I was cross today, and I cried when I went to bed. I made good resolutions, and felt better in my heart. If I only kept all I make, I should be the best girl in the world. But I don't, and so am very bad." An older and wiser Louisa reread that entry and wryly commented, "Poor little sinner! She says the same at fifty."

New residents trickled in that spring and summer to the farmhouse. It's hard to imagine a more peculiar household. One man turned his words inside out and "startled newcomers by blandly greeting them with 'good morning, damn you,' and other remarks of an equally mixed order." In her remembrance, Alcott described their bearded neighbor, farmer Joseph Palmer, "wearing white cotton raiment and shoes of untanned leather. This costume, with a snowy beard, gave him a venerable, and at the same time a somewhat bridal appearance."

Charles Lane laid down a new sheaf of rules, while Bronson set right to work plowing and planting. He worked ten to twelve hours a day, turning the land by hand to avoid using animal labor. They were a month behind before they began. It seemed impossible that they would catch up in time for harvest. The Consociates gave in and accepted the loan of an ox and cow from a neighbor. Drinking milk was forbidden, though the children spied some of the adults sneaking out to the barn for the contraband substance.

Early-morning cold baths were the norm. Louisa enthusiastically took part. She was never one to shy from physical challenges. Instead she met them head-on. "I rose at five and had my bath. I love cold water!" she boasted. She also took part in the weighty philosophical and ethical questions flying around her. "What is the difference between faith and hope?" "What are the most valuable kinds of self-denial?"

Sundays were spent with two hours of reading, followed by long sermons given by Bronson or Lane. More hours were devoted to philosophical discussions and self-criticism, while Abby kept the household going. Ten-year-old Louisa listened to the men talking, but later, as a grown woman she wrote, "All the philosophy in our house is not in the study, a good deal is in the kitchen, where a fine old lady thinks high thoughts and does kind deeds while she cooks and scrubs."

As summer wore on, Abby began to grow anxious. "The right people, with the right motives . . . do not come," she wrote. Despite their canvassing, Bronson Alcott and Charles Lane managed to convince only four others to join their Consociate utopia. Neighbors spread the rumor that Bronson ate only fruits and vegetables that grew above the ground, "reaching for heaven," and disdained root vegetables as too dank and earthly. Townsfolk in Harvard treated the whole experiment as a joke. Bronson became famous again, but this time for his foolishness.

It was a mild summer, luckily, and Bronson and his

small band of workers managed to plant close to a dozen acres with a variety of crops, including corn, oats, potatoes, peas, melons, and squash. Ever forward-thinking, Bronson Alcott nourished the soil with clover and buckwheat— a technique used by organic farmers today. According to biographer Harriet Reisen, "A stream of curious visitors passed through that summer." None offered to join or help. Emerson stopped by just once, on the Fourth of July, and shrewdly observed, "They look well in July. Let us see how they fare in December."

The Alcott girls pitched in to help with the endless rounds of chores. A daily routine had developed—waking at five, followed by the cold shower-bath. Next came singing lessons with Mr. Lane, then breakfast. After breakfast followed household chores, more lessons, intellectual discussions, fruit and bread for dinner, followed by more chores, discussion, and singing before bed. Asked what was God's noblest work, Anna suggested "men," but Louisa amended it: "Men are often bad; babies never are."

Their farmer neighbor Joseph Palmer offered welcome help around the farm. A devout Christian and antislavery advocate, Palmer knew more about farming than the rest of the Consociates put together—and he would prove one of Fruitlands' most loyal defenders. Long after the communal experiment, he would buy the property and turned it into a refuge for the homeless.

Lane had no qualms about saving his energies for

higher things, leaving the bulk of the farming to Alcott and Palmer, and all the household work to Abby. A visitor once asked, "Are there any beasts of burden on the place?" Abby answered tartly, "Only one woman!"

She wrote that she felt like "a noble horse harnessed in a yoke and made to drag and pull instead of trot and canter." Abby had a desire for freedom as keen as her daughter Louisa's—with less opportunity to exercise it. She grew anxious and cross with the girls, noting, "The mind yields, falters, and fails. . . . It unfits me for the society of my friends and husband and my children."

When Lane declared that Abby should be barred from all Consociate discussions except those about "carnal" matters, she went on strike. She refused to dine with the others, and stayed away till her daughters finally begged her back. She was the only female Consociate at Fruitlands till Ann Page put in an appearance, giving music lessons to the girls. Abby was elated, but Louisa wrote, "I hate her, she is so fussy." Page's stay did not last long. According to "Transcendental Wild Oats," she ate fish at a friend's house and was cast out for the sin. More likely, Abby's patience had worn thin. At the time Louisa merely noted happily, "Miss P. is gone."

As summer turned to chilly fall, more Consociates defected. One man left complaining that the whole Alcott family showed "too decided a tendency toward literature"! He resented the scarcity of fruit at Fruitlands. As Louisa later put it, the residents were instead offered "bowls of sunshine for breakfast" and "dishes from Plutarch's chaste table."

As summer ended, even the butterflies, Louisa mourned, "took flight." The Fruitlands residents had stored too little against the winter and could expect "precious little . . . beyond the satisfaction of a few months of holy living."

Among the long list of forbidden indulgences were: coffee, meat, warm water—and parenting. Back in England, Lane had wanted to do away with the institution of family. Then, he had been overruled. Now he tried again. The family, he argued, must be sacrificed in the name of the communal Family. Lane also opposed conjugal relations between husband and wife. Abby tried for a time to convince herself that abstaining from sex would lead to greater happiness. "To be truly quickened into spiritual life one must die a carnal death," she agreed—but she changed her mind when she saw the wedge driven between her and Bronson. By that fall she argued, "Even our passions herald a deep nature. A passionless person is to me a tame, half-whole animal." Bronson wavered wildly on the subject— one moment upholding the holiness of intimacy, the next rejecting it. A life-and-death tug-of-war began to shape itself, with Lane on one side and Abby on the other, each pulling with all their might.

The "perennial picnic" in Fruitlands came to a hungry

end. On August 28, 1843, Louisa wrote in her diary, "We had a dinner of bread and water." The family was back where it had started. This wasn't Louisa's only rude awakening. One day she opened the cold oven door and found a freedom seeker, a formerly enslaved man, hiding crouched inside, staring at her in terror. The vision made an everlasting impression. Historians theorize that Fruitlands may have been a stop along the Underground Railroad. The same has been said of Thoreau's cabin on Walden Pond. We know that the Alcotts housed this particular man for weeks around Christmastime—Abby suggests a longer period, Louisa a shorter one. It's likely that the adults would have kept him and other freedom seekers secret from the children as long as they could.

Bronson and Lane traveled again that fall, visiting nearby settlements to look at their options. A mile away lived a thriving Shaker community. The Shakers preached simplicity and abstinence. Lane found their way of life inviting; Abby disliked it. "There is a fat sleek comfortable look about the men," she observed, "and among the women . . . a stiff awkward reserve." Separation did not ensure equality, she argued. "Wherever I turn, I see the yoke on woman in some form or another."

Bronson and Lane embarked on a long recruiting mission, hoping to stir up new members for their utopia. They ended up penniless in New Haven, Connecticut. Bronson raised money for their passage home by conducting a

Conversation on board the steamer. Meanwhile, the two men had left Fruitlands unprotected, with its precious barley crop cut but uncollected on the ground.

Abby watched anxiously at Fruitlands as an autumn thunderstorm rolled in. She and the children—Anna, Louisa, Lizzie, and Lane's son, William—raced out to the fields. They filled baskets and bedsheets, even using their own clothing to carry grain to the barn. After working through that storm, every child came down sick, even the invincible Louisa.

She had always been the Alcotts' most expressive child. Now she created fantastical stories and plays, which she and her sisters acted out. The daring escapes they could not achieve in real life, they lived out onstage. She christened her family "the Pathetic Family," a name that stuck.

She also began having insomnia. She recited poetry at night to calm herself. Abby observed her second daughter struggling with "her peculiarities and moods of mind . . . uncommon for a child of her age." Louisa tried her hardest to "be very good." But tensions within the farmhouse kept rising. She and her sister Anna were bickering as they hadn't for years. Louisa wrote, "I hardly dare speak to Annie for fear she should speak unkindly and get me angry. O she is so very very cross I cannot love her it seems as if she did every thing to trouble me but I will try to love her better." Having turned eleven, Louisa fretted even more about her "bad temper."

Louisa reserved her hottest anger not for Charles Lane, the fleeing Consociates, or her own family, but for the friends back home who had deserted them. Visitors stopped coming by. Even the long-faithful Emerson stayed away.

Abby visited Boston that November, taking along only her gentlest daughter, Lizzie. When she returned, Fruitlands was no better, and the weather much worse. It was one of the harshest winters in New England history, bitterly cold, bringing more than one hundred inches of snow. Within the farmhouse, relations became equally frigid. Louisa felt the tension; so did the rest of the family. "Mr. Lane looks miserably and acts worse," noted Abby.

Bronson was cracking under the strain of being tugged between wife and friend. His journal from this time has disappeared—the only volume missing among thousands of pages. He later admitted that he feared he was losing his mind. Abby feared the same. One bitter cold night, a neighbor delivered a load of firewood. To his wife's despair, Bronson came inside a few hours later announcing that he had given it all away to a nearby family with a young baby. It was useless to point out that the Alcotts had a baby, too.

Bronson showed signs of acute mania and paranoia. He couldn't sleep, talked incessantly, and became uncharacteristically restless and irritable. Abby wrote to her brother, "That piercing thought flashes through my mind of insanity, and a grave, yawning to receive his precious body," yet the grave would be "a consolation" compared with the complete breakdown and madness she feared.

Abby hunted for some way out. She begged her brother Sam to withhold his promised November payment on the farm property. The minister was hard to convince. Abby insisted. She was fighting for the family's survival. "I do not wish you to put a cent here. I am sifting everything to its bottom. . . . I see no clear healthy safe course here in connexion with Mr. L."

Those words—*clear, healthy, safe*—sounded an alarm. By now it may well have occurred to Abby that Lane was in love with her husband. His behavior was more like a possessive lover than a friend. He was certainly determined to wrest Bronson away from the family. While Bronson and Lane looked about for other living situations, Abby made a decision of her own. She would leave Fruitlands, taking her children and the furniture with her. Lane saw his opening. He wrote hopefully to friends, "You will perceive a separation is possible."

In mid-December, with Lane away, an agonizing family discussion took place. Bronson warned his daughters he might be leaving them to go away with Charles Lane. One can only imagine the grief and shock of that night. A heartbroken young Louisa wrote, "I was very unhappy and we all cried. Anna and I cried in bed, and I prayed God to keep us all together."

Snow drifted against the door, and the wind howled

while the inmates struggled within. It was a miserable Christmas. Bronson spent it away in Boston. Lane was not speaking to the rest of the Alcotts—though they were the only ones left in the big rattling house. Their farmer neighbor, Joseph Palmer, was the only friend who still showed any interest in their survival. By New Year's Day, Abby played her trump card. She and the girls moved out of Fruitlands and found shelter with friends down the road in Still River, Massachusetts. Half-terrified, half-triumphant, Abby announced that she had "dissolved all connection with Fruitlands."

It took a few long, silent, nerve-racking days before Bronson decided to join them.

Six days later Charles Lane and his son, William, moved out to the Shaker settlement. Lane wrote bitterly to an English friend, "Mr. Alcott's constancy to his wife and family and his inconstancy to the Spirit have blurred his life forever."

Bronson had made his choice without choosing. Now he suffered a nervous collapse. He lay in his bed facing the wall, not eating, drinking, or speaking. These were his darkest days. He believed that demons were torturing him, that he hung between earth and hell. He had witnessed the failure of all his dreams: first his beloved Temple School, then his hope for a son, now the Fruitlands experiment. Emerson visited and observed, "Very sad, indeed, it was to see this half-god driven to the wall."

In "Transcendental Wild Oats," Louisa invents a scene in which her father determines to rise from his bed for the sake of his faithful wife and little girls, vowing, "They are mine by ties that none can break." That tearful, melodramatic scene never took place in real life. It suits the myth of the idealized Alcott family as Louisa perfected it over time.

Bronson's recovery was slower and spottier in fact than in fiction, with backslides so severe that Abby at one point begged Lane to come visit. But she had won the long war. She could not help crowing to her brother, "All Mr. Lane's efforts have been to disunite us. But Mr. Alcott's conjugal and paternal instincts were too strong for him. He comes away convinced that Mr. Lane and he were never truly united." This was key for Abby. Not only had Bronson stayed with the family—he had refuted his bond to Charles Lane. To her that meant such a bond had never existed.

The Alcotts would suffer other trials and misfortunes, but never again would husband and wife be torn apart. The balance of power in the Alcott family had also shifted. From now on, the future would rest on the women's shoulders—first Abby's, then Louisa's. Daily survival was up to them. The collapse of the Fruitlands experiment marked the end of the Alcott patriarchy.

CHAPTER SEVEN

Hillside and a Room of Her Own

It took a long time for Bronson to recover. "I am all alone again," he wrote to his brother, Junius. The rest of the Alcotts also moved forward in fits and starts. Louisa's perspective changed; she grew into a young woman while still a child. On her mother's birthday that year, eleven-year-old Louisa wrote, "I wish I was rich, I was good, and we were all a happy family this day." She would carry that goal a long, burdensome way—and would not rest till she'd made it a reality.

The Alcott girls found friends their own age nearby, and Abby took in a boarder to help with household expenses. This new resident was an orphaned young man named Frederick Llewellyn Willis. His arrival proved a true blessing. Fourteen years old, sensitive, bright, and eager, he became a lifelong friend to Anna and Louisa.

Abby sold her last remaining family heirloom, a silver cake slicer she'd received from her favorite aunt, Hannah Robie. Bronson went off exploring again in western New York in search of new opportunities. Abby must have been horrified when Bronson wrote to say that he had found another utopian community in Onondaga County. Her journal entries commenting on this period were carefully scissored from her book.

The Alcotts moved into their own small rented house. From there they moved into a slightly larger half house. Louisa had little privacy in either home. All the sisters shared bedrooms. Louisa learned how to signal her moods with pillows. If she placed one vertically, you could safely approach. But a pillow laid horizontally warned others to keep away—or suffer the consequences.

In the rented house—nicknamed Brick Ends for its brick siding—the Alcotts could breathe again. The house had five rooms in all, and an outdoor shower. Bronson began to garden. He seemed to gain strength from contact with the earth. Definite physical chores, especially tasks outdoors, revived him.

The girls attended public school. Their school friends gathered to jump rope, play ball, and roll hoops, all under Abby's cheerfully watchful eye. "Mrs. Alcott was like the guardian angel of the merry company," wrote one school-mate. Louisa resumed her role as leader of the pack. She was first among friends in courage, strength, and ferocity.

A friend described her as "witty and warm-hearted and earnest, indignant at wrongs, sympathetic, full of energy and shy daring." But when her temper overtook her, "let her best friend beware"! Louisa "married" her friend Walter Gardner that spring in an "old wood shed for a church," wearing an apron for a veil, but she slapped the young groom when he tried to kiss her. As she later commented, "Moods began early." They also became more pronounced, and the dark moods lasted longer when they came.

Her friend Annie Clark remembered Louisa as a "jolly girl" but when she "got mad . . . she *could* be severe." Louisa put to death by hanging a chair that bruised her leg when she bumped into it by dangling it outside her window. She lived adventures that were the stuff of fiction. In life, she resembled her famous fictional heroine, Jo: "A quick temper, sharp tongue, and restless spirit were always getting her into scrapes, and her life was a series of ups and downs, which were both comic and pathetic." Frederick Willis describes her as the perfect "Nut-Brown Maid; she was full of spirit and life; impulsive and moody, and at times irritable and nervous."

Like Jo, Louisa constantly knocked things over—including herself. One day she laminated her hair with lamp oil and smelled like "a young whale" for weeks. Around this time she began again to write plays. The four sisters put on dramatic shows for the neighbors. Abby encouraged them even when their performances demanded extreme measures. For instance, Louisa dressed up as a courageous Native American girl, her skin dyed with bloodroot. Sometimes they stayed up all night sewing costumes and fashioning props out of household items.

Emerson urged the Alcotts to come "home" to Concord. That year had been a time of change for Emerson as well. Many friends and neighbors had moved away; he was beginning to feel his age. Abby agreed to the move, thinking Emerson's friendship might have special healing power for Bronson. "I dread his falling into that solitary life he led last winter," she wrote. From a distance, Concord looked sweeter in retrospect, their old trials forgotten.

That November the Alcotts left Still River and headed back to Concord, traveling first by coach and then, thrillingly, by train. They sailed along at a wild twenty miles per hour. Train travel was still a rarity; the Alcotts were the only passengers disembarking at Concord.

The train was a sign of the oncoming age of speed and automation. The Gilded Age with its rich industrialists stood against everything the transcendentalists stood for. Thoreau raged against "the iron horse that makes the hills echo with his snort like thunder." Emerson, Alcott, and others protested the laying of tracks in Concord, but Emerson shrewdly invested in railroad stock.

Emerson found a house and land for the Alcotts a stone's throw from his own property. Bronson called the place Hillside for its sloping woods of pine, hemlock, and birch and fields below. There were nearby ponds, and a stream ran just across the road, between banks of flowers. Emerson and Samuel May took care of the arrangements, paying for the purchase out of Abby's inheritance. Bronson Alcott still rejected private ownership, so the transaction had to be arranged secretly, honoring "Mr. Alcott's wishes, that all feel welcome there, as to a common inheritance." One wonders at his lack of curiosity about where the new property had come from—or who was paying for it. As one Alcott expert notes, "At times his unworldliness was almost breathtaking."

Bronson set to work making repairs. There was nothing unworldly about his ability with real-life tasks. The Hillside house was old and badly out of date. Bronson undertook major renovations—dividing a wheelwright shop in two and placing one half at each end of the house as extending wings. He was ingenious in his designs and tireless in his labors. By the time Bronson was done renovating, the house had eight separate doors leading outside. When company came, three or four doors would come flying open at once to admit the guest. If Louisa was in one of her "moods," she fled out the back door into the woods. Bronson dug a new well and built an outdoor bathhouse. He "greatly beautified the place," Emerson's son Edward wrote, "by a little terracing of the sunny slope here and there, the planting of woodbine on the porch." He made a set of homemade enclosures, "out of sticks cut on the place . . . a rustic fence and gates, a seat around the spurs of the elm by the door, and pretty arbors and trellises . . . of gnarled pitch-pine boughs, over which the Concord grapevines should run." Those grapevines spill over the house to this day.

Bronson landscaped the whole property so marvelously that Emerson brought guests to tour Hillside's orchard and gardens. Even neighbors who had heard rumors of the odd Fruitlands experiment were impressed—though they didn't draw any closer. The cautious Concordians watched and waited. They hesitated to befriend the rest of the family as well. Bronson called his four daughters the "golden band" of sisters; in truth, they had no choice but to form their small inner circle. Just as they had made their own theatricals, their own doll clothing, playthings, and gifts, they created their own world of four. Louisa was commander of the golden band, leading in the fun and adventures. At the far edge of childhood, she had more ideas, more will, and more energy than anyone else.

An ecstatic Louisa helped Bronson with the weeding, working "like a Trojan" and galloping freely through the grounds. She had back her liberty, "freedom being the sauce best loved by the boyish soul," as Jo March declares. When stormy moods overtook her, she found her way out.

She would "whistle and make a great racket," driving decorous Anna to her wit's end.

Vigorous activity soothed Louisa—she was a great one for going out for a long "ramble" or run—and writing also became a solace. "I was very dismal," she wrote at age twelve, "and then went to walk and made a poem." Abby seemed to best understand her tumultuous daughter and observed that writing was "a safety valve to her smothered sorrow, which might otherwise consume her young and tender heart."

Louisa's journals show an early gift for self-reflection and self-sufficiency: "I wrote in my Imagination Book, and enjoyed it very much. Life is pleasanter than it used to be, and I don't care about dying any more. Had a splendid run, and got a box of cones to burn. Sat and heard the pines sing a long time. . . . Had good dreams, and woke now and then to think, and watch the moon. I had a pleasant time with my mind, for it was happy."

Solitude helped. She wrote in a wistful note to her mother, "Dearest Mother,—I have tried to be more contented, and I think I have been more so. I have been thinking about my little room, which I suppose I never shall have. I should want to be there about all the time, and I should go there and sing and think."

Bit by bit, all the Alcotts became sociable again. The family resumed its close friendship with Henry David Thoreau, who was building his famous cottage at Walden

Pond. Bronson helped with the framing and loaned Thoreau his ax. He was one of the few visitors Thoreau always welcomed.

For Louisa, those three years at Hillside were the happy essence of her youth, condensed, the way a perfume distills from flowers. Those years carried her from childhood to young-womanhood. Fred Llewellyn Willis, nearly a brother to the girls, provided cheerful male company—Louisa always preferred boys' activities to girls'. There were friends close by, games and pranks, theatricals, fields to roam in, family outings. Louisa would draw on all of it in the creation of *Little Women.*

The years from 1845 to 1848 at Hillside were also the family's most stable years. The Alcotts had seldom stayed in one place so long. Perhaps, too, there is some genuine literary magic about the place. Though Alcott fans flock to Orchard House next door, where Louisa lived as a grown woman and composed her most famous book, Hillside was where she *lived* it, as she'd later say—and the place maintains its air of mystery. The modest house has sheltered three world-famous authors: Louisa May Alcott, Nathaniel Hawthorne, and Margaret Sidney, author of the children's classic *Five Little Peppers and How They Grew.*

That first full autumn at Hillside, 1845, Louisa awoke before dawn, crept outside alone, and watched the sun rise over the Concord River. It was, she said, a moment of pure loveliness. The leaves were turning crimson and gold.

Louisa felt overwhelmed by nature's beauty. She tried to put the charged experience into words in her journal. "The moss was like velvet . . . I sang for joy, my heart was so bright and the world so beautiful." She felt transported to something spiritually alive. "It seemed like going through a dark life or grave into heaven beyond." For the first time, she wrote, "I *felt* God as I never did before, and I prayed in my heart that I might keep that happy sense of nearness all my life."

Despite joyful moments like these, the old struggle for financial stability invariably returned. Abby considered opening her own small school at Hillside. They needed the income. She brought in another boarder to help with expenses, the teacher and naturalist Sophia Ford.

The ever-growing group of Concord friends had the rowdy adventures that suited Louisa best. They waded across "a great big pond a mile long and half a mile wide . . . splashing along making the fishes run like mad." Then they came home soaked to the skin, "bawling and singing like crazy folks."

Louisa developed a schoolgirl's crush on a local boy named Augustus, who took her rowing in the golden days of summer and early fall. He invited her to go berry picking. Louisa accepted. Before they could have their first official date, the young man took ill and died. It was a season of false starts.

Bronson Alcott's eccentric reputation kept students

away from Abby's proposed school. The neighbors had felt alarm when the Alcotts moved back into staid Concord. They'd heard about Fruitlands and its peculiar goings-on. "We are dreadful wild people here in Concord," Louisa admitted to a friend. Since there was no longer any school to attend at home, the Alcott girls went to school with their friends. Anna was still the docile, well-behaved sister, Louisa the merry prankster. Though they no longer quarreled, Louisa was irritated by Anna's hammering away on her music at home, and Anna frequently "shocked" by her sister's "daring speech or deed." Fifteen-year-old Anna obeyed the rules. At age thirteen, Louisa was not above "borrowing" local horses and sleighs for joyrides.

Louisa was not the only rule breaker at Hillside. Abby shocked her neighbors by allowing her daughters to play card games of whist—a pastime frowned on by the local adults. Abby thought cards preferable to the popular "kissing games" at other parties. She need not have worried, for Louisa kept a sharp eye out for romantic trouble. When one local boy attempted to kiss the lovely Anna, Louisa "stormed about it." She made up mocking nicknames for the boy and never let him forget his impertinence.

Louisa played the protective part traditionally assigned to fathers and older brothers. She also began acting the male parts in the melodramas she wrote. Among other male roles, she played "Louis," a masculine version of Louisa, who protects his sister from her husband's neglect and cruelty.

Anna, a gifted young actress, admired Louisa for her bravery and creativity and despite their differences declared she was "so interesting and funny that other girls seem commonplace." Anna predicted, "She'll write something great one of these days." Not only did Louisa write the plays; she directed and produced them, played all the leading male roles, crafted props, designed sets, and sewed and embroidered elaborate costumes, including villain Roderigo's boots, cobbled from scraps of old golden-brown leather. Those russet-colored boots were nearly as popular as the play.

While Lizzie and May took on small parts as needed, Louisa and Anna played the leads, acting four or five parts each. This resulted in some unexpected and unlikely stage appearances and disappearances. The shaky theatrical illusion was enhanced by handcrafted costumes consisting, for instance, of "a velvet robe, a plumed hat adorned with silver, long yellow boots . . . and tinsel ornaments." These homegrown theatricals continued till the Alcott girls were well into their twenties, living next door in Orchard House. Abby joined in their games and concerns, and she tried to provide the local young folks with "quiet rational amusements that . . . would draw the young men away from bad places."

Not long after the Alcotts' move to Hillside, a penniless Charles Lane showed up on his way back home to England. Abby took pity on him, noting that he was "quiet and gentle, seeming saddened by something. The reunion between him and Mr. Alcott was quite affecting." Even Emerson took a softer view of his former adversary. Hard-hearted Louisa stayed firm. She distrusted Lane and his ilk and wrote in her diary, "I wish we could be together, and no one else."

Louisa's "moods" became ever more troubling. She turned to her mother for solace, confidence, and under-standing. This closeness between Abby and Louisa increased with time. Even when Louisa was ten years old, her mother noted, "You and I have always liked to be grouped together."

Their stormy natures matched—both women were pas-sionate, generous to a fault, loyal, and impatient. Bronson called them "two devils, as yet, I am not quite divine enough to vanquish." The unvanquished Abby assured Louisa, "Believe me, you are capable of ranking among the best." Abby gently encouraged Louisa to write, while Bronson, surprisingly, required it—one evening making Louisa eat dinner alone because she had neglected to write in her journal.

In the spring of 1846, Louisa's long-held wish came true. She finally got her own room, a luxury she'd talked about for years. Bronson did the carpentry; Abby dec-orated. Louisa's was a small bedroom leading out to the woods behind the house. "It does me good to be alone," she exulted, "and Mother has made it very pretty and neat for me. My work-basket and desk are by the window and my closet is full of dried herbs that smell very nice." When needing escape, she could "run off to the woods"—a trick that the reclusive author Nathaniel Hawthorne would adopt when he took up residence.

Like the fictional Jo March, Louisa was famous for her jokes and tricks, her use of slang, and rowdy, tomboyish manners. She was the "jolly one" among her friends. But she had a serious, philosophical side, too, which she confided in her journal: "I have made a plan for my life, as I am in my teens, and no more a child. I am old for my age, and don't care much for girls' things. People think I'm wild and queer; but Mother understands and helps me." For her birthday that year, Abby gave Louisa a fountain pen with this note: "Dearest, accept from your Mother this pen and for her sake as well as your own use it freely and worthily."

In her teens, Louisa entered what she called her "silly" phase. She indulged in a series of hopeless crushes, almost all on older men. "My romantic period began," she later wrote, "when I fell to writing poetry, keeping a heart-journal, and wandering by moonlight instead of sleeping quietly." Thoreau, her childhood chum, took on the aspects of a romantic hero, with his broad shoulders, brown beard, and easygoing ways. Trousers tucked into his boots, he cut a dashing figure.

Louisa also pined over the Great Friend, Ralph Waldo Emerson. He was an impressive man—larger than life, generous yet distant. Years after his death, Louisa wrote, "Pity he could not get a little nearer to people & love them more & let them love him. Like Hawthorne he seems like a beautiful soul in prison trying to reach his fellow beings through the bars, & sad because he cannot."

Young Louisa wrote him love letters, which she "wisely" never sent, and left bouquets of wild flowers secretly on his doorstep. She stalked his house, which was just down the road, hoping to catch a glimpse of him. One night she serenaded him with German love songs, in a voice too low to be heard. The hooting of an owl startled and chased her away.

Bronson had never fully recovered from the collapse of the Fruitlands dream. The failure haunted him; he had lost some of the elasticity of his youth. "I am looked upon with distrust," he wrote in his journal. "How am I to work?" He portrayed himself in Christ-like terms. "How long, O Lord! How long wilt thou try me?"

He felt unwelcome at planning meetings held by the Concord Teachers' Institute, led by the famous educator Horace Mann, Elizabeth Peabody's brother-in-law. No one showed any interest in employing Bronson as a school-teacher. When Emerson hired someone to school his own children, he chose the teenage Louisa rather than her father. She ran a summer school for a few local children in the Hillside barn, Emerson's daughter Ellen among her pupils.

But teaching did not suit impatient Louisa. She wanted

to make her mark on the world. In *Little Women*, Jo vows "to do something very splendid." Louisa made a similar promise: "I will write a good book, be famous, go abroad, and have plenty of money!"

Like a character in a fairy tale, she had neglected to wish for health and time to enjoy these lofty accomplishments—but she would make many of her youthful dreams come true. Louisa wanted security for her father, "a sunny corner" for her mother, opportunities for Anna and Lizzie, and a good education for the gifted May. "One of the most interesting tales in the world is the record of how resolutely Louisa kept that promise," notes biographer Cornelia Meigs, "and how, no matter what things were against her, she always refused to be beaten."

Louisa's conviction that it was her duty to rescue the family came to her early and stayed till the end. To achieve that rescue she had to do something splendid—be as famous as the great opera singer Jenny Lind; become a great writer or perhaps even an actress, despite the associated scandal. In Louisa's day, acting was considered one step above prostitution. If you were an actor, in some towns you could not be buried with "decent people" in a church graveyard. But as Louisa later declared, "I am not afraid of storms, for I am learning how to sail my ship."

Despite their poverty, the sisters never considered working in mills or factories. "Such work was not for the Alcott girls," writes Susan Cheever. "They might starve, but they would starve as gentlewomen and intellectuals." The girls ate Spartan meals and grew thin again in Concord, despite Emerson's patronage. The family subsisted again on hand-me-downs and handouts. Abby cut back on personal pleasures—she would not spend so much as a dollar on a carriage ride and purchased only absolutely necessary clothing, relying on her May relatives to supply the rest. Unfortunately, they often donated bits of finery too impractical to wear.

The family's diet barely kept them alive. Louisa was skinny, brown-skinned from her time out of doors, long-limbed, growing taller each month, but she rarely got enough to eat.

Louisa resolved again and again to "be good." At age thirteen she wrote in her journal, "I have not told any one about my plan; but I'm going to *be* good. I've made so many resolutions, and written sad notes, and cried over my sins, and it doesn't seem to do any good! Now I'm going to *work really*, for I feel a true desire to improve, and be a help and comfort, not a care and sorrow, to my dear mother." The girls were constantly reminded to always put others above themselves. More than any other Alcott, she took that lesson to heart. In his old age, Bronson composed a poem for Louisa, naming her "Duty's faithful child."

Abby was Louisa's great supporter, cheerleader, and champion, Bronson her most astute critic. "In looking over our journals, Father says, 'Anna's is about other people,

Louisa's about herself.' That is true, for I don't talk about myself; yet must always think of the willful, moody girl I try to manage." Small surprise that her first published novel would be titled *Moods*.

A neighbor in Concord described Louisa as possessing "a strange combination of kindness, shyness, and daring." She was a study in contrasts: "loving and spiteful, full of energy and perseverance, full of fun, with a keen sense of the ludicrous, apt speech and ready wit; a subject of moods." She loved jokes and was always the first to poke fun at herself.

Family expectations held her in check, insofar as it was possible to restrain her high spirits and low moods. Lofty adults surrounded her, setting impossible standards. Years later she commented, "To have had Mr. Emerson for an intellectual god all one's life is to be invested with a chain armor of propriety. . . . And what would my own good father think of me . . . if I set folks to doing the things I have a longing to see my people do?"

Sometimes, despite her jokes and tricks, she fell prey to depression—one of her earliest poems is titled "Despondency." A worried Abby confided to her brother that Louisa suffered "at times the greatest volatility and wretchedness of spirit . . . no hope, no heart for anything."

A childhood friend, Lydia Hosmer Wood, wrote that "Louisa and May were the unruly ones; Anna and Lizzie were by nature more quiet and subdued." Anna attracted the notice of admiring young men while Louisa stood at the gate to scare them off. One cannot imagine the ethereal Bronson stepping in to involve himself in his daughters' love lives. Lydia Hosmer Wood recorded that "the atmosphere of their house was almost sanctified"—which sounds pleasant for visitors, harder on the inmates. The Alcotts' methods were gentle for the times—but no less compelling for the absence of force.

Wood remembered that Bronson shamed his children for their transgressions rather than punishing bad behavior. It was consistent with his earlier tactics at the Temple School. When disappointed in one of his girls, Mr. Alcott would "serve a meal, and then, without eating anything himself, he would rise and leave the table." The child who had "caused her father sufficient unhappiness to make him lose his appetite would lose hers too, and until a reconciliation could be effected felt thoroughly ashamed and disgraced."

There was also the Alcott tradition of a family Bonbox—a new form of the family post office. If any of the girls had been "bon," good all day, "and hadn't disregarded a single rule of conduct," she could drop her name into the box with three marks after the name. Even friends asked to take part and work for the "distinction" of having their names in the Bon-box.

The Hillside barn, "scene of her first dramatic triumph," was where Louisa started her salaried life, thanks to Emerson. His daughter Ellen, only a few years younger than Louisa, adored her young teacher and spent as much time at Hillside as Louisa did at Emerson's house. Louisa composed fanciful stories for her student that later formed her very first book, *Flower Fables*. Emerson read the early stories and said prophetically, "She is, and is to be, the poet of children. She knows their angels."

Louisa was a popular teacher but was "too restless and impetuous" to spend her days indoors. She had never loved school as pupil. She was no fonder of it as teacher. Though teaching offered a way out of poverty, she could not embrace it as a career.

Abby suggested Louisa might prefer decorating small boxes and other knickknacks to be sold in "the fancy stores." It's unclear whether she really believed her restless daughter would enjoy that kind of fussy work, or wanted to make Louisa grateful for her teaching—or if she simply felt driven to desperate measures to keep Louisa employed.

The Alcotts now lived at the brink of disaster. Bronson had nearly given up trying to make money. "I submit to the decree of fate," he wrote. "They also serve who only stand and wait." Louisa's small school brought her neither fame nor fortune. Had she been the once-longed-for son, her prospects would have been greater—a thought that drove her to distraction.

If Louisa's teaching brought in too little income, Bronson's occasional lectures provided even less. He was hired to build a summerhouse for Emerson. What he then created was either a masterpiece or a monstrosity, depending on whom you asked. Bronson called the structure "sylvan," but amused friends and neighbors called it "a whirligig" or "Tumbledown Hall." Emerson worried that it would collapse, while Mrs. Emerson teasingly called it "the Ruin." Even Thoreau wondered if Alcott had ever even heard of geometry, "the relation of straight lines to curves." In any event, no further carpentry work came Bronson's way.

Abby left no stone unturned in looking for ways to survive. She and the girls took in sewing—the last resort of the genteel poor—but even this tedious labor failed to support them. The family's credit in Concord was running out. In desperation Abby took on another boarder, a girl Louisa's age "in a state of sad mental imbecility."

Finally, Abby's aunt Hannah Robie stepped in again. She galvanized her Boston family and friends to fund a job for her destitute niece. The Mays began plotting how to sponsor Abby in a respectable occupation. If her husband refused to work for a living, at least his desperate wife could.

After discarding several unlikely ideas, the family settled on one that made sense. Abby would be paid for the charity work she had long been doing voluntarily: visiting the poor and the sick. Her Boston relations called her a paid "missionary to the poor." Abby chose the more democratic title

"Sister." It was an early version of social work. But there was a price to pay for their upturn in fortune. Abby's charity work must be done in Boston, close to her relations.

The senior Alcotts made their decision without consulting their girls. What followed was a rushed move to a cramped house in the dingy South End of Boston. The family's peaceful years in Concord came abruptly to an end. The Alcotts made the moving arrangements while Louisa was away visiting friends for her birthday. The family held an anxious last-minute council, but the outcome was already clear. There was no use arguing. Much like her mother, Louisa preferred action to discussion anyway.

The fifteen-year-old "took a brisk run over the hill" to her favorite thinking place—in the well of an abandoned wagon wheel. There she sat wrapped in a red shawl against November's chill. She made a vow to the empty field: "I *will* do something by-and-by. Don't care what, teach, sew, act, write, anything to help the family; and I'll be rich and famous and happy before I die, see if I won't!"

CHAPTER EIGHT

Heaven's So Far Away

The girls had treasured their life in Concord, but Abby called the town "a cold, heartless, Brainless, soulless place." Always for Abby, the *next* thing sparkled with promise. Now it was Boston. Even Bronson allowed himself to dream of renewal: "Possibly a school may grow up—a reading room, a church, a Journal, a press, a Club."

The reality proved less than the dream—especially for the girls, who'd had other hopes for life in the big city. Their South End neighborhood was crowded and dirty, caught in a tale of two cities. If Louisa walked a few blocks in one direction, she arrived at the stately homes of her May relatives. But a few steps opposite led to poverty and squalor.

Either way, she felt trapped. She missed the open countryside, her friends, and most of all her freedom to roam, to think, and to write. The luxury of her own room had vanished. The Alcotts crammed a family of six into four sunless rooms, and Louisa's job was keeping house alone—work for which she was singularly ill-suited.

"I . . . [felt] like a caged seagull as I washed dishes and cooked in the basement kitchen, where my prospect was limited to a procession of muddy boots," she wrote. In close quarters, with nothing stimulating or promising in view, Louisa stopped thinking and dreaming.

"I don't get on at all," she noted sadly. She tried not to complain but confided to her journal, "The bustle and dirt and change send all lovely images and restful feelings away. Among my hills and woods, I had fine free times alone . . . they helped to keep me happy and good. . . . But heaven's so far away in the city, and I so heavy I can't fly up."

Abby wrote Louisa a poem, urging her toward "Duty's clear but tedious way." It was not an easy path for a lively teenage girl. Bronson would similarly honor—or corner—her in his poem where he named her "Duty's faithful child." Both parents' expectations were as "clear but tedious" as duty itself.

Each morning, Louisa kept house while the family went their separate ways, to work and school. This fracturing was one of many prices paid in the move. Abby, now the financial mainstay of the household, worked to the brink of exhaustion. She tramped all over the city till her head and feet ached, ministering to the needy, begging her sponsors to give her the necessary resources to help those she had promised to serve.

"They suffer, I know they suffer," Abby wrote of her clients. Her wealthy benefactors allotted her only thirty dollars a month—enough to keep them all in poverty. Bronson held his Conversations in Boston, but the meager earnings had become at best a side act to the family's survival. Lizzie and May attended school while Anna labored unhappily as a governess in nearby Roxbury.

Louisa settled into a dreary round of chores. It was a sad time, with few friends nearby and even fewer visitors. Before and after work, Abby depended on Louisa's sympathetic ear, convincing herself that Louisa in turn relied on her mother: "She must have retirement, agreeable occupation, and protective, provident care about her. . . . Nothing can exceed the strength of her attachments, particularly for her mother."

Abby's letters to her eldest daughter, Anna, during this period are full of gentle maternal advice. Her notes to Louisa reveal more. She wrote, "What is time doing to us? Oh my daughter . . . shall we only lament its loss?" Louisa began to know what she later described as "something of the pathetic side of life with its hard facts, irksome duties, many temptations and daily sacrifice of self."

Old-fashioned Boston was no longer the city of

Louisa's toddlerhood. In her infancy, 95 percent of Boston's population had been native-born. Now, immigrants made up half the population, many of them Irish and desperately poor. Times were hard, divisions between classes more extreme. The rich had grown richer, but the poor became destitute, living in squalid shanties down by Boston's wharf. Only the very rich had indoor plumbing. The Alcotts made do with chamber pots and outdoor toilets.

Abby understood poverty only too well. Her views on social justice and economic equality were advanced for her time—they would be considered radical even today.

In her "Reports While Visitor to the Poor of Boston," she wrote, "Never until society looks upon poverty as an incident of man's condition, not as a crime of his nature, shall we see any permanent or beautiful results." The poor didn't need just handouts—they needed skills and equal opportunities. To do right by them was not charity, but justice. "Do the poor justice, and no alms giving would be required." Her monthly reports shocked her well-meaning relations but did not inspire any increased financial backing.

In letters to her brother Sam, Abby was even more outspoken. "Our charitable societies are too complex, the poor are freezing and starving, while wrapped in our sables and picnicking on tea and toast we discuss resolutions." Abby lived these contradictions day after day. And her fiercest daughter took the lessons to heart. Louisa, more than any of her sisters, was outraged by the gulf between rich and poor.

Boston provided more torments for the Alcott girls than pleasures. Window-shopping was a painful exercise—costly things displayed were as far out of reach as planets and stars. Louisa wrote, "We found ourselves in a small house at the South End with not a tree in sight . . . and no money to buy any of the splendors before us." The city held temptations they'd never had to resist in Concord. Louisa compared her ragged hand-me-downs to the luxury around her.

Her wealthy relatives had extras of everything. The Alcotts, never enough of anything. "My moodiness makes it hard to be cheerful when I think how poor we are, how much worry it is to live, and how many things I long to do I never can."

She and Anna toyed with the notion of going onstage, which seemed a quick and painless way out of their dismal situation. "We could make plenty of money perhaps," Louisa wrote hopefully, "and it is a very gay life." It also would have cut off all connection to the proper May relations. Only a successful, wealthy actor could hope for any kind of acceptance in "good" society.

Walking through the city, Louisa fought against vanity, remembering her father's old alphabet lessons about "the egoist, I." When she looked at her own window reflection, she noted, "I try to keep down vanity about my long hair, my well-shaped head, and my good nose. In the street I try not to covet fine things. My quick tongue is always getting me into trouble."

Louisa never saw a photograph of herself that pleased her. She considered herself plain, but Edward Emerson, for one, found her beautiful. "Louisa was fine looking, had the most regular features of the family." Her hair was long, thick, and wavy like her mother's, a rich, glossy brown. She was tall and shapely. But womanhood also suggested servitude, and Louisa rejected both—as did her character Jo. "Round shoulders had Jo, big hands and feet, a fly-away look to her clothes, and the uncomfortable appearance of a girl who was rapidly shooting up into a woman, and didn't like it."

Louisa, like Jo, hid her beauty behind two masks: comedy and masculinity. "She had always a rather masculine air, and a twinkle woke constantly in her eye at the comic side of things." Nevertheless, according to friends and neighbors, she attracted the attention of a handful of suitors—whom she lightly and humorously dismissed. Few encounters even made it into her surviving journals, letters, or reminiscences.

In June 1849, the teenaged Louisa shipped off to vacation in Leicester, Massachusetts, with some wealthy cousins and her youngest sister, May. Golden-haired May Alcott knew how to charm. Her manners were naturally graceful and easy. She got along beautifully with her relatives, while Louisa blundered ahead—a real-life Jo, who "upset an inkstand, broken both boot-lacings and sat down upon her hat."

Her visits to wealthy Boston relations only added to her misery. These were command performances. They summoned; Louisa obeyed. She was expected to perform favors graciously while effusively thanking her benefactors. Abby had felt like an outsider as a girl; Louisa was *made* to feel like one. The "poor relation" among her mother's rich relatives, she was alternately snubbed and patronized. Between household drudgery and uncomfortable social occasions, Louisa read books for escape—and began to work in earnest at her own writing.

She completed a first novel titled *The Inheritance*, modeled on popular romances of the time. It features a poor but virtuous orphan named Edith Adelon who is (of course) rewarded for her courage and talent by winning the heart of Lord Percy. She gains a "stately home" in the bargain.

Cooking, cleaning, and scrubbing in her dim South End apartment, the seventeen-year-old Louisa concocted a hybrid "half castle, and half mansion" with arches, balconies, and stone towers rising "here and there" like weeds. Despite the odd architecture, gaping holes in the plot, and an unbearably saintly heroine, Alcott created vivid characters in *The Inheritance*. The most complex of these is the resentful spinster Ida. There is more than a touch of Louisa to Ida's sharp edge. "There should always be one old maid in a family," the author commented tartly. She generally included at least one old maid in each of her books.

The writing in *The Inheritance* is crisp and lively—the work of a real writer. She used all the old literary chestnuts—hidden identities, long-kept secrets, and unsurprising plot "surprises." Louisa never tried to publish *The Inheritance*—but she was addicted to romance novels like it. She wrote nearly as much gothic and romantic "rubbish" as stories for young readers—and she kept writing them longer than she let her readership know, working under one pseudonym after another. The two styles mirrored her two sides: moody and cheerful, pessimistic and hopeful, wild and domestic.

Louisa's reading taste ran toward the dramatic and the melodramatic. "I fancy 'lurid' things, if true and strong also." She admired the work of her future neighbor, Nathaniel Hawthorne, his dark novel *The Scarlet Letter* in particular. She relished adventures, danger, narrow escapes, mystery. Such reading was a welcome outlet for a young woman subjected to "the cold neglect, the crude inferences, the silent reproach of those who profess to love us," as Abby wrote.

Abby Alcott, too, was suffering in Boston. Nonetheless she pushed on—distributing food and clothing to the poor, dispensing sensible advice on health and family hygiene.

She begged, scolded, and harangued her wealthy patrons till she had another fifty dollars per month to establish a homeless shelter, a "relief room" for those with no place else to go.

Those she came in contact with were desperate; many had turned to petty crime, drugs, or alcohol. More than once, Abby housed young prostitutes no older than Louisa, despite the horrified disapproval of her relatives. If Louisa felt uneasy around these houseguests, she held her tongue. "I can't talk to anyone but Mother about my troubles, and she has so many to bear now I try not to add any more."

Occasionally, Louisa attended plays and parties with wealthy relatives, wearing their hand-me-down clothes. Just as often, she spent evenings volunteering—teaching destitute immigrants and Black women how to read and do simple sums. The work sharpened her hunger for justice and prepared her to become a lifelong philanthropist. She would always reserve the bulk of her charity for children, struggling mothers, and penniless young women.

After eighteen months of laboring in the poorest sections of Boston, Abby had exhausted her reserves of strength. She'd never learned the art of diplomacy, much less flattery. Instead, she scolded her own supporters. The poor needed more than charity baskets, she argued—they needed skills, jobs, and decent wages. Her time as a "sister of charity" ended on a sour note. As her final thank-you,

Abby delivered one last angry report to a handful of bewildered Ladies of the South End Friendly Society.

Louisa sympathized with her mother's tribulations. And she couldn't help tracing many of her mother's hardships back to her father. She wrote in her journal, "What a hard life she has had since she married,—so full of wandering and all sorts of worry!"

With Abby out of work, the Alcott family closed ranks against the world, as they always did in times of crisis. Lizzie dropped out of school and took up the housekeeping, to Louisa's relief. May showed a talent for art that the family believed might lead to something that could support her. Anna was the main source of income, from her little school on Canton Street. Louisa came along to assist, though she disliked the teaching as much as ever. She was feeling old, worn-out before her time. "School is hard work," she admitted. "I get very little time to write or think, for my working days have begun."

Louisa feared she might be stuck forever with uncongenial, unfulfilling work. She took stock of her limited options and began haunting local theaters looking for an entry into dramatic life. She took on even more sewing jobs, working pillowcases and sheets, handkerchiefs and neckties late into the night. It was hard and unrewarding labor, but she preferred it to teaching. "Sewing won't make my fortune; but I can plan my stories while I work," she explained.

Louisa celebrated one small but wondrous success that

year. Her old friend Frederick Llewellyn Willis had come again to board with the family while attending Harvard University. He and Louisa rekindled their old closeness. They shared a love of ideas and books, as well as a penchant for fun and adventure. Louisa had shown Frederick a few of her literary efforts—including a poem, "Sunlight." He admired it enough to submit it to *Peterson's*, a new women's magazine. He kept the submission secret from Louisa, to spare her disappointment. She was amazed when *Peterson's* accepted the poem and paid her the glorious sum of five dollars—her first earnings as a writer. It was half what she made that year by sewing, only a tenth of her teaching income—but it was a start. She published under the flowery pseudonym Flora Fairfield—the first but not last time she would invent a nom de plume. The money and encouragement, however, were very real.

Anna taught twenty students at her school, earning barely enough to keep the family afloat. Abby's generous brother Sam made donations whenever possible to what Louisa tartly called "the Alcott Sinking Fund." But even Sam no longer risked giving cash to the Alcotts. They were as likely to spend it on some new scheme, or to give it away. Sam set up an account at a local grocery store, donating thirty dollars a month to keep the Alcotts fed. Louisa described their life succinctly: "Poor as poverty but bound to make things go."

The family spent time that summer of 1851 at the

home of one of Abby's patrons, a Mrs. Savage, who had left her house on Boston Common empty for the season. Louisa began an Alcott newspaper she called the *Olive Leaf*, taking a page from Charles Dickens's famous *Pickwick Papers*. That Alcott family newsletter is a model for the March family's *Pickwick Portfolio*. Its first real-life issue contained an ode to cats, a botanical essay by Lizzie, a serial by Louisa, and a family "report card": "Annie, bad; Louisa, bad; Elizabeth, bad; Abby [May], bad." At least they were all evenly matched!

They had just settled in at the mansion when, one after another, each member of the family took ill. Louisa called it "the small-pox summer." Abby claimed she had no idea how the Alcotts had been exposed, but Louisa wrote that they'd all caught the disease from "some poor immigrants whom mother took into our garden and fed one day."

Years later Abby would blame herself. "I dare not dwell on the fever which I conveyed to my home." At the time, however, she insisted that her girls had been touched only "lightly." Bronson came down with a full-fledged case of smallpox. The family isolated itself and turned to their preferred homeopathic remedies instead of traditional medicine. As if she had an inkling of future sorrows, Louisa called it "a curious time of exile, danger and trouble."

For Bronson, that summer in Boston was darker still. Bronson's spirits leaped and dropped at a terrifying rate. He felt isolated in the big city, leading "a solitary life, passing an evening occasionally with Mr. Emerson and a circle of young people." Bronson felt "scoffed at" by the world. His hair had gone prematurely gray; his thin shoulders were now permanently stooped. His dreaminess escalated to a point of near madness. Bronson suffered from hallucinations that summer and fall, tormented by his "demons" to the point that he considered suicide. (Three years later his gentle brother, Junius, would in fact descend into madness and kill himself.)

Bronson's frightening behavior was not confined to the family. He showed up unannounced at a friend's doorstep one day, declaring "I am God. I am greater than God. God is one of my ideas." He ate poorly, slept poorly, and spoke incomprehensibly—all symptoms of mania. His journal from this time contains lines from a poem he wrote: "Possessed, insane / Tormenting demons drove him from the gate." The details of his struggles in Boston were later deleted from all family records. Abby packed him off to Concord, where he could find solace with old friends like Emerson and Thoreau.

Louisa sent care packages of food and other comforts to her father, as if he'd gone off to summer camp rather than to a much-needed rest cure. To relatives in Boston, it looked as if Bronson had gone on a summer lark, abandoning his family. But Abby knew it was a crisis. In their long marriage, Abby and Bronson took turns alternately bearing the family's heavy burdens and collapsing. Soon it would be Abby's turn to break.

Bronson wrote about his wife's frail state of mind just a few months later: "Quite dejected, feeble, weeps from anxiety . . . cannot be comforted." She cast about for any way to keep the family from starvation. A few of her ideas were outlandish. She concocted a scheme for Louisa to learn to cast figurines and thus make her living as a sculptress. Abby thought of heading west to join the gold rush. Sam calmed her down and urged her instead to open her own small employment office in Boston. "Employment is needed," Abby responded enthusiastically, "but just compensation is more needed." She entered into this new venture with her usual high hopes.

"Any person paying the subscription of $1," a flyer read, "shall be furnished with a ticket, entitling her to a choice of help for six months from Mrs. Alcott's rooms." She ran an informal employment agency, paid for by subscription. Jobs available ranged from cook to parlor maid and dressmaker. The Alcotts moved from their borrowed summer mansion to a house on the edge of one of Boston's worst slums.

This brief chapter in Abby's work life is best known for its unintended effect on her daughter Louisa. The eighteen-year-old was at her mother's office when a tall, handsome thirty-five-year-old lawyer stopped by, looking to hire a companion for his sister. The man's name was James Richardson.

Richardson is fictionalized and villainized in one of Louisa May Alcott's best-known pieces, "How I Went Out to Service." The sketch based on her first job away from home is both hilarious and heartbreaking. It was also, according to friends and family, uncomfortably close to truth.

Louisa had been at loose ends and in need of employment. "The Pathetic Family," she noted, was "poor as rats & apparently quite forgotten by every one but the Lord." In "How I Went Out to Service," Louisa thinly disguises the real-life Richardson and turns him into smug Reverend Josephus: "He possessed an impressive nose, a fine flow of language, and a pair of large hands, encased in black kid gloves." Those "large hands" in "black kid gloves" are the stuff of which horror and gothic novels are made; Louisa uses her background in both literary genres to put a comic spin on the debacle.

The female narrator of the piece initially thinks of her employer as a godsend. Reverend Josephus takes advantage of her innocence. He paints a tempting picture of the offered employment, promising only light work and many advantages—among them access to fine music and to a large library. As one Alcott heroine reflects, "I'll put my pride in my pocket, and go out to service. Housework I like, and can do well. . . . I never thought it degradation to do it . . . so why should I mind doing it for others?" Josephus cleverly emphasizes all the comforts of home, leaving out its real-life problems. The trap is set. "When my mother turned to me, asking if I could suggest any one, I became red as a poppy and said abruptly: 'Only myself.'"

The promised mansion turns out to be a house in utter neglect, with only one livable room in it—the study of Reverend Josephus. This sanctuary is "full of the warm glow of firelight, the balmy breath of hyacinths and roses, the white glimmer of piano keys and tempting rows of books." The reverend tries to woo his young employee by prattling "all manner of philosophic, metaphysical, and sentimental rubbish." His attempts at seduction are repulsive. The heroine soon realizes that she has been hired not as the sister's but as her employer's romantic companion.

The minute she rejects the reverend's advances, he treats her like "a true Cinderella," and gives her the roughest work. Louisa encountered in real life the same courtship and then the same hard labor. "I . . . dug paths [in the snow], brought water from the well, split kindlings, made fires, and sifted ashes." After seven weeks she was sent home with four dollars' pay for two months of backbreaking labor. As an elderly servant reminds the heroine, "Some folks is liberal and some ain't."

In Louisa's "How I Went Out to Service," the narrator's outraged father returns the insulting four dollars. Louisa and her family could not afford that gesture of defiance.

Louisa made brilliant comedy out of those two months, but her friend Maria Porter said that years later Louisa couldn't speak about the episode without choking up. "This experience . . . at eighteen made so painful an impression upon her that she rarely referred to it, and when she did so it was with heightened color and tearful eyes." In Louisa's journal she noted tersely her time in Dedham, Massachusetts, "as a servant . . . starved & frozen . . . $4.00."

CHAPTER NINE

The Door Is Opened

Louisa returned home to a life of few options. She could be a teacher, a seamstress, or a governess—nothing else offered itself. Anna had tried her hand at being a governess a long way from home but was dismissed and sent home after a month for crying and being too homesick. Anna made the grand gesture that Louisa could not afford: she left her twelve dollars' salary behind in her employer's sewing basket.

Now, and for years to come, Louisa would teach and sweep floors, clean houses, dust, and sew—but always, now, she was also writing. She wrote as much as twelve or fourteen hours a day. The same year she went "out to service," she sold her story "The Masked Marriage"—for *ten* dollars! It was more than twice what she'd earned for seven weeks of hard labor in Dedham. That Christmas, her mother scraped up the money for a desk for Louisa, telling her husband, "She is a fine bright girl [who] only needs encouragement to be a brave woman." Abby observed that while Anna longed for order and elegance, "gentles and genteel surroundings," Lizzie and Louisa were made of "rather higher metal."

Louisa hated debt as much as had her maternal grandfather. She dreaded debt "more than the devil!" she declared. Her indebtedness to others was not merely financial. Wealthy relatives called on her to do favors and then treated her with contempt and pity. Unlike her gracious sister May, Louisa could neither refuse the favors nor do them with a smile. She "longed for a crust in a garret with freedom and a pen." At a low financial point, Louisa had one desperate plan in reserve—to sell her long, beautiful chestnut-brown hair.

She asked a barber what price her hair would fetch. He named an amount that seemed astronomical—but still she could not bring herself to do the deed. She would wait seven days, she promised herself, and then if nothing came through, she would sell her hair for the cash. On the seventh day a family friend stepped in at last to help. Louisa used the incident to great effect in one of the most stirring moments in *Little Women*. Jo did lose her fine head of hair, and Louisa didn't. But then—Jo surrendered her life as a single woman, and Louisa held fast to her independence.

In 1852, Nathaniel Hawthorne took a fancy to Hillside, the Alcotts' former home, which had been up for sale ever since the Alcotts had left Concord for Boston. Hawthorne's book *The Scarlet Letter* had made him a wealthy man. He paid $1,500 for the house and crowed over the "bargain" he'd struck with the desperate Alcotts: Hawthorne bragged, "Mr. Alcott . . . wasted a good deal of money in fitting it up to suit his own taste, all which improvements I get for little or nothing." The Hawthornes began their own renovations, including an immense three-story tower, housing Nathaniel's lofty third-floor study, which he called his "sky parlor."

Louisa had increased her writing income, though at a much slower rate than Mr. Hawthorne. "The Rival Painters: A Tale of Rome," written when she was sixteen, was published by the *Olive Branch*, a magazine she had long admired—even naming the Alcott family newsletter after it.

With the proceeds from the sale of Hillside, the Alcotts moved to a better part of Boston, on Beacon Hill. Abby scouted for boarders to help with household expenses. But money never lasted long among them. Christmas of 1852 would have been a dismal one if not for the charity of relatives. Louisa wrote to her cousin Charlotte: "Mother broke down entirely over your letter, and *we* like dutiful children followed her example for we felt somewhat forlorn and forgotten among the giving and receiving of presents going on all around us, and it was so cheering to find . . . someone had remembered the existence of the 'Pathetic Family.'"

Abby plodded along with her employment agency, a job she now found "full of responsibilities, and petty perplexities." All this hard work earned her "hardly . . . 5 c a day." Louisa looked on in dismay while her mother struggled to achieve the impossible. Still, Louisa acknowledged, "it paid," and her mother "always did what came to her in the way of duty or charity, and let pride, taste, and comfort suffer for love's sake."

The household adjusted itself around Abby's new job. Wrote Louisa, "Our poor little home had much love and happiness in it, and was a shelter for lost girls, abused wives, friendless children, and weak or wicked men." What the family lacked in resources they made up for in compassion. "Father and Mother had no money to give, but gave . . . time, sympathy, help,—and if blessings would make them rich, they would be millionaires." She added, "This is practical Christianity."

Louisa made a list of her favorite books, including Carlyle's *The French Revolution*, *Plutarch's Lives*, and Milton's *Paradise Lost*. As usual, she tried to live up to her parents' lofty ideals. She excluded from her list all the "trashy" melodramas she had been devouring in secret. The Alcotts would not have approved of those.

Louisa honed her writing skills through trial and error.

In many ways her single-minded ambition cut short her adolescence. She looked on wonderingly at Anna's flirtations and romances, much as Jo March watched Meg "drifting away from her into a world where she could not follow." While a blushing Anna rode the usual waves of social hopes and dreams, Louisa held to her goals. She created heart-throbbing gothic fantasies in fiction—courtships, betrayals, lunacy, and intrigues—but rejected real-life romance. There is no record of a courtship or romantic outing during her later teenage years, though a few such adventures must have happened.

Watching her mother "suffer for love's sake" surely strengthened Louisa's resolve to remain single and independent. She read voraciously, and though she promised herself to "read fewer novels, and those only of the best," it is doubtful that she kept her promise.

She recorded all of her literary earnings with pride, even while she dismissed her first paid story, "The Rival Painters," as "great rubbish." Rubbish, perhaps, but profitable. It provided a glimmer of hope that she might one day make her living by her pen rather than needle or broom. Encouraged by the publishers' checks, she continued to write her romantic and "lurid" tales in private.

Bronson Alcott's financial contribution to the household by this point was barely discernible. That burden had passed on to the women. Even with Abby, Anna, and Louisa working as hard as they could, the annual family income never rose above $700 total—low enough to "keep them all in poverty." That January, Anna left for New Hampshire to work as a mother's helper for a cousin. Louisa opened a small school in the new Beacon Hill house. The pupils loved her, Abby noted with satisfaction, but Louisa still resisted the long hours of sitting still indoors and worse still, the need to set an example in good behavior.

She aspired to do more and better—much better. After reading a biography of Charlotte Brontë, author of *Jane Eyre*, Louisa wrote glumly, "Wonder if I shall ever be famous enough for people to care to read my story." That summer she went "out to service" again, this time to her wealthy uncle's house, at a fixed rate of two dollars per week. She "needed the change," and was happy to do the wash, even if the work kept her below her relatives, physically and socially. Laundry was hot, hard, heavy work, but easy compared with her seven weeks laboring for James Richardson in Dedham while repelling his advances. Still, it was not a happy time in Louisa's life.

Of 1853 she wrote, "A hard year. Summer distasteful and lonely, winter tiresome with school and people I didn't like. I miss Anna, my one bosom friend and comforter." Her mother wrote in a letter, "Keep up dearest!" She understood that Louisa's spirits were low, but pretended to think otherwise. "I am pleased to hear you say that your mind is quite at ease, and you get happiness out of writing and reading letters." Her uncle's house in Boston might have provided social interaction—though given Louisa's role as chambermaid that seems unlikely—but Abby wisely urged her to rely on her own resources. "Get all the enjoyment you can from intercourse with others, but your best and most enduring, will be that of your own character."

Little or no help came from "others." The Mays and the Sewalls had given up trying to keep the Alcotts employed. They advised Abby instead to push her husband into salaried employment. Even brother Sam, the Alcotts' long-suffering supporter, wrote, "It does seem to me, as well as to everybody else, that he might find something to do, for which he would receive something toward the support of his family."

Finally, even the oblivious Bronson felt the pressure. Debt, he declared, was ruining his family's peace and harmony. He proposed returning to Concord and taking up farming again. He considered other options: working with his brother, Junius, at a mill in New York, heading out west to California, even returning to his childhood home at Spindle Hill, Connecticut, to care for his "aged mother." He was ready, in fact, to do almost anything other than the obvious—stay with his family and get a job. Salaried work was still to him "that slavery by which an estate is accumulated." Instead he forged on with his unsuccessful Conversations, offering his services as speaker in Boston and elsewhere in New England.

During this time, Bronson became vulnerable to flirtations. While lecturing, he often caught the eye of a female admirer. Ednah Dow Littlehale, a beautiful and wealthy young woman, became a regular attendee at his lectures. Bronson seems to have fallen in love with Ednah, and she—to some degree—returned his affection. It would not be the last time Bronson was smitten by a young admirer. But Ednah Dow Littlehale was the first, and he fell for her hardest. Bronson wrote rapturously about Ednah in his private journals—under the initial *E*. He composed love poems for her. They went on walks together, took romantic picnics, climbed mountains, and gathered flowers.

It's unclear whether things ever went further than that. We don't know if Abby or the girls knew just how much the two spent together—but Louisa apparently had her suspicions. A friend described how Louisa once sat silently staring at Ednah, her dark eyes fixed on the other woman's face.

Likely the romance was mostly one-sided. But it was a love affair from Bronson's point of view—and he clung to Ednah's memory. He wrote longingly about her for many years afterward, even after she'd married the artist Seth Cheney. By a strange twist of fate, Cheney created one of the few likenesses done of Bronson Alcott. And Ednah

Dow Cheney became Louisa May Alcott's first serious biographer.

Bronson's love life was not creating the only turmoil at home. At the age of thirty-two, his unstable but gentle young brother, Junius, threw himself into the wheel of the mill where he worked, dying instantly. Junius had bidden goodbye to his mother that morning, telling her only that he was "going away." Bronson worried that his brother's depression might be genetic. Insanity, he feared, was in "the blood." He set out to prove himself wrong. He began to elaborate on his old theories of "angelic" and "demonic" races. He maintained light-haired, blue-eyed people—like himself—were angelic beings, while dark-haired, dark-eyed people—like his wife, Abby, and daughter Louisa—could never entirely be trusted.

Emerson provided the usual ballast to the troubled "man up in a balloon." Fresh from speaking tours abroad, he reestablished his friendship with Bronson and resumed his patronage. He was touched by Bronson's steadfast loyalty to transcendentalist beliefs. "He has no obligation to old or new, but is as free as a newborn," declared Emerson

He organized a speaking tour for Bronson, "along the great Canal towns, west, Syracuse, Rochester, Buffalo, perhaps Cleveland." Bronson was enchanted—and once again became the Hoper. "The West is a new field for me," he enthused in his journal, "and Autumn an auspicious season." Louisa's mood lifted too, perhaps cheered by her father's new prospects. She wrote in her journal, "Slowly coming out of the Slough of Despond."

On October 30, 1853, just a month shy of his fifty-fifth and Louisa's twenty-first birthday, Bronson headed west by train on his speaking tour. Emerson had provided him with the train fare and a new suit costing twenty-eight dollars.

Bronson carried along a prospectus of his Conversations. The former peddler of mugs and buttons had become a peddler of words. Bronson visited all the cities outlined in advance by Emerson, pushing as far west as Cincinnati, Ohio. Audiences in city after city welcomed him. He sent home a bank draft for $150—an immense sum for the usually insolvent Bronson. The family rejoiced at the change. Bronson bragged that he was at last providing "that sum of solid support for all and sundry inmates" of his household.

The world around the Alcotts was also changing, especially on the national and political front. The split over American slavery intensified. North and South edged closer toward civil war. All the Alcotts were passionate abolitionists and suffragists, supporting two of the most ferociously debated issues of their times. Massachusetts women petitioned their legislature for female suffrage, "that their votes shall be counted as of equal value and potency with those of men," and Abby Alcott led the fight. The Massachusetts legislature turned them down flat—but years later, Louisa proudly wrote, "Was the first woman to register my name as a voter."

While Bronson was away on his speaking tour, sister Lizzie suffered some sort of collapse. It may have been a teenage heartbreak—Louisa noted in her journal that her beloved "Betty" had "had a little romance with C." No one knows who "C" was. But most likely the problem had a physical basis as well. During this time, Lizzie suffered from fits of catatonia, when she would become "immoveable—almost senseless." Abby added, "There is a great struggle going on in her mind about something."

This quiet third daughter, Elizabeth, is the least-known real-life sister among the Alcott daughters. She is widely recognized as the gentle Beth in *Little Women*. Only a single image of her survives, in a photograph taken when she was in her late teens. She has a round face, dark hair, and a mysterious *Mona Lisa* smile. Lizzie's mental collapse may have also been the warning shot before her physical illness fully revealed itself. It wasn't the only time the Alcott family misread each other's urgent cues.

If Lizzie experienced some "little romance," the older Alcott girls had their romantic adventures as well—Anna certainly, Louisa debatably. The usually levelheaded Anna fell easy prey to heartbreaks. Abby wrote to Bronson, "I think she feels better about the heart pang. . . . It was severe while it lasted—but the inevitable soon quiets inflammation."

Both Louisa's future neighbor Julian Hawthorne and sister Anna surmised that Louisa had her heart pangs as well. If she ever had these heartfelt romantic encounters, she censored them all after she became famous enough to be scrutinized. Louisa ruthlessly censored her private material—diaries, letters, other people's accounts. At her direction, every member of the family deleted sections from their diaries and letters, editing the past, destroying passages. Anna only later in life revealed that Louisa may have had had "various adorers" in "her youthful days."

Louisa had more urgent concerns, pressing family needs, and demands. Bronson's tour in the Midwest rekindled interest in transcendentalism but did little to restore the family fortunes. In the end, Bronson spent more than he earned on his speaking tour, counting on opportunities that dissolved into thin air. "I think Anna and Lizzie are a good deal oppressed," Abby wrote to Bronson, pointing out the chronic poverty and the uncertainty of their future.

Louisa rushed in to meet all challenges head-on. Abby praised her second daughter's resilience. "Louisa feels stronger and braver—to meet or to bear whatever destiny may have in store for us." At twenty-one, her health was sturdy, her outlook more optimistic. Louisa threw a "masquerade ball . . . in fancy costume" on little or no funds. Abby bragged, "You can predict its brilliancy and success."

Louisa still played the clown in public, the philosopher in private. She wrote in her journal, "I began to see the strong contrasts and the fun and follies in every day life about this time."

Louisa records her father's homecoming from his long tour out west the winter of 1854. Everyone in the family flew downstairs to greet "the half-frozen wanderer." Bronson was "hungry, tired, cold, and disappointed, but smiling bravely and as serene as ever." Only bold May, the baby of the family, was brave enough to ask, "Well, did people pay you?" According to Louisa's journal entry, "With a queer look, he opened his pocket-book and showed one single dollar, saying with a smile that made our eyes fill, 'Only that!'" "His overcoat had been stolen," writes Harriet Reisen, his travel expenses high, and "promises of large audiences or generous payment were not kept." Bronson had been gone longer than Louisa's seven weeks of servitude, and had managed to bring home even less than four dollars.

"Another year, I shall do better," Bronson murmured. There was a stunned silence. Then Abby kissed him, saying, "I call that doing *very well*." Louisa later described the scene in her journal, calling it "lesson in love . . . half tragic, and comic"—the essence of her own genius.

Louisa earned five dollars that fall—five times her father's profit—from the sale of a new story, "The Rival Prima Donnas." Published under her pseudonym Flora Fairfield, it recalled her old theater melodramas, featuring a disastrous love triangle. The faithful Frederick Willis negotiated the deal. Five dollars was a tidy sum, and the *Saturday Evening Gazette* became a regular outlet for Louisa's stories—sometimes under the pseudonym Flora Fairfield, sometimes not. Frederick came home from this success triumphant, handed her the five dollars, and said, "Now, Lu, the door is open, go in and win."

But most of her earnings still came from work she disliked. She continued, reluctantly, to teach: "School for me month after month," she moaned to her diary. After the long teaching day was done, she sewed in the evenings and "earned a good deal" from the added work. To her family she acted as if all this labor were a grand lark. Writing to Anna she joked that she was "grubbing away as usual." But her earnings weren't spent for her own pleasure or purchases. She crowed about "eleven dollars, all my own earnings," which she used "to buy Mother a nice warm shawl." With the rest, she declared, she would adorn May, the golden-haired baby of the family.

May was "so graceful and pretty and loves beauty so much, it is hard for her to be poor and wear other people's ugly things," Louisa wrote. She didn't mind the "ugly things." In *Little Women*, the four March sisters divide into two matched pairs: Meg partners with the spoiled baby, Amy. Jo defends and protects timid Beth. In real life, Louisa took care of *all* of her sisters. She was as generous in small things—a new beribboned hat—as in the large. Louisa put an old talent to good use: "I got a crimson ribbon for a bonnet for May, and I took my straw and fixed it nicely with some little duds I had. Her old one has haunted me all winter, and I want her to look neat." She does not report on how she managed without her own straw hat. She considered herself too homely and awkward to "smarten up." May was the graceful, poised "snow maiden," at ease anywhere. Louisa was hopelessly clumsy in every public situation, and she captured that in her fictional counterpart, Jo March, "blundering away to the dining-room . . . Making a dive at the table, she secured the coffee, which she immediately spilt, thereby making the front of her dress as bad as the back."

Louisa always wrote year-end notes in her journal, summing up the annual triumphs and losses. Money was always at the forefront of her mind. At the end of 1854, she recorded fifty dollars earned from teaching, fifty dollars from sewing—and only twenty dollars from her writing, usually five dollars at a time. It was better than nothing. She kept submitting poems, stories, and plays and hoping, working for the best. "I want more fives and mean to have them too," she told sister Anna. Soon her writing became not only her own personal "salvation," but the family's rescue, even though Louisa would have been the last to predict her future fame and glory.

December 1854 marked an exciting new milestone: Louisa published her first "real book" under her own name. It was *Flower Fables*, a version of the fanciful stories she had created as a teenaged teacher to entertain her young friend and pupil, Ellen Emerson. Even then, Ellen's father had made his famous prophecy: "She is, and is to be, the poet of children."

Louisa gifted her very first copy of *Flower Fables* to her mother, inscribing it as "the first fruits of my genius." She immediately crossed out the word *genius* and amended it to *little talent*. (The egoist "I" must not strut!) She thanked Abby for her constant, loving support and offered the slim volume "merely as an earnest of what I may yet do."

As modest as she aimed to be, she felt proud when the book appeared. Here at last was concrete evidence of her status as a writer. She was only twenty-two. Yet a publisher valued her work enough to bring it out into the world. Vanity was publicly discouraged in the Alcott household, but there was little danger for Louisa. She was too awkward, too tall, she declared, hopelessly ungainly around strangers. Her eyes were too deep-set, giving her a perpetually angry or sad look. The slim book of published fables gave her something to point to with pride. She confided to her journal, "People began to think that topsey-turvey Louisa would amount to something after all. . . . Perhaps she may."

In her early twenties, she still felt uncertain. What direction should she take? At what lofty goal should she be aiming? Should she become a writer, an actress—or something else altogether? Her writing had just begun to sell more and to command higher prices. Her parents approved of her literary efforts as long as her standards remained high. Louisa's goals were more down-to-earth. She declared in her journal with obvious satisfaction, "Prices go up, as people like the tales and ask who wrote them."

Flower Fables sold better than Louisa had dared hope. The book earned good reviews and even turned a small profit. Louisa declared in her first entry of 1855, "I feel quite proud that the little tales that I wrote for Ellen E. when I was sixteen should now bring money and fame. . . . Mothers are always foolish over their first-born." Thirty years later she would contrast the income from *Flower Fables* with her recent royalties, ruefully noting, "I was prouder over the $32 than the $8000."

In spring of 1855, Louisa made an even more startling debut—this time onstage. She had once dreamed of making "easy money" from acting. For a church benefit that spring, she played the comical character Oronthy Bluggage, spouting a nonsensical lecture on "Woman, and her Position." A famous comedian happened to attend the show and was impressed enough to invite Louisa to repeat her performance at the Howard Athenaeum—this time for pay.

That same summer two of her favorite cousins, Ham and Lu Willis, invited her to join them in the fashionable village of Walpole, New Hampshire. The town hosted a

Shakespeare Club and the new Walpole Amateur Dramatic Company. The Willises had contributed generously to the Alcott Sinking Fund, giving Abby gifts of money and Louisa valuable introductions to editors. That summer fed Louisa's theatrical dreams. When the Alcotts' Boston landlord gave last-minute notice for them to move out, the Willises offered a house in Walpole, rent-free.

By this time Abby was eager to leave Boston. When life and plans went wrong, Abby blamed places and people, almost never herself. Walpole would also earn her disdain eventually—but for now, the change felt welcome.

Louisa left Boston first, traveling ahead of the family by train and stagecoach, hauling along the hand-me-downs she had updated with trimmings she'd paid for herself. Happily ensconced with cousins Ham and Lu, she woke each day at five and went for a long run, watching "the woods wake." She spent her mornings writing, afternoons gardening with cousin Lu, and evenings swept up in the excitement of Walpole's summer theater season. It was a rare time for Louisa, so used to carrying the burden of the family.

They soon trailed her to Walpole. Bronson set to work gardening, while Abby enjoyed the luxury of her free time. Anna joined Louisa onstage, playing ingenue roles while Louisa stuck to comedy. A Concord friend remembered Anna as the more gifted actress. She completely disappeared inside a role, while Louisa's "acting had this peculiarity, that she seemed always to be herself and the character she was representing at the same time."

It was a rare easy summer, and the whole family thrived—including Lizzie. A neighboring pastor became so fond of the shy twenty-year-old that he presented her with a piano—a gift that Louisa would later immortalize in *Little Women*.

The Walpole theatrical productions drew fine reviews and large audiences that summer. A Boston newspaper singled Louisa out for her "superior ability." But while these events raised considerable money for charity, the young actresses earned nothing at all, and when summer ended, Louisa cast about for something more lucrative. She began a second book of children's stories, *Christmas Elves*, and asked fifteen-year-old May to illustrate it.

Young May was sought after by girls and boys, young and old alike. The first ball gown she ever wore came from Louisa's own nimble hands. The word Louisa used most often about her youngest sister was *proud*. "My tall, blonde, graceful girl! I was proud of her." May came as close to being spoiled as any Alcott could ever be. May and Louisa were alike in many ways—sensitive, willful, fun-loving, and artistic. But Louisa had been trained early to stifle her own desires and to think of others first. As Cheever points out, "No wonder her early work is studded with passionate storms, murders, and melodramas." May had an easier time indulging herself. Everyone stepped forward to assist May, noted Louisa, "an amiable, engaging girl with something very agreeable about her."

By November, the empty summer colony of Walpole felt drab and dull. Louisa left for Boston to live with an aunt and perform endless unpleasant chores for her room and board. Try as she might, she could find no better work. She dragged herself through November, "'the month of suicides,' as they call it in Paris," she wrote in her gothic romance *A Long Fatal Love Chase*. She told her father on their birthday, celebrated miles apart, "Birthdays are dismal times to me." She had just turned twenty-three. He was fifty-six. She penned a revealing self-portrait, comparing the "serene & placid" baby her father must have been with her own "topsey turvey" self:

"I was a crass crying baby, bawling at the disagreeable old world . . . scrambled up into childhood . . . fell with a crash into girlhood & continued falling over fences, out of trees, uphill & down stairs tumbling from one year to another till . . . the topsey turvey girl shot up into a topsey turvey woman who now twenty-three years after sits big brown & brave, crying not because she has come into the world but because she must go out of it before she has done half she wants to."

She declared she would emerge "queen of herself tho not of the world." That autumn she decided that she lacked the genius needed to be a great actress—and saw that acting didn't necessarily result in a "gay" and prosperous life. Acting was grinding work, with long hours and little pay or security. She wanted not merely to survive but to shine. When she created a heroine for her early novel *Work*, she declared that her Louisa-like character possessed "no dramatic genius . . . had no talent except . . . lively fancy, sympathetic nature, and ambitious spirit." Another, more experienced character in the book agrees that she would only "make a clever actress, never a great one."

Louisa felt happier being in the audience than onstage. Now and again she toyed with the idea of "trying a new life" as an actress, but the "stagestruck fit" was fading. "Worked off my stage fever in writing a story, and felt better," Louisa noted in her journal. But she hadn't given up yet on all art. "Nature must have a vent somehow," she wrote.

ORCHARD HOUSE

CHAPTER TEN

Well at Last

Back in the big city, Louisa took advantage of Boston's free events. Between her chores and efforts to find new employment, she sometimes accompanied wealthy relatives or friends to concerts and plays, or lectures. She eagerly accepted a free pass to the Boston Theatre. Sunday evenings she walked into town to hear her father's old companion, the respected minister Theodore Parker. There in his parlor she sat "in a corner listening" to the great minds and political voices of her day argue the great issues: abolition, women's rights, social justice. The speakers included the infamous and the famous, and of course Theodore Parker himself. Louisa was too reticent to engage in the spirited debates. "I stared, blushed, & sat in a mass of enjoyment the whole evening," she confided to a friend.

Her contemporary, the novelist Henry James once said, "Be one on whom nothing is lost." Nothing was lost on Louisa. Of the crowd gathered at Parker's, she observed wryly, "The talk lasted until two, and then the hungry philosophers remembered they had bodies and rushed away, still talking."

No one guessed that the silent girl in the corner was busily taking mental notes. They would have been horrified by her shrewd observations. Louisa's sharp eyes spared no one. She described Julia Ward Howe, who wrote "The Battle Hymn of the Republic," as "a straw colored supercilious lady with pale eyes & a green gown in which she looked like a faded lettuce." In dozens of notes in her journal and letters, Louisa was already flexing her muscles as an author.

She kept on writing and sometimes publishing stories in journals and newspapers, especially the *Saturday Evening Gazette*, where her great friend and cousin Ham Willis worked. Her next published story, "The Sisters' Trial"— which features a four-member sisterhood—earned the proud author *six* dollars rather than five, and the next story, "Bertha" paid ten!

At last she began to see a way out of the family's woes. "I feel hopeful in my mind & more determined than ever to try my experiment & be independent of everyone but my own two hands & busy head."

She wrote with an eye on pleasing the publishers and gleefully welcomed each new check. Her aims were monetary rather than literary. She called her own productions "rubbish, a mercenary consideration," as she worked to expand her market, always hunting for new and better-paying venues. "Money is the principle object of my life just now," she wrote bluntly. "I want to add another string or two to my bow." To an editor who sent a check for twenty dollars along with some criticisms, she replied politely, "I find it difficult to make them interesting & yet short enough to suit your paper. But hope to improve in both points."

She kept anxiously comparing her writing income against her other earnings, as her journal glumly reports: "Sewed a great deal and got very tired; one job for Mr. G. of a dozen pillow-cases, one dozen sheets, six fine cambric neckties, and two dozen handkerchiefs, at which I had to work all night to get them done. . . . I got only $4."

Anna raced home from her lonely teaching work in Syracuse, New York, to rejoin the family in Walpole. Abby realized that her eldest daughter was done venturing into the world alone—"at least to be separated from Louisa for whom she has a passionate attachment." Louisa was equally devoted to Anna, but she hesitated to rejoin the family in wintertime New Hampshire. She clung to the remnants of an independent life in Boston till June, when the next theater season would begin.

She arrived in Walpole only to be met with heart-wrenching news. Her mild sister, Lizzie, had fallen ill with scarlet fever, "caught from some poor children Mother nursed when they fell sick, living over a cellar where pigs had been kept." Five years earlier, the family had caught smallpox "from some poor children." Then, they had come through unscathed. The Alcotts generally chose alternative treatments such as homeopathy and herbs over Western medicine. They had no reason to think their methods would not work again.

Sixteen-year-old May bounced back quickly from her bout of scarlet fever—but Lizzie's illness grew worse. She may have been weakened by depression and disappointment over some new "small love affair which had not gone properly." Louisa and Anna took turns sitting by Lizzie, relieving Abby of some household chores. There would be no gay theatricals that summer. It was, as Louisa noted in her journal, "an anxious time."

They welcomed a rare visit from Bronson's mother, who seldom left Connecticut. The old lady shed new light on Bronson's childhood and youth and made Louisa feel closer to her father. Still years away from writing her famous novel, Louisa mused, "The trials and triumphs of the Pathetic Family would make a capital book." She saw resemblances not only between Bronson and his feisty mother but between her father and herself. They had survived challenging childhoods and poverty; both had struggled to reshape their fates. "As we sat talking over Father's boyhood, I never realized so plainly before how much he has done for himself."

To "do for herself," Louisa kept churning out her dramatic tales—gothic horror, romance, and high adventure—using any time she could steal away from sewing and teaching. She told a friend, "Though my tales are silly, they are not bad, and my sinners always have a good spot somewhere." The stories were nearly as complete an escape from reality as her childhood theatricals. She was free in fiction as she had never been in real life—free to write about everything from infidelity to murder, revenge, madness, incest, and drugs. In 1856, she announced she was producing nearly "a story a month." Under the cover of one pseudonym and another, she explored the darker, seamy side of humanity. She began publishing these "lurid" stories. This work she did not show to her family, selecting instead to share the few stories they might like.

Even before Lizzie's illness, Abby had grown restless in Walpole, which she called "a dark valley of selfish propriety." She urged Bronson to look for a more congenial place. Louisa fled back to Boston as soon as Lizzie showed signs of recovering. She was at last declaring her need for independence—in action, if not in open speech.

Louisa settled in Mrs. Reed's boardinghouse, popular among what biographer Harriet Reisen describes as "Boston's best and brightest youth." Louisa spent cheery time with people her own age. Her stories now paid ten dollars apiece, and her "queer pie shaped" attic room and board cost only three dollars a week. If she supplemented her writing with sewing and part-time governess work, she could just about scrape by, with money left over to give to the family.

"I took my little talent in hand and forced the world again, braver than before and wiser for my failures," she declared. She was relieved to be away from "the still life of Walpole" and back in the city. "Boston is nicer and noisier than ever," she declared. "The sidewalks are perfect rainbows in point of color." From this time forward she would use the city of Boston as she used her noms de plume—as a place to escape reality and grinding family responsibility, dashing back and forth between two worlds.

Her cozy attic room in the city boardinghouse, she informed Anna, was "nicely carpeted, with two bureaus, (for which I give praise), a dormer window with a table & a rocking chair for my private benefit." This boardinghouse planted the seed for Jo's New York sojourn in *Little Women*. Often Louisa felt lonely there, even in her private haven. On her twenty-fourth birthday in 1856, she wrote to her father: "Your little parcel was very welcome to me as I sat alone in my room, with snow falling fast outside, and a few tears in."

She despaired of the future. She was barely scraping by. No one in the city of Boston seemed to care whether

Louisa lived or died. One day she found herself standing on Boston's Back Bay staring down into the water. Had she not believed it cowardice to give up, she later admitted, she would have thrown herself into the oily black waves. But even when she suffered her blackest moods, she would not stay gloomy. The smallest delights could buoy her spirits. She and her cousin Lu Willis attended plays, and Louisa went wrapped in her cousin's gift of a red silk shawl that made her feel "illuminated." She met famous actors and politicians, and continued to attend the weekly salons thrown by her father's old friend Theodore Parker. Her parents might not have approved of the extravagant red shawl, but they liked her to keep visiting Parker's salons to learn all she could.

Reverend Parker was not only a speaker and host; he lived his beliefs. He was an active abolitionist—like Louisa's own daring uncle Samuel May. Parker had integrated a school and hidden a woman fleeing slavery in his house. He wrote his sermons with a loaded pistol at his side, in case anyone should try to re-enslave her. He'd helped a pair of fugitives from slavery escape to England. Parker performed the illegal wedding ceremony before the couple sailed away. He gave them two farewell gifts: a Bible, "for the defense of your soul," and a hunting knife, "for the defense of your body."

Parker now befriended Louisa. He was a man of few words, but no less impressive because of his silence. He welcomed her with a hearty "Well, child, how goes it?" "Pretty well, sir." "That's brave." On parting, he said, "God bless you, Louisa, come again." She did, many times.

Louisa to spent more time writing than sleeping. She declared, "Though not an easy life, it is a free one, and I enjoy it." She would sometimes bump into her wealthy relatives around town, but she felt uneasy asking for help, noting, "When I do they are so busy about their own affairs that my concerns seem a bother." Only Lu and Ham Willis offered constant friendship and acceptance. Beyond that, she was conducting a heady experiment "to be independent of everyone but my own two hands & busy head."

This independence extended even from her father now. When he gave her the gift of an elegant cloak pin, she wrote a double-edged thank-you note that must have stung even the serene Bronson: "I think I shall come out all right and prove that though an Alcott I can support myself." Bronson was still struggling to eke out a living with his Conversations back in Walpole. Louisa wrote, "I will make a battering-ram of my head and make a way through this rough-and-tumble world."

Home-loving Anna resisted Louisa's invitations to come to Boston. Lu Willis tried to tempt her with an extra theater ticket to any performance she liked. Anna politely declined. Not even the theater could tempt her from the family hearth.

Instead, sixteen-year-old May glided into town to stay

with an aunt and study art in the city. May and Louisa lived in two separate Bostons—Louisa in her homely boarding room, May in the embrace of wealthy relatives. Their aunt Bond had given Louisa a dozen chores in exchange for her housing—sewing, mending, reading aloud, visiting sick relatives, and more. May performed no such work. She had her room and board for free, with tuition to art school thrown in besides. May had grown serious about her art— and she was truly gifted. Somehow the conservative branch of the family didn't mind May's ambitions. Louisa's odd ways inspired suspicion. Her sister May, Louisa noted enviously, "could inspire outright gifts."

May's looks were fairy-princess-like and regal. Her complexion was fair, her eyes bright blue, her wavy hair golden. She had an air of confidence that Louisa lacked except when onstage playing some outrageous character. Offstage, Louisa would retreat into a haughty-seeming silence or fall back on unladylike slang. Nine years her junior, May had too much dignity for such behavior. Men fell in love with her; old ladies praised her.

Louisa spent that Christmas in Boston, her first apart from home and family. She welcomed her mother's package of homemade gingerbread, a flannel cap, and a yellow butterfly holder. Privately, she expressed delight over luxuries from friends and relations. Lu Willis sent "a handsome silk gown the first I ever had." Others bestowed gifts of handkerchiefs and perfume, but none were as precious as her

161

independence. "I love luxury, but freedom and independence better," she exclaimed.

She attended a lively round of holiday parties. Now and then she crossed paths with the May. "As I sat in a corner I enjoyed the remarks her relations made about her for they seemed astonished that an Alcott should dance & talk like other people."

Louisa herself neither danced nor talked "like other people." Ill at ease, tongue-tied, clownish or serious, she confused outsiders. She bequeathed these same contradictions to her character Jo. Her mind kept busy with new stories, making wry observations, and laying plans for the Pathetic Family's survival. She vowed that year to find the family a new home—away from "Mount Blank," as they'd all taken to calling Walpole. How she would manage all this was unclear. She possessed only "eight cents in the bank . . . & a fortune in prospect."

Louisa paid a surprise visit to her family in Walpole that February. She laid out her plans to relocate the family closer to Boston. Abby was swept up in her daughter's optimism. She was sick of Walpole and eager to move nearer to her most kindred daughter. "She is quite intent on getting us nearer Boston," Abby enthused. That winter Louisa noted her progress with satisfaction: "I have done what I planned—supported myself, written eight stories, taught four months, earned a hundred dollars, and sent money home."

Lizzie—Louisa preferred to use the nickname Betty—rose and fell in health, but she was always losing ground. Her ailments were mysterious and shifting. She suffered from stomachaches, hair loss, nausea, weight loss, breathlessness, and headaches. Her old scarlet fever probably triggered rheumatic fever, which led slowly but surely to fatal congestive heart failure. The Alcotts continued for a long time to blame a lack of "cheerful society" for "this sad wrench of her frame."

Though the Alcotts preferred unconventional medicine, in desperation now they consulted doctors, who offered contradictory but equally unhelpful suggestions. One doctor diagnosed Lizzie with tuberculosis and ordered her to the seaside. The next confidently declared she had no such thing. Meanwhile, Lizzie just grew sicker. "The system of medicine is a prolonged Guess," wrote Abby in despair. Even Bronson confided in his journal, "The case is a critical one, and there is . . . a dark side to the prospect."

In light of Abby's anxiety over Lizzie, Bronson took charge again. He moved the family away from Walpole that spring, back to sympathetic and friend-filled Concord. Louisa had hoped to have them closer to Boston, but she noted with tender resignation, "He is never happy far from Emerson, the one true friend who loves and understands and helps him." She may have also recognized that the family would need support from all sides in the heartbreaking months ahead.

Louisa followed the family to Concord, reluctantly sacrificing her Boston freedom. The call of family came first. Each family member was hurried to Concord, set on nursing Lizzie back to health. The prospects were grim. "Find Betty a shadow, but sweet and patient always," Louisa wrote.

The Alcotts' "true friend" Emerson paid a $400 deposit that September on a house next door to their beloved old Hillside home, where the Hawthornes now lived. From her window Louisa could gaze next door as if looking directly into the past. There the ghost of her happiest memories lived—when young folks had gathered to play games, and her dear Lizzie still thrived.

The Alcotts' new piece of property came with ten acres of beautiful apple orchards and not much else. The house itself was so dilapidated that the farmer threw it in for free. Bronson named the place Orchard House. The foundation had shifted, leaving the old floors to slant. Wise-cracking Louisa nicknamed it Apple Slump, after a then-popular dessert.

Bronson restored the orchard and gardens and was again renewed by his labors out of doors. Louisa and Anna cleaned and scrubbed, organized closets and cupboards, and turned every available corner into bookcases. Abby stayed close by with Lizzie in a quieter house while the construction work at Orchard House was underway. The gifted

May painted decorative wall panels in many rooms, beautifying them with delicate birds and flowers. Her sense of whimsy transformed the plain walls into objects of mystery. "Owls blink at you and faces peep from the most unexpected places," wrote a Concord friend. Visitors to Orchard House still see young May Alcott's original owls and flowers peering down on modern passersby.

The Alcotts resumed a more sociable life than they had known in a long time—with dinners, tea, nut cracking, with games of whist, chess, casino (Louisa's favorite), and old maid. The Alcott sisters gave theatricals again, in the downstairs sitting room separated by a doorway from the dining room. A curtain hung between the two, one side serving as theater seating, the other their stage. Hours of work went into these homemade productions, which occupied the spare hours of the golden band, even when Louisa and Anna were well into their twenties.

Guests were treated to picnics and games of croquet on the lawn. Whenever Louisa was around, there were jokes and laughter. She was "a comic, bright, talented extravaganza of a girl," as a friend described her. Louisa used physical comedy, slang, and a touch of the shocking— "Excuse me if I appear to flop!" she exclaimed, tumbling into a room. "Louy" kept her guests "in fits of laughter for two hours with the jolliest kind of talk." Her use of slang, so familiar to her readers, shocks no one now but startled her less daring friends. The Alcotts gave generously of what they had—beautiful natural surroundings, fun, and friendship.

Author Nathaniel Hawthorne, living next door, was a distant neighbor, shy as a skittish deer. Louisa caught only "glimpses of a dark mysterious looking man in a big hat and red slippers darting over the hills or skimming by as if he expected the house of Alcott were about to rush out and claim him." They gave Mr. Hawthorne a wide berth but soon grew close with the young folks of the family. Julian Hawthorne became a dear lifetime friend. Poor Julian seems to have developed a mad, unrequited crush on each of the Alcott girls in turn.

The regal Hawthornes brought out Louisa's wicked sense of humor. After a rare occasion when all three of the Hawthorne offspring could be persuaded to visit them next door, Louisa escorted them home. On her way back to Orchard House, her mocking spirit got the best of her. She stopped every few steps, curtsying deeply toward her old Hillside house, "squatting down on the sidewalk," before dashing off again.

Nathaniel's wife, Sophia—Bronson's former Temple School assistant—helped the Alcott family as best she could, though Louisa mocked her in private. The elegant Mrs. Hawthorne, she wrote to a friend, was "sentimental and muffing," wearing her "crimson silk jackets, a rosary from Jerusalem, fire-flies in her hair and dirty white skirts with the sacred mud of London still extant." Louisa dismissed the eldest Hawthorne girl as hopelessly dull. Julian fared better in Louisa's opinion and was deemed "a worthy boy." Louisa collected "worthy boys" the way other girls collect dolls or pets. But she teased her boys at least as often as she petted them.

Julian, still guileless enough to be "full of pictures, fishing rods and fun," nourished a long crush on the golden-haired May Alcott. Louisa tormented Julian with tales of a wealthy, aristocratic cousin who planned to sweep May off her feet, marry her, and cart her off to live in the lap of luxury. Desperately, Julian tried to dismiss it all as a lie. Louisa only piled on more details about the eligible suitor.

One April afternoon Julian stopped by only to spy May standing and chatting with a handsome mustachioed youth, dressed like a dandy. Wrote Julian, "He was slender and dark, and wore a black broad-cloth suit and soft black felt hat. His waistcoat and cravat, however, were rather too decorative for my taste; he twirled an absurd switch cane and occasionally caressed the points of a tiny black mustache." Julian's blood boiled. Worse still, at one point this stranger put his arm around May's waist and called Julian "child." The insult!

"Oh, I say, don't be in a hurry, my dear child," drawled

this intolerable stranger, flourishing his cane. "Do you know, I find you quite amusing." He kept his arm tight around May's waist—scandalous behavior, Julian thought.

The young man, dark eyes dancing, exclaimed, "Well, well, so this is our young friend Julian; quite a well-grown boy!"

When Julian drew closer, the stranger twirled his cane directly in his face. Julian scowled, his hands curled into fists, and May fled to the house, apparently overcome.

The stranger took one step forward, tore off his mustache, and threw it over Julian's head, tossing after it his black felt hat. A cascade of rich brown hair came tumbling down, and as Julian later reported, both Alcott sisters yelled back over their shoulders, "April Fool's!"

From Julian's written reminiscences come many of our best and liveliest descriptions of the author: "Louisa, when I first saw her, was a black-haired, red-cheeked, long-legged hobbledehoy." According to Julian, "We naturally fraternized with our neighbors, and my two sisters and myself and the Alcott girls were in and out of one another's houses all the time, almost forming one family." The three Emerson children—Ellen, Edward, and Edith—lived ten minutes down the road. It's easy to see shades of the fictional neighbor Laurie in Julian's friendship with Louisa. He was slightly younger than Louisa, intelligent and artistic. She teased and ordered him around like a kid brother even when he longed to be taken seriously. Like the fictional

Laurie, he courted the youngest Alcott sister. Even if he had wanted to try his luck with Louisa—and there's good evidence that he did—he stood in awe of her. "There was power in her jaw and control in her black eyes," wrote Julian, "good nature in her generous mouth . . . in short, she was a leader, and, in a place like Concord, she stood out."

Louisa stood out even in her eccentric family. In her early twenties she began describing herself as one of the permanently unpartnered, and to write comically about her "benighted spinsterhood." Her single state and her self-declared role of "the man of the house" went hand in hand—she felt responsible for everybody's welfare but her own. When she earned thirty-five dollars from her writing, she spent it on "a second-hand carpet for the little parlor" at Orchard House, a new bonnet for Anna, treats for the others, and only the plainest shoes and stockings for herself. "If any of my fortune is left, will invest it in the Alcott Sinking Fund," she wrote.

Julian describes her with affection and admiration. "In no young woman that ever I knew was strength of character more manifest than in Louisa Alcott. Ellen Emerson, of the Concord girls, was nearest her in that respect; but Ellen was aristocratic, while Louisa was a true democrat." The "true democrat" was not concerned only with the family. She was caught up in the larger questions of her time. Her sense of justice and injustice had only sharpened over the years. "Ellen was deep, but narrow," wrote Julian. "Louisa was both deep and broad; her sympathies were world-wide. Ellen, for all her noble self-dedication to her father, was always conscious of herself; Louisa—aside from her dignity of womanhood—never considered herself at all."

Louisa was facing two imminent losses. One came from sister Anna's courtship with suitor John Pratt, a kind, serious young man who fit right in with the Alcott family. He'd even been a member at the commune at Brook Farm. Pratt and Anna met each other playing onstage lovers in the Concord Dramatic Union. Nearness inspired affection. Offstage, their romance grew serious. Unlike her early lighthearted courtships, this time Anna, too, was in love.

A younger Louisa would have raged against her sister's defection, but now she was too brokenhearted over Lizzie. Her younger sister was failing and begged to have Louisa stay close by. "It makes me feel strong," Lizzie said gratefully. Louisa devoted herself to her care. Lizzie's long, ruthless illness had taken its toll. Louisa mourned that her beautiful young sister looked middle-aged, ravaged by suffering. Her cheeks were drawn and thin. Her soft brown hair was all but completely gone, replaced by a cloth cap. Louisa put on a brave, cheerful, hopeful face while nursing Lizzie. All the Alcotts pretended that Lizzie would soon get well again. Only Lizzie did not pretend.

She had never felt she was part of the big, busy world. Lizzie's life was domestic, self-contained. She had wanted it that way. Her resemblance to the gentlest sister of all the little women is unmistakable. Now she resigned herself to fate, even while her family—especially Louisa—raged against it.

"I can best be spared of the four," Lizzie confided to her grieving father. She gave up looking for cures. A month before her death she began to refuse all medicine. None of it had helped her; some only made her feel weaker. As Lizzie's caregiver, Louisa tried to stay upbeat, gathering spring branches and flowers to brighten the sickroom, reading aloud to her weary patient.

Louisa's brief onstage career had prepared her well for comedic acting. Usually she succeeded. Only rarely did the smiling mask slip. Louisa's dear friend Alf Whitman— another of her favorite "boys"—described her caretaking: "Louisa would be backwards and forwards from the upstairs room, making everybody feel happy and cheerful, yet at all times ready to answer a call from Lizzie." He and John Pratt often visited Orchard House in those last sad days. Alf wrote about Louisa's tender nursing: "No written words can convey an adequate idea of the love and care which Louisa . . . lavished upon Elizabeth."

Alf glimpsed Louisa's private and well-hidden state of mind when he dropped by Orchard House unannounced one Sunday. Louisa sat hunched over some bit of sewing work. "I opened the door of the little sitting-room, found Louisa there alone. She had turned her back to the door as she heard me come in. Before I could speak, she threw down the white garment upon which she was sewing . . . burst into tears, and with the words, 'It is Lizzie's shroud,' hurried out of the room."

Julian Hawthorne, the shrewd observer who lived next door, saw through Louisa's high-jinks as well. He wrote, "Her spirit was high and courageous. She was great in comedy, laughed and inspired laughter, but for a heart so tender as hers tragedy was always near, though she was res-olute to smile her tears down."

In nineteenth-century America, birth and dying hap-pened in the home. Abby and Louisa took turns watching over Lizzie in her last days. It was not an easy death. Lizzie struggled painfully for her last breaths. Nothing they did helped. Louisa wrote bleakly, "For two days, she suffered much, begging for ether though its effect was gone." On March 12, 1858, Lizzie called the family together around her and kissed each one of them tenderly. That farewell was her last fully conscious gesture. By the next day at midnight, Lizzie fell unconscious, then, wrote a grieving Louisa, "with one last look of the beautiful eyes, she was gone."

While they still yet stood over the bed, it was not the last they saw of Lizzie. A strange thing happened next. Within a few minutes after Lizzie's death, Louisa observed a light mist sparkling and rising up from her sister's body. Startled, she looked at her mother and said, "What did you see?" Abby instantly described the same airy figure floating up. It was one mysterious comfort in the midst of grief.

Louisa and Abby washed and dressed Lizzie's body, preparing it for burial. The funeral was small and simple, as Lizzie would have wished. Her trusted friends Emerson and Thoreau were among her pallbearers. Family and friends sang Lizzie's favorite hymn. We know so little about Lizzie that even the name of the hymn remains a mystery.

A few weeks later, Anna announced her engagement to John Pratt. The senior Alcotts tried to rejoice, even while Louisa further mourned the breaking apart of the family. Lizzie had left them; soon Anna would follow. Her older sister's departure felt like another death. As Jo March tells Marmee on the eve of Meg's marriage, "I just wish I could marry Meg myself, and keep her safe in the family." Louisa had counted all her life on Anna's steady companionship.

Louisa had ample reason to feel downhearted. Selfish motives played little part in Louisa's life, but she must have known that her own life would grow even harder and lonelier without her older sister's presence. Anna had provided peace and "sensible" conversation in a sometimes-chaotic household. Louisa would now become solely responsible for her family's happiness as well as its financial security. Her prospects seemed frighteningly narrow.

As the petted youngest child, May was free to pursue her own education, her art, and even her whims. Louisa and Anna had early on harnessed themselves to the family wagon. Anna's affectionate aunt Lucretia fretted over Anna's self-sacrifice, observing that her young niece kept none of her wages for herself. (She added tartly of Mrs. Alcott, "Abba as usual was full of debt & in want of money.") Anna had been contributing to the Pathetic Family's Sinking Fund since age fifteen, working difficult jobs to help the family. Gentle Lizzie had done the house-keeping without complaint. Now both burdens would fall on Louisa.

She faced her prospects head-on. As usual, humor was her tool of choice. She was "rather tired," she admitted, "of living like a spider,—spinning my brains out for money," but her sense of humor kept her going. She rejoiced that "the inside of my head can at least cover the outside." The opposite was also true. She covered her inner sadness with an outwardly smiling face.

Louisa wrote of Lizzie's death, "She is well at last"—a phrase she would use again in *Little Women*. But no amount of self-comfort could disguise her true heartbreak. "So the first break comes," Louisa mourned in her journal, "and I know what death means."

Anna's marriage and Lizzie's death were the two major "events that change[d] my life," Louisa wrote. She fought each day against despair. Her lifelong struggle with moods, those "fitful changes of sunshine & shade," became more chronic and serious.

She turned now to the consolation of writing. "I am learning that work . . . is my salvation when disappointment or weariness burden and darken my soul." Twenty-six-year-old Louisa received few birthday gifts that sad year. As she would later note, "I never seem to have many presents."

It was also a time of introspection and change. Grief had softened some of her sharp edges. Her life fueled her writing, and she was slowly but surely finding her voice. She sensed, too, that she was moving closer to her true material. Her best stories were not to be found among turreted castles or exotic foreign cities. Instead, she wrote, "The nearer I keep to nature the better the work is." Grief and disappointment were hard but effective teachers. "I feel," she wrote in her journal, "as if I could write better now,— more truly of things I have felt and therefore *know*."

While Louisa turned a brave face to the world and still "romped" when she could, she was beginning to feel the weight of her responsibilities. She could not share the burden with anyone, not even her mother. "I feel my quarter of a century rather heavy on my shoulders just now," she confided to her journal earlier. "I lead two lives. One seems gay with plays, etc., the other very sad,—in Betty's room." Louisa settled in now to her role as the spinster of the family and its source of support.

Louisa always disliked Orchard House after this glum

period, remembering it as when and where she lost two beloved sisters. Her youth was fading—and along with it, her brightest prospects. She could not simply abandon the family and return to independence in Boston. She had to stay put in Concord.

Most of us confront our old ghosts now and again. Louisa lived right next door to them. A few steps away sat Hillside, the house that held her happiest memories. It had been a decade since the Alcotts lived there. She could look out her window onto Hillside House—renamed Wayside—but she could not turn back time or return to a family unbroken. Nor could she regain her lost youth. As biographer Harriet Reisen notes, "In Boston she was a writer and an actress. Concord offered just one role: spinster family caretaker."

Louisa traveled between Concord and Boston as she considered her prospects. Boston tempted her. But time, circumstance, and duty drew her back to Concord and family. The theater was always her "great joy," but she no longer believed it was her destiny. "I'll try again, by-and-by, and see if I have the gift."

In her effort to "have a vent somehow," Louisa acted out in unexpected ways. She was considered the strange daughter of the strange Bronson Alcott. After her terrible year of loss, Louisa's moods vacillated wildly. Her behavior became erratic. A Concord neighbor described her as "breezy and snappy and using a lot of slang." That use of "slang" was more serious than it sounds now—like regularly using foul language.

She couldn't trouble herself to behave. With Lizzie gone, the impending loss of her sister Anna became almost unbearable. Louisa stormed and raged, as she had done years earlier when an impudent boy had kissed her sister at a party—but this time Anna would not send her suitor packing. Anna and John had a long engagement—nearly two years in the end—but Louisa felt the time slipping away.

Years earlier, she had contemplated suicide and stood on the bridge at the base of the Charles River. In the end she forced herself to live. It would have been, she declared, too "cowardly to run away before the battle was over." The moment of temptation on the bridge was a secret she finally disclosed now in a letter home. She had never revealed her near escape before.

"My courage most gave out, for everyone was so busy, & cared so little whether I got work or jumped into the river that I thought seriously of doing the latter. In fact did go over the Mill Dam & look at the water."

Though Louisa tried to make light of her despair, it had gone deeper and lasted longer than she would admit. Only her sense of duty had kept her from doing something desperate. "I said firmly, 'There *is* work for me, and I'll have it,' and went home resolved to take Fate by the throat and shake a living out of her."

A scene in her novel *Work* provides some of the grisly details Louisa left out—the bay bubbling "like a cauldron" beneath her and the smell of sewage rising to the bridge.

Her life again felt like one failure after another. She had long struggled to find lucrative work and failed. She had fought to keep all her family together under one roof and had failed there as well. Disappointment, Louisa declared, must have been good for her, she got "so much of it." She kept her head down, putting one boot in front of the other, teaching, writing, sewing, and learning all she could from lectures. Further education was not an option. "Life is my college," Louisa announced.

On the morning of May 23, 1860, Anna Alcott married John Pratt in the front parlor of Orchard House. According to Anna, "Louisa had adorned the house with wreaths & flowers, and never seemed more beautiful to me." The same minister uncle who long ago had married Bronson and Abby now performed the ceremony for Anna and John, on the very same date in May.

Anna wrote, "About ten o'clock the few friends whom we had invited begun to assemble & poor mother to look sad, for now all began to realize that it was to be." The bride was rewarded by a kiss from Ralph Waldo Emerson himself, reported Louisa, "the god of my idolatry . . . has been for years." The kiss was almost but not quite enough, she wrote, jokingly, to make "matrimony endurable."

Just before Anna's wedding service, Louisa arranged a wreath of wild violets around a portrait of Lizzie. With tears in her eyes she told Abby, "I am trying to keep Lizzie's memory inviolate [in violet]." May and Louisa wore gray to match Anna's silvery silk bridal gown. Louisa commented, "Sackcloth I called it, and ashes of roses, for I mourn for the loss of my Nan [Anna], and am not comforted."

Anna thrived in married life, though John Pratt made a small salary and the couple moved into a cheap boarding-house just as the senior Alcotts had done thirty years earlier. Anna found marriage an escape from a life filled with uncertainty. John Pratt was steady and kind. Within a few months, Anna noted, "I did not think I should be so entirely tranquil, so peaceful and content, so full of a quiet happiness that for many years I have not known."

She looked back at her childhood: "In a household like my father's where poverty & trial & disappointment have been continually trying the tempers & hearts, very quick tempers, very warm hearts, there has necessarily been much disquiet & great clashing of wills, & tho' we have always dearly loved & gladly labored for each other, there has been a want of that harmony which is the great charm of family life."

Louisa visited the newlyweds to see for herself "the great charm" of Anna's new life. Anna and John Pratt were absorbed in one another's perfections, as Louisa shrewdly

179

noted in a letter to her cousin Adeline—"which amiable delusion I admire and wonder at from the darkness of my benighted spinsterhood." She famously concluded, "Very sweet and pretty; but I would rather be a free spinster and paddle my own canoe." She also declared, "Liberty is a better husband than love." It's poignant that she felt she had to choose between the two.

Louisa had her own romantic chances, though she spoke less of her love affairs than most young women before her or since. She carefully and sometimes sweepingly destroyed any journal entries and letters that might prove too revealing.

Anna noted that there were always men in love with Louisa, hanging hopefully around. A family friend asked Louisa why she had spurned an attentive suitor. "Ah he is too blew," Louisa drawled in response, "and too prewdent for me. I should shock him constantly."

Julian Hawthorne, her friend next door, mused on Louisa's personal life while recognizing that she had erected a wall no neighbor would ever breach. In his written reminiscence, Julian wondered, "Did she ever have a love affair? We never knew; yet how could a nature so imaginative, romantic and passionate escape it?" His question feeds a hope that she did not "escape" romance and love entirely.

We know that in the spring of 1860, with marriage and death on either side, she "had a funny lover who met [her] in the cars, and said he lost his heart at once." Louisa felt no such loss, and the experience was "soon ended." While Anna always dreamed of marriage, Louisa had ample evidence that her mother had suffered since her marriage, enduring poverty, miscarriages, debts, and near desertion. None of this escaped her second daughter's watchful eye. Louisa was determined not to suffer a similar fate. Around young men during her eligible teenage years, she had played the clown, the outlaw, and the tomboy. Now in her twenties, she was apt to tease and lecture them like a sister or mother.

Even so, Louisa received at least one other proposal that year, from a Mr. Condit, a prosperous manufacturer of silk hats who lived in Somerville, Massachusetts. Nothing further is known about the man, other than his good taste in women. Louisa considered his proposal seriously enough to consult her mother. There were obvious advantages to the match. Mr. Condit offered financial security and creature comforts for the entire Alcott family. This was his main virtue. But when Abby asked if Louisa had feelings for her suitor and Louisa said no, she advised Louisa to give him up. This Louisa did quickly and offhandedly in the following note: "I have decided it be best for me not to accept your proposal, In haste, L. M. Alcott."

Afterward she commented, "My adorers are all queer." She would say the same of her adoring fans, calling them "rampant infants" and "so cracked." Her favorite subject for mockery was herself, and she saved her sharpest barbs for Louisa May Alcott.

On the literary front, things were looking up. For the first time she could glimpse the possibility of an independent writer's life. She earned a grand seventy-five dollars for one of her stories, "A Modern Cinderella"—a fortune in its time, about the equivalent of $2,000 today. Another story brought in fifty dollars. The windfalls were enough to purchase some peace of mind, as well as new summer outfits and hats for her sisters and mother. She allowed herself a new claret-colored dress, "having mended my six-year-old silk till it is more patch and tear than gown."

The year 1860 was full of changes, a turning point for Louisa as an individual, an Alcott, and a writer. That August she began working on her first serious novel, *Moods*, in which two male characters fight for the love of the heroine. One hero looks and acts suspiciously like Ralph Waldo Emerson; the other the rugged Henry David Thoreau. Most readers then and now find *Moods* a scrambled, sentimental failure, even as early novels go, but Louisa was swept up in its creation.

It's not clear whether she fell in love with her material or with the image of herself as a writer. Her usual modesty disappeared. "Genius burned so fiercely that for four weeks I wrote all day and planned nearly all night, being quite possessed by my work." She added, "I was perfectly happy, and seemed to have no wants." *The Inheritance*, her earlier teenaged attempt, had actually been her first—and better—attempt at a full-length novel, but Louisa dismissed that book and never spoke of it.

She had higher aspirations for *Moods*, which she considered a serious work of fiction. Its manner of composition was new as well. This was Louisa's first experience with what she would later call her writing "vortex." During a vortex, she disappeared into her work like Alice down the rabbit hole. The Alcott family encouraged these creative bursts. Immersed in her writing, Louisa was briefly spared her role as servant. Abby delivered meals and tea to her on a tray. Her father kept a respectful distance, not wishing to disturb.

After weeks of feverish writing, she emerged from *Moods* and threw herself just as violently into household tasks at Orchard House. She gardened, painted, and papered, while Bronson created innovative household devices such as the drying rack that swung out from the fireplace into the kitchen, and a well-rigged enclosed outdoor shower.

Abby escaped to Syracuse for a visit with her brother Sam, and Louisa rolled up her sleeves and added the role of cook to her other chores. "We won't move again for twenty years if I can help it," she wrote, but it's not clear what "we" she meant, since she returned to Boston that October, "on my usual hunt for employment," noting both proudly and ruefully that she seemed to be "the only bread-winner just now."

That November, Bronson turned sixty-one, Louisa twenty-eight. She felt at the edge of middle age, while young May was just coming into bloom. A friend sent money so that May could continue art lessons in Boston. Louisa, watching from the sidelines, wrote, "She is one of the fortunate ones, and gets what she wants easily. I have to grub for my help, or go without it. . . . Cheer up, Louisa," she concluded, "and grind away!" Fortune continued to smile on the youngest, most charming Alcott. May was offered a job teaching art in Syracuse, and without May that winter Louisa sorely missed "our lively girl."

Christmas of 1860 proved a subdued and melancholy holiday. "A quiet Christmas," Louisa commented in her journal, "no presents but apples and flowers." She alone of all the Alcott offspring was still living at home. It made a sad contrast to her independent days in Boston. There was reason for the quiet: "No merry-making; for Nan and May were gone, and Betty under the snow."

CHAPTER ELEVEN

Turned Nurse

That year's somber Christmas was followed by an unexpected flurry of social activity and gifts from friends at New Year's. Louisa wrote, "I was blessed with all manner of nice things, from a gold and ivory pen to a mince-pie and a bonnet." It marked a welcome relief from her usual sense of loneliness and isolation in Concord.

Even while creating *Moods*, she had felt another story "simmering." This was her second novel, initially titled *Success*. At the start of 1861 Louisa disappeared yet again into her vortex, up in her second floor bedroom at Orchard House. Bronson had built a little wooden half-moon desk in front of her window that looked out onto Concord's main road. Nothing passed by without parading before her eyes. Clothed in a green-and-red party wrap—she called it her "glory cloak"—her "simmering" brain topped by a green silk cap with a red bow, she looked like a great Christmas tree as she sat scribbling away on *Success*. Yet to many readers it is, if possible, a worse book than *Moods*. The novel jumps from scene to scene to scene, from tragic event to tragic event, its heroine dragged from one crisis to the next, as if on a world tour of disaster. The original title, *Success*, may have seemed too ironic even to its author. Years later it would finally be published under the title *Work*.

In the midst of this "grove of manuscripts, 'living for immortality'" as May described the scene, mortality reared its ugly head again and interrupted Louisa's creative life. Abby collapsed, from either mental or physical strain. Louisa changed back in a flash from writer to nurse.

Abby had been depressed and listless ever since Lizzie's death, which she called "the trial of my life." She had put her strength into nursing Lizzie back to health. When that failed, Abby lost her fierce, lifelong will to struggle on. "I had done what I could," she wrote. "Since then I have made little or no effort to earn."

Louisa flew to her mother's side to "cure" her. It was just as her mother had once pictured—the faithful daughter nursing her mother. As soon as Abby fell ill, Louisa wrote, "I corked up my inkstand and turned nurse." Bronson, who was traveling again, praised Louisa for her efforts to lighten "the load with which she is so burdened."

Abby understood the burden she was placing on her

second daughter. "My frequent sick-turns interrupt her too much. It is with real sorrow I find her compelled . . . to leave her desk for the kitchen"—something Abby had been doing all her life—"but," she added tellingly, "life is full of sacrifice for women." Louisa was less accepting of those sacrifices expected of women. At least, she was less accepting in theory; this was practice. Louisa hurried to be by her mother's side and stayed there. Abby no longer possessed the reserves to fight on alone. "My health is not firm and my heart less valiant," Abby wrote.

These nursing experiences would soon, at great cost, turn Louisa into a Civil War nurse—her wildest, and most dangerous, adventure. The nursing experiences with Abby and Lizzie led to her war work. Guiding her mother back to health, Louisa wondered "if I ought not to be a nurse, as I seem to have a gift for it." She determined, "if I couldn't act or write" she'd try nursing. "May yet," she added prophetically.

Close as she was to her mother, Louisa kept her internal struggles to herself. "Now that Mother is too tired to be wearied with my moods," she wrote, "I have to manage them alone." There was nowhere else to turn. She was learning that her work could be "salvation when disappointment or weariness burden and darken my soul."

As soon as Abby was well again, Louisa resumed writing. But she did not take up the new novel *Work*, which she had recently abandoned. Instead she returned to her earlier novel, *Moods*. For three weeks she did nothing but write and occasionally escape outdoors for a run. According to her own account, she neither ate nor slept and barely got up from her writing desk.

Bronson approved "and brought his reddest apples and hardest cider." And "Mother wandered in and out with cordial cups of tea, worried because I couldn't eat." As the newly crowned genius of the household, Louisa was now praised and petted by the parents who had left her half-starved through much of her childhood.

The "pleasant and queer" experience, as she described it, finally ended. While it lasted, she exhibited many of the symptoms of her father's mania—she was unable to stop working, wholly obsessed. "My mind was too rampant for my body, as my head was dizzy, legs shaky, and no sleep would come."

When these creative spells were over, they left Louisa depleted and downhearted. Her black moods deepened. She resumed her role as self-sacrificing pauper. It was hard, lonely work. Anna was married, Lizzie dead, but May as pampered and carefree as ever.

Away from home, young May responded with nonchalance to her father's advice and exhortations. At twenty-one, she answered one of his letters airily: "I received your moral lecture . . . and did read it over twice as I was bid, but for all that I am afraid it didn't have the desired quieting effect as I immediately went to ride with a young gallant, of which I don't believe you would of approved or even allowed if you had been here." She had all of Louisa's bravery—without her penchant toward self-sacrifice.

Anna, the eldest of their golden band, lamented, "Lu herself is as poor as a rat & I could not help crying when I saw her ragged clothes and shabby things." As usual, Louisa had given away her best belongings to May. Anna secretly made up a "parcel of underclothes for dear Lu," since she lacked even those bare necessities. While May's letters to Anna were "full of gaity, delight at her trunk full of new clothes, anticipations of a happy summer, & the happy dreams of young folks," Louisa's letters struck Anna as "sober" and lonely.

On one gloomy Sunday, Louisa went to hear Theodore Parker preach. Parker himself was ill, and as it turned out, Louisa witnessed one of his very last sermons. His subject was "Laborious Young Women"—about women who worked hard and long while receiving little pay or encouragement. He might have been speaking directly to the heart of his hungry listener.

Louisa shyly approached Parker's wife after the lecture and asked if she knew of any work she could do to make a difference in the world. Mrs. Parker, strangely, suggested Louisa go to a girls' reform school to sew ten hours a day mending sheets and uniforms. Louisa was horrified by the prospect. Yet she considered it seriously.

As she had in the matter of shearing off her hair and

selling it, she delayed her answer—and at the eleventh hour was offered a position teaching a young invalid named Alice, at a salary that allowed her to stay on in Boston. Sewing for ten hours a day in an institution, she recognized, was not her life's destiny. "Louisa," declared Theodore Parker, "will succeed." Mrs. Parker told her, rather mysteriously, "It was a test, my dear, and you stood it."

Louisa's story melodramas continued to sell. She relished both the escapism of the work and the pay. She had recently finished what she hoped might be two solid literary novels. "I hope I shall yet do my great book," she told herself, "for that seems to be my work, and I am growing up to it."

Everyone around her appeared to have found their place. Even Bronson had been appointed superintendent of the Concord schools—a job he enjoyed for the few years it lasted. Anna was absorbed in her happy marriage. Louisa observed, "The world is composed of John and John is composed of all the virtues ever known." May lived for her "crayons and dancing, father for his garden, mother for the world in general and I," she added, almost as an afterthought, "for my pen and ink, and there you have a brief account of the 'pathetic family.'"

She had nothing to show for the "pen and ink effort" she had invested in her novel *Moods*. "Daresay nothing will come of it," she noted in her journal, "but it *had* to be done." At least she still had plenty of encouragement at home. After reading the novel, Bronson had asked in wonder, "Where did you get your metaphysics?" Her mother "pronounced it wonderful" while Anna "laughed and cried" as Louisa read the book aloud.

Bronson offered to show the manuscript to the mighty Emerson, who agreed to read it, but no word survives as to whether or not Louisa's intellectual idol actually read *Moods*—or if he did, what he thought of it. The manuscript lay in her room untouched. Louisa vowed to return to it and perfect it when she had more freedom—her eternal hope—"when duty no longer orders me to make a burnt-offering of myself."

"Duty's clear and tedious way" called on all her energies. She couldn't spare the time or money for a visit to New Hampshire, to see her friend and cousin Lu Willis. She possessed, she wrote ruefully, "one dollar, no bonnet, half a gown and a discontented mind." As for life in Concord, she declared, "Nothing [was] stirring but the wind."

Louisa was nearly thirty. Her Concord friends and neighbors considered her fit only to settle down to the lifelong work of housekeeping and caring for her aging parents. But Louisa still allowed herself the occasional fantasy of running away. She wrote to Alf Whitman with a mix of brotherly affection and something bordering on flirtation, that she herself had been "born with a boy's nature" and fought her battles "with a boy's spirit . . . and a boy's wrath." She invited him to drop everything and go abroad

with her. The proposal was not only bold but shocking.
"Lets you and I go as sailors & work our passage over," she
suggests teasingly. But then she added, in a more tender
and appealing tone, that they might find work "all over
Europe having a nice time—Will you go?" The answer,
apparently, was a silent no—and soon Louisa's attention,
like most country folk, was consumed by the driving issue
of whether the country could continue with North and
South so bitterly divided.

The Alcotts had always been passionately opposed to
slavery. On one occasion, Bronson was part of an angry
crowd that had gathered to protest. He kept pushing forward even after police began firing on the crowd and others
ran for their lives. A friend finally had to drag him away.
The Alcotts had grieved over the death of the radical abolitionist John Brown as for a family member. They knew and
loved Brown's daughter, Annie. Louisa was a proud Yankee.
She witnessed the start of the new war with a mixture of
enthusiasm, fear, awe—and envy.

In Concord, the local soldiers were marching off to
battle. Enthusiastic crowds gathered to cheer them on.
Louisa longed to join these brave young soldiers. Her character Jo March fumes because she can't join her father and
help in the fight. Louisa herself exclaimed, "I was born with
a boy's spirit under my bib and tucker. I can't wait when I
can work." She marched down to Concord's town hall and
volunteered to sew uniforms and roll bandages.

The first years of the Civil War went badly for the North, with battle after battle lost and thousands of young men killed. The Alcott family watched anxiously as the war progressed, their minds on little else. Abby fell asleep one day in front of the fireplace, startled awake, and announced drowsily, "I've enlisted."

Louisa took the same action wide awake. She wrote to her father's old teaching assistant, Dorothea Dix, who now led the nursing effort for the war, and begged for a place as a nurse. If Louisa could be patient a little longer, Dix told her, she would help. Louisa was not yet thirty, the required minimum age for army nursing. She reluctantly agreed to wait.

After war was declared, the town of Concord became "a sight to behold," as Louisa reported to Alf. Young men drilled on the commons in their dashing blue wool uniforms. Emerson's eldest son, Edward, organized a company of cadets, and the town raised more than $4,000 in a week toward military expenses. "I long to be a man," Louisa groaned in her journal, "but as I can't fight, I will content myself with working for those who can."

She studied the care and treatment of gunshot wounds and harbored dreams of nursing the wounded. But for the time being, 1861 was mostly a time of waiting and more waiting. Louisa tried to make light of her struggles in letters to Anna. "We three mull along wearing our nightcaps to keep us warm all day like three old witches."

While May pursued her own interests with everyone else's support and approval, Louisa stayed home making pretty outfits for her vivacious youngest sister. An observant Anna commented, "Louy has almost sewed her dear old fingers off getting the child's things ready, & together we selected many pretty articles for her, & I think she will be what an Alcott never was before, 'handsomely attired.'"

The sole mainstay of her parents' household, Louisa had her work cut out for her—but it was not the world-affecting work she craved. That summer, she received an invitation to visit the White Mountains of New Hampshire—something she had always longed to do. Her family urged her to make the trip. The Alcotts had done a great deal of moving but little traveling. Louisa did not know when another opportunity would come. Once she said yes, she felt sure some catastrophe would intervene. As Anna observed, "She always seems to feel the moment she is having a good time that she is doing wrong & that her duty in this life consists in doing exactly what she doesn't want to do."

Despite Louisa's worries and dire predictions, the mountain vacation went off smoothly. In preparation, Louisa made over her old clothes, creating "pretty things . . . out of nothing." She borrowed a veil from sister Anna and set off in a new traveling suit—a rare indulgence for any Alcott.

Otherwise, it was a time of domestic chores and waiting. "Wrote, read, sewed and wanted something to do," Louisa recorded at the end of the year. By "something to do," she meant something grand and dramatic. Louisa watched the enlisted men of Concord marching off to war, departing to the music of church bells and "huzzahs." "I've often longed to see a war, and now I have," she wrote—innocent of the real horrors ahead.

While she waited to contribute to the war effort, she summoned her courage and paid a momentous visit to the famous Boston publisher James Fields. His wife Annie Fields was her distant cousin. James Fields was bookseller, editor, and head of the new *Atlantic Monthly*. Full of hope, Louisa brought him the manuscript of her tragicomic essay on her hard and unappreciated housework for a stranger, "How I Went Out to Service."

Beside Fields sat a quiet young assistant named Thomas Niles. Niles said nothing but watched what ensued. James Fields took stock of the aspiring writer and asked a few desultory questions about Louisa's previous work. He paged through her essay as Louisa sat waiting for his verdict. When he'd finished reading, he told her bluntly, "Stick to your teaching—you can't write."

In a journal entry she described her rage: "Being willful, I said, 'I won't teach, and I can write, and I'll prove it.'"

A few months later that year, Fields added insult to

injury by offering Louisa forty dollars to start her own small school—the detested teaching he said she should "stick to." The loan needn't be paid back, he added jokingly, till she'd won her own "pot of gold."

James and Annie Fields also offered Louisa room and board at their large, luxurious house overlooking the Charles River. Their mansion was a hub for the rich, the famous, and the successful. In return, Louisa was expected to perform various chores, help Annie entertain her guests, and run errands. Louisa was singularly unsuited to the work. She felt ill-used and patronized, just as she had among her wealthy May relatives.

But she was older now, and even less willing to please. The school supported by Fields ended up costing her more money and precious time. Louisa abandoned the teaching—along with her bedroom at the Fields mansion—and handed both over to her obliging sister May. "Hate to visit people who only ask me to help amuse others," she fumed. "I never knew before what insolent things a hostess can do, nor what false positions poverty can push one into."

She consoled herself by selling a story for thirty dollars to the new *Concord Monitor*, though that was not yet enough to repay James Fields. "A wasted winter and a debt of $40," she fretted, "to be paid if I sell my hair to do it."

Louisa did not forget the Fields' loan. She returned the money almost immediately after she became a success, publishing *Little Women* not with Fields but with his quiet former assistant, Thomas Niles. She included with her check to James Fields this triumphant note: "Once upon a time you lent me forty dollars, kindly saying that I might return them when I had made 'a pot of gold.' As the miracle has been unexpectedly wrought I wish to fulfil my part of the bargain & herewith repay my debt with many thanks, Very Truly Yours, L. M. Alcott."

Fields had rejected her best essay to date, and Louisa no doubt knew it. Very well then, she would write what she could sell. She churned out pulp fiction she described to Alf Whitman as "easy to 'compoze,'" and "better paid than moral & elaborate works of Shakespeare," boasting and apologizing for the work in one breath. She informed Alf her published "drivel" was likely to contain "Indians, pirates, wolves, bears & distressed damsels." These stories, she joked, bore titles like "The Maniac Bride" and "The Bath of Blood. A thrilling tale of passion."

To be sure, hers was an eclectic apprenticeship. Louisa honed her craft, writing essays, songs, poems, thrillers, sentimental romances, war stories, and fairy tales. No genre or plot was beneath her notice. She called herself a "thinking machine in full operation."

In May 1862 her childhood friend, heartthrob, and first science teacher Henry David Thoreau died after a long, hard struggle with tuberculosis. It was one more sign that Louisa's girlhood had ended. Bronson visited his naturalist friend at home a few days earlier, finding Thoreau ill and frail. Thoreau, he reported, was resigned to his fate, lying "patiently & cheerfully," remarking to Bronson only that it was taking "Nature a long time to do her work."

Louisa knew that Thoreau would have disliked the ornate funeral service that Emerson organized—and the formal church setting—but she acknowledged that Emerson's "sorrow was so great he wanted all the world to mourn with him." A few Concord worthies objected to an unbeliever like Thoreau being honored in church. Louisa wrote, "If ever a man was a real Christian it was Henry." The day of his funeral, Louisa wrote, was "lovely . . . clear, & calm, & spring like." She followed after the funeral procession with flowers falling from her arms. Outside in the churchyard, she mournfully observed, "birds were singing, early violets blooming in the grass."

Thoreau's grave was up on a wooded ridge in Concord's Sleepy Hollow Cemetery, between his father and his beloved brother John—only a few paces from where Lizzie Alcott was buried. Louisa placed a wreath of Thoreau's beloved andromeda on his grave.

She later tried to put into words her feelings for him in a poem titled "Thoreau's Flute." The poem was published by James Fields ("Stick to your teaching")—only after pressure from neighbor Sophia Hawthorne. Sophia wrote to Annie Fields, "I am sure you will both agree with me that it is worthy . . . I hope Mr. Fields will let it go into the

Atlantic that Louisa may have the honor as well as the pecuniary benefit." In her elegy, Thoreau is "the Genius of the wood," "large-hearted child," nature's "darling," his name written "in violets." (*Inviolate* again.) "O lonely friend!" she wrote poignantly.

Louisa insisted in a letter, "I never can mourn for such men because they never seem lost to me but nearer & dearer for the solemn change." Despite these brave words, her spirits sank. She was exhausted, depleted, and depressed.

Around this same sad time, Louisa attended a reading given by the popular author Rebecca Harding Davis. Davis provides us a glimpse of the author before the world knew her. She describes Louisa as a "tall, thin young woman standing alone in a corner. She was plainly dressed, and had that watchful defiant air with which the woman whose youth is slipping away is apt to face the world which has offered no place to her."

Louisa approached Davis and introduced herself. In blunt language she told the visiting author that though many of the gathered crowd "may say pleasant things to you . . . not one of them would have gone to Concord and back to see you, as I did today. I went [back home] for this gown. It's the only decent one I have. I'm very poor. . . . My name," she added, "is Louisa Alcott."

Louisa often walked the twenty miles from Concord to Boston; that day she'd traveled from Boston to Concord, changed her clothes, and walked back again—a long and wearisome journey. So much is revealed in her awkward stab at conversation with a famous literary stranger: her hope and despair, humility and defiance.

A still-unknown young woman, her publications at that point existed chiefly under a series of masks and disguises. Her best work to date had been rejected out of hand by a famous publisher. Her life looked insubstantial. She had no money and no reputation. She had accomplished little for the great national cause of freedom. Everywhere she turned, more obstacles arose.

Civil War nurses, she knew, must be thirty years old. According to the regulations of the Union army nursing corps, nurses also had to be "plain looking" and married. Louisa May Alcott was neither.

But Dix knew the Alcott family well. Louisa was a naturally gifted nurse. "Thirty years old," she jotted in her journal in November 1862. "Decided to go to Washington. . . . Help needed, and I love nursing, and *must* let out my pent-up energy in some new way. Winter is always a hard and a dull time, and if I am away there is one less to feed and warm and worry over." This last note may have been intended to placate her worried parents.

On a brighter note she added, "I want new experiences, and am sure to get 'em if I go." Her life that year was composed of tiny triumphs amid many defeats. With typical thoughtfulness and care, she'd bought Abby a handsome new hairbrush for her birthday along with a note confiding, "It has troubled me for a long while to see such an old brush on the toilette table of the lady who possessed the handsomest head of hair in the house, so here is a new one with loving wishes for many more happier brighter birthdays."

She understood her mother's gloomy introspections. On her sixty-first birthday, Abby spent the day quietly thinking "how little I had been to this family, and really how little I was in myself." It was a crushing self-assessment.

Louisa submitted her official nursing application days before her thirtieth birthday and began her preparations in earnest. She "mended up" her old clothes, noting with satisfaction, "Nurses don't need nice things, thank Heaven!" She wrote cheerfully to her male friends on the front lines if wounded in the war, to "just put it off till I get to Washington to mend you up." There is something touchingly childlike in these references to "mending," as if soldiers could be sewn back up like her dolls or hats. Reports from the battlefront trickled home, with few of the grisly details. Like many young people safely at a distance, Louisa thought of the war as a grand occasion—and to some degree, as a grand lark.

She had watched Concord's young men march off as heroes. At last her time had come. "The blood of the Mays is up," she exclaimed. "I must go."

CHAPTER TWELVE

Union Hotel Hospital

Just before she left Concord, Louisa entered a writing contest at *Frank Leslie's Illustrated Newspaper.* The prize was a whopping one hundred dollars. She submitted "Pauline's Passion and Punishment," a story featuring a strong but dangerous character: "To and fro, like a wild creature in its cage, paced that handsome woman, with bent head, locked hands and restless steps." It could have been a self-portrait of Louisa that autumn, trapped in Orchard House, waiting for release.

Her army orders lagged till December 11. Then she was thrown into action with amazing speed. She had only one day to pack her things. Her mother and sisters helped, as did their long-mocked neighbor Sophia Hawthorne. Louisa packed only the necessities, saving space for her pens and paper, her diary, and works by her favorite author, Charles Dickens, to read aloud to her soldier patients. Her mother supplied sandwiches, apples, and gingerbread for the long journey from Concord to Washington, DC.

We know about Louisa's nursing days chiefly from her own letters, diary entries, and above all, her semifictional account, *Hospital Sketches*. The author—who narrates the story under the name "Nurse Periwinkle"—gives a bird's-eye view of the Civil War. Nineteenth-century Americans had little access to what was happening on the front. *Hospital Sketches* gave readers a glimpse from the inside. It became Alcott's first true success. As with *Little Women,* she'd "lived it."

At the verge of leaving for her nursing stint, Louisa choked down a last cup of tea she'd stirred by accident with salt instead of sugar. Her courage failed at the sight of her aging mother waiting to say goodbye. "I had taken my life in my hand, and might never see them all again," she realized. Abby, who had lost one daughter to scarlet fever, could not hide her fear. The stricken Louisa asked, "Shall I stay, Mother?" Abby answered firmly, "No, go! And the Lord be with you."

It was the kind of gallantly "boyish" farewell scene Louisa had been dreaming of all her life. Her mother waved a damp handkerchief at the door, and Louisa "set forth in the December twilight, with May and Julian Hawthorne as escort, feeling as if I was the son of the house going to war."

Louisa was too practical to linger in a state of high drama. She set off to get a tooth filled, bought a traveling veil, and tried to claim her free nurse's rail ticket. It took her half the day to get it. She ran back and forth between railway clerks and officials, comparing herself to "an energetic fly in a very large cobweb." Finally, ticket in hand, she ate a quick supper with her sister Anna and gentle brother-in-law, John Pratt, survived one last farewell, and departed "full of hope and sorrow, courage and plans."

Louisa caught a steamship to New Jersey, worrying that her usual accident-prone "bad luck" would bring disaster down on everyone on board. She was surprised to see the sun rising peacefully over the Long Island Sound the next morning, with "mist wreaths slowly furling off, and a pale pink sky above us." She rode a train through Philadelphia on south through Baltimore. There came the mishap she'd been waiting for—suddenly her train car came uncoupled, sending objects flying everywhere. "No journey in America would be complete," she noted with satisfaction, without incident.

As a lone traveler, she looked to the other women on

board for clues of what to do. When one woman suggested to a friend that they secure their berths, Louisa darted at one and peeked out to find what came next: "Several ladies draw the curtains that hang in a semicircle before each nest—instantly I whisk mine smartly together, and then peep out to see what next. Gradually, on hooks above the blue and yellow drapery, appear the coats and bonnets of my neighbors, while their boots and shoes, in every imaginable attitude, assert themselves below, as if their owners had committed suicide in a body."

For humor, sharp observation, and character, nothing Louisa May Alcott wrote quite compares to her *Hospital Sketches*, not even *Little Women*. That may be a *greater* book, but it is less consistently adept.

The train flew south, past strangers "looking as if they had come out of a picture book, or off the stage," alongside military encampments "gay with blue coats and the glitter of buttons." From the safe distance of the train, war looked like an exciting spectacle, where young boys "threw up their caps and cut capers as we passed."

The farther south they rode, the less she liked it. The sight of a place where a Massachusetts regiment had been fired upon by rebel soldiers made her want to throw "a stone at somebody, hard." She had not come to make friends, nor to win fame or fortune but, as she said with breathtaking foresight, "I'm here to fulfill my destiny."

The immensity of Washington, DC, she wrote, "quite took my breath away," but the Capitol Building reminded her that Cinderella labored in a castle—and Pennsylvania Avenue made her feel as if she'd "crossed the water and landed somewhere in Carnival time." She saw fashionable ladies dressed in "three story bonnets, with overhanging balconies of flowers" and decided "that they dressed in the worst possible taste, and walked like ducks."

Whenever Louisa felt lost she made fun: her way of whistling in the dark. The shabby Union Hotel had been hastily upended into a wartime hospital. Louisa's arrival in the dead of night made the place look even more frightening. Armed guards blocked the front door, along with "a very trying quantity of men lounging about." She wrote, "It struck me that I was very far from home."

A tour inside did little to cheer her. Louisa's room was poorly lit and unventilated, her windows nailed shut. Where window glass had broken, curtains hung in a vain attempt to keep out the cold. She shared her cramped room with one other nurse. Two bare iron bedsteads were the only furniture. Her tiny closet held cockroaches and rats. She was warned not to leave her things out in plain sight—someone in the hospital would likely steal them.

Her ward was no better than her living quarters, with iron cots, hard pillows, dirty mattresses, filthy floors, and unwashed windows. Many nurses quickly fled in dismay, leaving the Union Hotel Hospital desperately understaffed.

Louisa later described the chaos: "Some dozen women did double duty; and then were blamed for breaking down. If any hospital director fancies this a good and economical arrangement, allow one used up nurse to tell him it isn't, and beg him to spare the sisterhood . . . who forget that they are mortal, and run the risk of being made immortal sooner than is agreeable to their partial friends." Louisa, with no medical background or real-life training, quickly became superintendent of a ward of forty beds.

At the start of her adventure she'd written, "I'm a woman's rights woman, and if any man had offered help . . . I should have condescendingly refused it, sure that I could do everything as well, if not better, myself." Here was a chance to test her own theory.

Everything at the Union Hotel Hospital was in a state of confusion. Ailing patients, sickly and weak, were expected to perform hard tasks as soon as they were able to get out of bed. A soldier with a bad heart did so much heavy lifting that he was closer to dying when he left than when he'd come. Another injured young soldier with a bad back scrubbed the floors, his lips white with pain. After she'd finished her twelve-hour nursing shift, Louisa got on her hands and knees and washed the floor to spare him.

She wrote home to joke that signs of the Union Hotel's former existence remained. Her ward of forty sick soldiers "was in truth a ball-room, if gun-shot wounds could christen it."

The conditions were not conducive to good health. Her first patients were sick, not war-wounded; men with measles, diphtheria, typhoid, and pneumonia all slept in the same room. Louisa herself replaced a nurse who had fallen ill. Life in the Union Hotel Hospital was not the glorious work she'd expected. "Rheumatism wasn't heroic, neither was liver complaint, or measles." She waited impatiently for the new soldier patients to arrive. Three days later she got her wish.

Louisa was wakened at dawn by a pounding at her door, and the call; "They've come, they've come! Hurry up ladies—you're wanted." In her confusion Louisa thought rebel soldiers were attacking the hospital, but the uproar came from Yankee casualties pouring in from the battle at nearby Fredericksburg, Virginia. The carnage was worse than anyone could have imagined. Fredericksburg marked a terrible loss for the North. Within the space of five days, thirteen thousand Union soldiers had been captured, wounded, or killed.

Louisa's hospital sat close by the center of the coming storm, and forty carts of the injured and dying unloaded "their sad freight at our door." She admitted that she had once "rather longed for the wounded to arrive." The numbers of the dead and dying froze her on the spot: "My ardor experienced a sudden chill, and I indulged in a most unpatriotic wish that I was safe at home again." Her light tone disguises the horror of the moment. She was inexperienced, new at the job—and in charge.

Crowds of men swarmed inside, some carted on stretchers, others limping on crutches, still others staggering in alone or shuffling a wounded comrade toward the converted ballroom. Even for Louisa, who had done her share of home nursing, the scene was overwhelming. "All was hurry and confusion; the hall was full of these wrecks of humanity."

Safe in Concord she had once written in her journal, "It seems as if a few energetic women could carry on the war better than the men do it so far." If so, they needed to work fast. There was no system in place to care for these men. Each patient, however badly wounded, had to be stopped, lined up, and "duly ticketed and registered" before they could be helped. Men propped themselves up against the walls, while the worst injured lay on the floor. A knot of soldiers tried to warm themselves around the stove: "ragged, gaunt and pale, mud to the knees, with bloody bandages untouched since put on days before." All of them, she observed, were "wearing that disheartened look which proclaimed defeat."

But Louisa barely had time to think. The hospital

matron, Hannah Ropes, handed her a basin, a sponge, and a block of brown soap and told her to begin washing the men. "If she had requested me to shave them all," sputtered Louisa, "or dance a hornpipe on the stove funnel, I should have been less staggered; but to scrub some dozen lords of creation at a moment's notice, was really—really—."

Louisa set to work, trying to look as if she knew what she was doing. This was probably her first physical contact with undressed and half-dressed men. It was certainly the first time she'd had to bathe one. Her first patient—or experiment—was an "old withered Irishman" who enjoyed Louisa's attentions and blessed her aloud. His teasing and laughter gave her courage to continue. For the next twelve hours she cleaned and comforted soldiers, using her limited tools at hand. She tended to young boys who had lost their arms or legs or minds, and handsome men with faces disfigured by bullets. A few words and a gentle touch were often all she had to offer; it was heart-wrenching to see how gratefully these were received. A soldier from New England gave her a pair of earrings meant for a friend's widow, because, he said, Louisa looked like the dead man's bride. One wounded soldier asked for a glass of water. Louisa ran to fetch it; by the time she came back "something in the tired white face caused me to listen at his lips for a breath. None came."

The next day, Louisa was thrown into even more horrifying duties. She assisted at the bloody amputations—undertaken without ether—and tested her ability to dress real-life wounds. The men's courage lent her strength. Many nurse volunteers ran from the ghastly work; Louisa held her own. After her hospital shift was done, she recalled, "the next task was to minister to their minds." Louisa sat beside the men and wrote letters to their loved ones, listened to their stories and confessions. She delivered money and valuables to the matron for safekeeping. At five o'clock the men had their supper. Even the worst wounded ate so much that Louisa feared the hospital would run out of food.

"Bless their hearts, why shouldn't they eat?" warmly demanded the matron, Hannah Ropes. "It's their only amusement; so fill every one, and, if there's not enough ready to-night, I'll lend my share to the Lord by giving it to the boys." Hannah Ropes's self-sacrifice was what Louisa had been used to all her life; it made Louisa feel closer to the "large-hearted old lady."

Louisa offered to take on the job of night nurse. She didn't mind the "topsy-turvy" hours. "I learned to know these men better by night than through any intercourse by day." She read the soldiers' sleeping faces and "found many things to amuse, instruct, and interest." "The snores alone were quite a study."

By day she explored the city of Washington, occasionally in the company of a young surgeon named Dr. John Winslow. His attentions, invitations, poetry recitations (he knew reams of Browning by heart), and his habit of giving "confidences in the twilight" alarmed Louisa. She may have switched to night duty partly to avoid the good doctor, whom she dismissed as "amiably amusing, & exceedingly young." Her night-long duties created "a strange life." She slept by day, but somehow still found time for long, relieving morning runs. She napped a few hours, then ate dinner at five with the staff. At nine p.m. the night bell rang; the gas was turned down, and as the day staff went off duty, her night watch came on.

Louisa divided her ward into three areas: "'my duty room,' my 'pleasure room,' and my 'pathetic room.'" This last room—given the nickname used for her own Alcott family—got her closest attention. "Wherever the sickest or most helpless man chanced to be, there I held my watch."

While the men slept or dozed she guarded them, "hovering, like a massive cherubim, in a red rigolette, over the slumbering sons of man." Sometimes a few patients would wake at the same time, and she'd run back and forth, "like an agitated pendulum." Of the nursing work itself she said simply, "I liked it." She tried to keep things merry, believing "that he who laughed most was surest of recovery." The men's faces brightened when Louisa arrived each evening, and she allowed herself a flush of pleasure in their welcome, "enjoying that moment heartily" before settling down to business.

She did not find her "owling" life lonely. She came to

know the hospital's night watchman, though she "never fairly saw his face." One night attendant whom she called "goblin" insisted on sharing his strong coffee with her. She dubbed his concoction "mud soup," served "scalding hot . . . rich in an all-pervading flavor of molasses, scorch and tin pot." She'd pretend to accept the "fearful beverage" gratefully, and the instant the attendant's back was turned, whip it into the nearest slop jar.

At thirty, Louisa was tender, vibrant, and affectionate. Dying men reached for her hand. They confided their last secrets to her. She in turn was deeply touched by them. Her first love affairs happened on that hospital ward—none of them typical, but Louisa was not typical. She drew close to "her boys" without having to manage a full, real-life relationship.

Strongest of all her attachments was to a Virginia blacksmith known to readers of *Hospital Sketches* simply as John. His real-life name was John Sulie, and he was Louisa's age. He is the unlikely romantic hero of *Hospital Sketches*. His story serves as the emotional climax of the book. John may be partly invented, but if so, he is one of Alcott's best creations. There is not a false step, no sentiment, no tidy ending. John is made of the earth, and to the earth he returns.

The fatally wounded hero is "a large, fair man, with a fine face, and the serenest eyes I ever met"—a description that might aptly fit Bronson Alcott. But John was a romantic figure in all the ways Bronson wasn't. He was strong, silent, universally admired. He was also young, and fated to die on Louisa's watch.

John had been wounded in battle while rescuing a young comrade. The narrator Nurse Periwinkle/Louisa admits, "I was a little afraid of the stately looking man, whose bed had to be lengthened to accommodate his commanding stature; who seldom spoke, uttered no complaint . . . as he lay high upon his pillows, no picture of dying statesman or warrior was ever fuller of real dignity than this Virginia blacksmith."

John had been shot in the back. He could not see his wound and did not understand how deadly it was. He struggled for breath and suffered more than any other patient in her "pathetic room," but he never said a word of self-pity or complaint. His death would not be easy, his doctor predicted grimly: "It will be a hard struggle, and a long one, for he possesses great vitality." To Louisa fell the bitter task of telling John he could not recover.

She kept her distance from her most pitiful patient at first, despite—or perhaps even because of—his beauty. "A most attractive face . . . framed in brown hair and beard, comely featured and full of vigor." Louisa was feminine yet boyish, John tough yet tender. She wrote of him, "His mouth was grave and firm, with plenty of will and courage in its lines, but a smile could make it as sweet as any woman's."

One night she stood nearby while his terrible wound was dressed. John's pain was so intense that she saw "great tears roll down and drop to the floor." Her shyness vanished. She supported the large man in her arms. He responded fervently, "This is right good! This is what I wanted!" Louisa kept close to John till the very end. On his deathbed he grasped her hand so tightly that when she drew away at last, her hand "was strangely cold and stiff, and four white marks remained across its back." The blacksmith left his imprint on her heart as well. She claimed that no death except her beloved sister Lizzie's ever made her "heart ache as it did then."

Soon after John died, Louisa's head began to ache. She tried to shrug it off as a cold. A sturdy New Englander, Louisa was accustomed to working through exhaustion and illness. For the next few days she felt well enough to go about the city and watch Washington's "mammoth masquerade." She wrote about men in "painfully tight uniforms" and little caps looking "like stuffed fowls" and others adorned with "Spanish hats, scarlet lined riding cloaks, swords and sashes, high boots and bright spurs, beards and mustaches, which made plain faces comely, and comely faces heroic." It was as if the Alcott girls' exotic childhood plays had sprung to life and walked about on city streets. Even after Louisa developed a racking cough, she continued to work her night shift and to go for morning runs in the cold.

She wrote in her journal on January 1, 1863, "I never began the year in a stranger place than this . . . alone, among strangers . . . surrounded by three or four hundred men in all stages of suffering, disease, and death." She did not realize she was about to join their ranks. Instead she tried to "cork up" her own exhaustion, hoping to be "motherly" to her patients. She began her new year by "seeing a poor man die at dawn, and sitting all day between a boy with pneumonia and a man shot through the lungs."

Just after the New Year she learned that she had won the hundred-dollar award in Frank Leslie's contest for her story "Pauline's Passion and Punishment." Her work was chosen from over two hundred entries. Not even the uplift of good news and good fortune could restore her constitution. She had been fighting off sickness for days. Mrs. Ropes, the kindly hospital matron, was diagnosed with typhoid pneumonia, and the outlook grew grim. Typhoid pneumonia was a dangerous, often fatal disease.

Soon after Mrs. Ropes fell ill, one of the doctors— probably the young John Winslow—found Louisa slumped on a staircase, trying to cool her forehead on the iron banister. At last, under pressure, she took to her bed. "Sharp pain in the side, cough, fever & dizziness," she wrote tersely. "A pleasant prospect for a lonely soul five hundred miles from home."

Louisa's condition grew worse. It was soon clear that she too had typhoid pneumonia—with the same dire prognosis. The Union Hospital was overrun with the wounded and dying. It was a terrible place to be sick. Even Louisa's friends on the staff begged her to leave the hospital in order to get well. She wrote in her journal: "Feel too miserable to care much. . . . Nurses fussy & anxious, matron dying, & everything very gloomy. They want me to go home but I *won't* yet."

She worried more about the lonely isolation of a sickbed than surviving pneumonia. But to her grateful surprise, the hospital staff took care of her. Even the head of the Union Army of Nurses, Dorothea Dix herself, visited every day to check on Louisa. A stream of doctors, including her unsuccessful suitor, Dr. John Winslow, kept stopping by. One evening she saw Winslow down on his knees on the floor, trying to coax her fireplace to life.

Every doctor on the ward, meaning to be helpful, dosed Louisa with quantities of calomel, a powerful mercury compound. In the mid-nineteenth century, calomel was considered a miracle drug. It turned out to be a deadly poison, now known to be so toxic that doctors wear protective gloves when handling it. Nothing destroyed Louisa's health and strength more thoroughly than the repeated mercury doses she was given to "cure" her. For the rest of her life she would suffer from the calomel's terrible side effects, including memory loss, tremors, shortness of breath, headaches, loose teeth, dizziness, hair loss, and damage to her kidneys and brain.

Louisa refused the doctors' orders to go home. She was determined to finish her three-month stint for the Union army. Dorothea Dix offered to move Louisa to her private apartments, but Louisa refused special treatment. Fevered and delirious, she argued that she'd so far served only one month out of the three and must stay on, even as she grew sicker and weaker each day.

She scribbled in her diary, "Dream awfully, & wake unrefreshed, think of home, & wonder if I am to die here as Mrs. R., the matron, is likely to do." The desperately ill Mrs. Ropes insisted a telegram be sent to Concord, begging the family to fetch Louisa home.

Bronson Alcott, against his usual impractical and dreamy nature, sprang into action. He left on a noon train and arrived in Washington the next day. But with all his powers of persuasion he couldn't convince Louisa to leave the Union Hospital. Bronson made the rounds of the place and was horrified by the human price of war. Though he passionately supported the Union cause, he never forgot his lesson on the wards. Later he wrote, "One sees its horrors in hospitals if anywhere." He toyed with the idea of arranging to meet his hero, President Lincoln. But his attention for once remained focused on his daughter. He kept begging Louisa to come home with him. She kept refusing.

The hospital's good-hearted matron, Mrs. Ropes, passed away on January 20. The next day, when Bronson pleaded his case again, Louisa finally agreed.

Had it not been for the calomel "cure" she received, she might have recovered from her bout of pneumonia completely. She had always possessed a strong constitution and an invincible spirit. But the damage, once set in motion, could not be undone. The effects of mercury poisoning would not fully show themselves for decades—and even then, doctors would keep missing the clues.

Julian Hawthorne remembered how his vibrant next-door neighbor, Louisa May Alcott, had set off for wartime Washington a "tender-hearted, generous girl, with black hair, thick and long, and flashing, humorous eyes." She was carried back home a "white tragic mask of what she had been." Abby was shocked at her daughter's appearance. Even after doctors declared her well, Julian observed "there were occasional tones in her voice and expressions of eyes and mouth that indicated depths of which she could not speak." Louisa had been floundering for years at the edge of adulthood, looking for a sense of purpose. She had found it as a nurse in some of the darkest days of the war, and she had held her own as bravely as any soldier. She left Concord a comical girl—one who had known hardship to be sure—but she returned home a heroine.

CHAPTER THIRTEEN

Tribulation Periwinkle

Louisa did not recover her strength all at once. She barely remembered the journey north with her anxious father. Once home, she continued to experience fevers, chills, and delirium. She believed at first that Orchard House was "roofless"—an apt metaphor for unprotected Alcott family life. Louisa suffered hallucinations over the next three weeks, a jumble of things she had recently seen, felt, or heard. "The most vivid & enduring," she wrote, was that she had married "a stout, handsome Spaniard, dressed in black velvet with very soft hands & a voice that was continually saying 'Lie still, my dear.' This was mother, I suspect."

The "mammoth masquerade" of Washington's streets had been transformed in her fever dreams; men in their

"Spanish hats, scarlet lined riding cloaks, swords and sashes, high boots and bright spurs" melded into one figure who pursued and constrained Louisa, till she found herself pleading for help and forgiveness. "I appealed to the Pope, & really got up & made a touching plea in something meant for Latin." She imagined she was being "hung for a witch, burned, stoned, & otherwise maltreated," and that she was urged to join Dr. Winslow and two other nurses "in worshipping the Devil." In another dream she thought she'd died and gone to heaven. She found it a "dismal" and "ordinary" place and wished she hadn't come. One feverish delusion carried her back to the Union Hotel Hospital, "tending millions of sick men who never died or got well." This last nightmare was so distressing that she flung herself out of bed to escape and crashed onto the floor.

In early February, after three weeks of disorientation, Louisa returned at last to her senses, if not to full health. She spied in the mirror "a queer, thin, big-eyed face" staring back. Her long, luxuriant brown hair, her "one beauty" and only vanity, was gone, shaved off by the doctors. Louisa had sometimes thought of selling her long hair for money. Instead she had sacrificed it to the war. For months she covered her head with a cap or wig while her own hair grew back, and she tried hard not to care. Always the most robust of the Alcotts, she did not willingly take on the role of invalid. As she would later say, "The life of an invalid is best left to silence."

Her mother wrote, "Poor Louy left us a brave, handsome woman . . . and returned almost a wreck of body and mind." Had the family known in advance, Abby admitted, the sacrifice "should not have been made willingly." "Never mind," Louisa joked. "It might have been my head & a wig outside is better than a loss of wits inside." By March, her appetite had returned a little, and she could sit up in bed. She received ten dollars for her work in the Union Hospital, which closed that chapter of her life. She began thinking again about books and her own writing.

A sparkle of good news on March 28, 1863, brought joy to the Alcotts—and Bronson in particular. Anna had given birth to a healthy baby—at last, the long-awaited baby boy! Bronson delivered the joyful news to Louisa, Abby, and May. Louisa later wrote, "With one accord we three opened our mouths & screamed for about two minutes; then mother began to cry."

Louisa had been hoping for a niece, but Bronson went around Concord in a daze of happiness, saying to "every one he met from Emerson to the coach driver . . . 'Anna's boy, yes, yes, Anna's boy.'" The still-frail Louisa pulled on a white cap to cover her bald head and tottered down the Lexington Road to meet her newborn nephew. She celebrated being upright and walking again. The town of Concord looked "beautiful and new," she gratefully declared.

"A good fit of illness proves the value of health," she

noted, "and self-sacrifice sweetens character"—that old, lifelong Alcott refrain. Abby forever mourned her daughter's loss of vitality, but Louisa wrote, "I shall never regret the going . . . for one may live and learn much in a month."

That spring a regiment of Union soldiers stopped outside Orchard House and presented arms in honor of their wartime nurse. With her old scarlet hospital rigolette thrown over her short hair, she went out to walk among them with tears in her eyes. Julian Hawthorne claimed it was the only time he saw Louisa cry.

In a quiet moment, she reflected, "To go very near to death teaches one to value life, & this winter will always be a very memorable one to me." The fields outside Orchard House were covered in snow when she first arrived home; they were carpeted with mayflowers before she came fully back to herself, and still the Civil War raged on.

That war—infinitely more drawn-out and deadly than anyone had dreamed—resulted in new work for the women at home. They took on jobs never before open to them—working in hospitals, government offices, and publishing houses. Even women's fashion changed. Feminists and physicians alike rejected the use of crinolines and tight corsets. War nurses gave up their hoop skirts for the sake of practicality. Pantalets, the first popular form of women's trousers, appeared.

New opportunities came Louisa's way as well. She reworked the letters home she had written from the hospital. She altered details to protect the identity of others, naming her alter-ego narrator "Tribulation Periwinkle." Though she called it fiction, those sketches stayed close to the truth—or at least, to the truth as she had reported it in her journals and letters home.

Frank Sanborn printed excerpts in his magazine, the *Boston Commonwealth*. Its first installment appeared in May 1863, after a crushing loss at the battle at Chancellorsville. Alcott's wartime writing sparked immediate interest among American readers and editors. Louisa dismissed her sketches at first: "They thought them witty & pathetic . . . I didn't, but I wanted money."

In the end, two editors vied for what would become the book known as *Hospital Sketches*. One was Thomas Niles, that silent young editor who sat beside James Fields when he told Louisa, "You can't write." Apparently Niles suspected that she could. But his publishing company was known for photographic books rather than for literature. Louisa chose a fiery lifelong abolitionist as her publisher instead. James Redpath produced an edition of one thousand copies and paid the author a royalty of five cents per copy.

On August 25, 1863, the day that *Hospital Sketches* appeared, Louisa noted that her "first morning-glory bloomed" in her room, "a hopeful blue." The paperback book appeared between green covers—not the army-drab Louisa would have liked, but she nonetheless called the production "quite a neat little affair." It could not compete with Anna's handsome baby boy, of course—but it would do. "I sell *my* children," Louisa wrote ruefully, "and though they feed me, they don't love me as hers do."

If her stories didn't love her, her readers did. *Hospital Sketches* won Louisa enthusiastic readers and reviewers. The sketches were praised as "fluent and sparkling, with touches of quiet humor and lively wit." Louisa was amazed. "Much to my surprise they made a great hit," she celebrated in her journal. "I find I've done a good thing without knowing it." She downplayed her own accomplishment, modestly insisting "'John Sulie' was the hero, & the praise belonged to him.'"

She was also bewildered—this was not the way she had expected to win fame. She had been raised to write serious literature, filled with grand ideas. "I cannot see why people like a few extracts from topsey turvey letters written on inverted tea kettles," she mused. Those "topsey turvey" letters were the first things she had published in her own, clear, witty voice. It was a change from both her gothic thrillers and her attempts at fictional Genius. Much later—it was fifteen years later in fact—she finally admitted, "[*Hospital Sketches*] showed me 'my style,' and taking the hint, I went where glory waited me."

Buoyed by the "praise and glory," she wrote, "I have the satisfaction of seeing my town folk buying, reading, laughing & crying over it wherever I go." Abby was ecstatic, and Bronson proud in his own way. "Nothing could be more surprising," he wrote, than this public "appreciation of Louisa's merits as a woman and a writer." It is typical of Bronson that he emphasized her merits "as a woman" first. Frank Sanborn, on the other hand, informed Louisa, "Any publisher this side of Baltimore would be glad to get a book from Louisa May Alcott."

With this encouragement, Louisa thought immediately of *Moods*, which she considered her *real* literary debut. Now that her "topsey turvey letters" had been met with enthusiasm, surely there would be a place for her novels *Moods* and *Work*. Even Louisa, who complained that "everything goes by contraries with me," gave in to moments of optimism. She crowed in her journal in October 1863, "Fifteen years of hard grubbing may be coming to something after all, & I may yet 'pay all the debts, fix the house, send May to Italy & keep the old folks cosy,' as I've said I would so long yet so hopelessly."

Moods did find a publisher, though her new editor, A. K. Loring, insisted on a raft of cuts and changes. He admired her characters—and no doubt, her newfound fame—but he made her boil the novel down to 286 pages. A family friend, the young novelist Henry James, promised Louisa a warm review as soon as the novel appeared.

Initially Louisa resisted Loring's editorial suggestions, turning from *Moods* to her second novel, *Work*. Then one night she had an "inspired" idea of how to rewrite *Moods*. In two weeks, Louisa slashed ten chapters from the book, sacrificing many of her favorite scenes. As when she first composed the book, she descended into a mad "vortex" of creativity. "The fit was on strong & for a fortnight I hardly ate slept or stirred but wrote, wrote like a thinking machine in full operation." She hadn't yet learned that her frenzies didn't necessarily lead her to greatness. She rode on the vision of her own genius, believing that she had sharpened and improved the manuscript.

But Louisa was too sharp to fool herself for long. Regret set in. She had cut too much, she moaned, too hastily—and all the wrong things. She had ruined the book, and what remained was "small, stupid & no more my own."

Louisa never stopped mourning her first creation. At age forty-nine, she'd revise *Moods* yet again, changing the ending one more time. Louisa blamed the world for the disappointing reception of *Moods*. She blamed herself for not standing her ground. She blamed the publisher and editor, A. K. Loring, for demanding bad revisions. She even advised a young writer never to work with Loring, calling him "neither honest nor polite." In its shrunken, chopped-up condition, the novel was published in 1864, to far less acclaim than her "topsey turvey" *Hospital Sketches*.

A few critics did praise her "lively wit and clear observation," but more attacked *Moods*'s style, topic, and plot.

The novel's stance on women and marriage brought New England wrath down on her head—and worse still, contempt. One reviewer called Alcott one of those "maiden reformers . . . who knew nothing of marriage by experience."

The twenty-one-year-old novelist Henry James, who had promised Louisa a fine review, tore *Moods* to shreds—attacking "the author's ignorance of human nature, and her self-confidence in spite of this ignorance." His father, Henry James Sr., called the book "the Dumps." It's a wonder the Alcotts ever spoke to the James family again.

Abby Alcott remained her daughter's greatest fan. "Her powers are greater than she knows," she insisted. Abby predicted in her 1863 journal, "It may take years, but she will have no mean ranks assigned her now. She is in the vestibule of the Temple, but the high Altar is not far off." In this assessment she was farsighted—though less accurate in judging her daughter's flagging health.

Abby took a desperately hopeful view: "She has great recuperative powers," she wrote to Dorothea Dix. Louisa's strong constitution, she wrote, "has often stood the test of sudden attacks and left her but superficially damaged." Louisa showed early symptoms of her illness from the moment she came home from her hospital. As she declared later, "I was never ill before this time, and never well afterward."

Though *Moods* fell short of Louisa's ambitions, she continued to publish stories both under her own name and under pseudonyms. Praise for *Hospital Sketches* continued to pour in. "A sort of perpetual surprise-party," she called it, and was especially touched when soldiers wrote to thank her. But she also began to see the darker side of fame. She he found it embarrassing to be the center of public attention. "Admire the books, but let the woman alone, if you please, dear public!" she declared—a hint of what was to come when fame arrived. She bolted from success the way most people run from failure. "People are very kind & very easily pleased & I'm much obliged, but don't understand it at all & probably never shall."

She turned down social invitations she would have eagerly accepted a few years earlier: "I refused being too busy & too bashful to be made a lion of even in a very small way." She offered her second novel, *Success* (published under the title *Work*), to James Redpath, who was eager to bring out another sparkling, realistic Alcott book. He balked at *Success*, though Louisa did her best to persuade him. "I don't wish to be obstinate," she wrote to Redpath, "but I still feel that I'd rather have 'Success' come first." It proved a losing battle.

But she had more successes than failures now. For the first time, magazines approached *her*. "A year ago I had no publisher & went begging with my wares; now *three* have asked me for something," she cheered. In the same journal of 1863, she began to invent a new myth about her past, claiming she'd "had a literary friend to lend a helping hand!" Thoreau himself had tutored her; Emerson lent his books and warm encouragement; James Fields gave her money and a place to live—the list goes on and on. But she told the hard luck story of a fully self-made woman.

With her earnings, she reshingled the roof at Orchard House, bought rugs and carpeting, paid debts "as usual," and splurged for "hat, boots, gloves, ribbons & other little matters" for May—acting very much the "man of the family." She turned down a teaching job, telling her prospective employer with understandable glee, "My time is fully occupied with my pen & I find story writing not only pleasanter than teaching but far more profitable, so I am glad to change the work which I have done for fifteen years for more congenial employment."

There was talk of another book to be written in the style of *Hospital Sketches*, this time a lighthearted travelogue about her vacation in the New Hampshire mountains with her Willis cousins. But after a few segments were published, she stopped short, declaring she was "heartily ashamed of them." If she only wrote for laughs, she was afraid she "should be rowdy & nothing more," noting, "I'm glad of the lesson & hope it will do me good." She was becoming a sharper critic of her work in general. Poetry, she finally decided, "is not my forte." She tried to write a war story, "but couldn't make it go," and refused an editing job: "was afraid to try," she confessed in her journal. She did agree to write a Christmas tale, which James Redpath published, "so there was another little help for this incapable family." That word *incapable* seemed harsh, so she crossed it out and substituted the word *rising*. Louisa's revisions were as revealing as her first drafts.

Frank Leslie's new publication, *Chimney Corner*, sought Louisa out as a regular contributor, offering fifty dollars in advance for each story. Biographer Cornelia Meigs explains how initially, Louisa literally could not believe her good fortune: "She was only worn-out Louisa Alcott, a total failure." Success confused her. "I don't know who I am," she wrote, point-blank.

There were new projects on other fronts. She had not abandoned her passion for the Northern cause, and she tried to use her small dose of fame to help. She arranged a trip down to Port Royal, South Carolina, to tutor contrabands—the African Americans who had fled slavery and joined the Union army. She planned to chronicle in letter form all that she witnessed.

She wrote to the head of the organization in Port Royal, "I should like of all things to go South & help the blacks as I am no longer allowed to nurse the whites." Lest she be misunderstood she added, "The former seems the greater work, and . . . most interesting to me." Without a male escort to chaperone her, however, the trip to Port Royal was torpedoed. Undaunted by the setback, she helped in other ways, editing and publishing a collection of letters called "Colored Soldiers' Letters." She ran the refreshment tables at a "Fair for Colored Orphans." And she wrote stories that strongly expressed her political views.

A family photo taken at this time shows Louisa sitting cross-legged on the ground, surrounded by standing family. It is the only natural-looking picture of Louisa in existence. The photo shows Orchard House to be sturdy, if shabby. Repairs were "proudly paid out of my story money," Louisa remarked, adding, "I call the old house 'the sinking fund' as it swallows up all I can earn."

It was a period touched with troubles as well as joy. Louisa began to suffer from toothaches, fatigue, and "blue devils." Bronson's mother, Grandmother Alcott, passed away at age eighty-nine, and Louisa's elusive neighbor Nathaniel Hawthorne died in his sleep while away on a camping trip in the White Mountains. His death was shockingly sudden. Bronson Alcott and Emerson served as pallbearers. Hawthorne was buried in Sleepy Hollow Cemetery on Author's Ridge, close to Thoreau's grave and Lizzie Alcott's. Only once had Louisa been able to trick her way into Hawthorne's third-floor "sky parlor" study. She'd pretended to need a particular book, and while the famous author was distracted, she had "wandered in."

With the flurry of fame from *Hospital Sketches* behind her, life resumed its lifeless pace. At the end of 1863 Louisa wrote in her journal, "Christmas a very quiet day, no presents." Life had returned to its dreary round of chores. It seemed certain that nothing exciting would ever happen again. As she noted, rereading those sad diary entries long after the fact, "Short-sighted Louisa! Little did you dream . . . [you were] to make your fortune a few years later."

In *Jo's Boys*, the last of her books about the March family, the author wrote—taking the words almost verbatim from one of her own letters—"Things always went by contraries with Jo. Her first book, labored over for years, and launched full of the high hopes and ambitious dreams of youth, foundered on its voyage, though the wreck continued to float long afterward, to the profit of the publisher at least." In *Jo's Boys* she referred to the failure of a *Moods*-like novel, contrasting it with the unexpected, overwhelming real-life success of a fictional work resembling *Little Women*. "The hastily written story, sent away with no thought beyond the few dollars it might bring, sailed with a fair wind and a wise pilot at the helm straight into public favor, and came home heavily laden with an unexpected cargo of gold and glory." But she had a few more capsizes and dunkings ahead before that ship would sail in.

CHAPTER FOURTEEN

A Little Romance

In the mid-1860s, on a quiet New Year's Day, Louisa and Anna attended a dance to benefit the Soldiers' Aid Society. The two sisters sat up in the gallery "and watched the young people dance the old year out." Louisa no longer counted herself among young people. She had settled into dull domestic routine: "Sewed, cleaned house & wrote." She was back where she'd started, as if she'd never published *Hospital Sketches* or *Moods*. "Nothing stirring but the wind," she once wrote of life in Concord, "nothing to see but dust. . . . If I think of my woes, I fall into a vortex of debts, dishpans and despondency awful to see." She was waiting "for the Lord to give me a lift," she added, only half joking.

Two major events threw her dreary personal routine out of orbit, one domestic, the other national. First came the birth of a second nephew, John Pratt. The other was the shocking assassination of President Lincoln. "The city went into mourning," observed Louisa. All that lifted her low spirits was the sight of a Black man walking in Lincoln's funeral procession "arm in arm with a white gentleman."

She had nearly resigned herself to being an eternal onlooker when an unexpected invitation fell into her lap. A well-to-do Boston shipping merchant, William Fletcher Weld, had heard that Louisa "was something of a nurse & wanted to travel." He invited her to become a traveling companion for his frail daughter, Anna Weld, and make the so-called grand tour of Europe. It was the offer of a lifetime, and just the "lift" Louisa had been praying for. She had always longed to see the world, and to visit Europe was her most cherished dream. But she hesitated to part with her "dear home faces," especially her mother's, whose health and spirits were still flagging.

In her private journal, Abby compared herself to "a boat much buffeted about by adverse winds and rough tides." She wished fair sailing for her second daughter; everyone in Louisa's family urged her to go. It was no small sacrifice. Louisa was pledged to serve as nurse and companion for a full year, traveling through England, France, Germany, and Switzerland—the traditional grand tour for elegant young ladies of the time. Louisa would not be one of those elegant creatures herself, of course—she was only a paid companion. In a sense she was again "going out to service."

But she had spent too many days in Concord quietly sitting "with the old folks," as she sometimes called them—sewing, cleaning, and writing. Pressed by her loved ones, Louisa seized the chance. As usual, she threw herself into a whirlwind of activity. She took less than one week to organize, pack, and ready the household for her absence.

Her passport registered her as thirty-two years old and five foot six in height. She did not know any of the Welds, and her courage wavered as she waved goodbye to her best-loved, familiar folk at the dock. As usual, her gentle brother-in-law, John Pratt—whom she had finally ceased to call "that man"—was there to support and cheer her on. She watched the city of Boston vanish with a pang at her heart. What might happen while she was away? Her parents were no longer young and strong. Her favorite uncle Samuel's health had been failing. Even Anna had taken ill only the year before, and her beloved nephews, the "fine boy" Freddy and baby John, could fall prey to common childhood diseases. Louisa worried about whether she would see "all the dear home faces when I came back."

Louisa, who was hired to play nurse, proved the sickest of her party of three travelers aboard the steamer. It was an inauspicious beginning. Her semi-invalid ward, Anna Minot Weld, "was not ill at all," and Anna's older brother George "scorned the idea" as it would turn out, he scorned most things. He was less interested in his sister or Louisa than in his own adventures. The seasick Louisa took what comfort she could resting in the ladies' lounge, but even there she found "no pleasant people on board," so she "read & whiled away the long days" as best she could.

Anna Weld often behaved like a spoiled young heiress— which was what she had been raised to be. The real nature of her illness never was made clear, but she outlived Louisa by more than thirty years, living on almost into her nineties. She mothered six children and grandmothered many more.

As a twenty-nine-year-old invalid, however, she was querulous and demanding. The two traveling companions had little in common—not interests, tastes, background, or beliefs. Louisa enjoyed hearing Anna's stories about her father's travels in the Far East, but most of the time she found Anna's conversation silly and pointless. Each exasperated the other, though Louisa had to make all the accommodations.

As biographer Harriet Reisen points out, Louisa's role as lady's companion "had the status of a governess, the function of a chaperone, and duties to be performed under the pretense of being a helpful friend of equal social rank but lesser wealth." Anna and Louisa were neither friends nor equals. In the course of time they formed an affectionate if unreliable truce as they traveled the world together.

On July 29, 1865, after a sickening nine days of sea travel, Louisa finally set foot on solid ground, at Liverpool, England. Liverpool was a shipping city, dirty and unglamorous—home to more beggars than Louisa had ever seen in her life, and "such desperate looking ones." From Liverpool they headed for rainy London. Here Anna Weld did take ill, and her brother George abandoned the two women as quickly as he could, setting out on his own escapades. Louisa escaped the sickroom when she was able, visiting a few parks, palaces, and Westminster Abbey, taking notes and sending long letters home.

In her journal she confessed to having spent "four dull, drizzly days" in London. To her parents, however, who had sacrificed so much to let her go, she waxed enthusiastic. She even lied about the weather: "We emerged into sunshine and a gallery of lovely pictures." Westminster Abbey, she admitted, was "a gloomy old place with tombs and statues," but she hurried to reassure her father, "one does not forget it and feels the richer all his life, for having seen it."

She would not be a true child of transcendentalists if she hadn't preferred countryside to city. Cities were always suspect to Louisa—the bigger they were, the more suspicious. Only a pastoral landscape felt like home. Louisa loved the bright green English countryside and hailed its beauties in letters home: "The farmhouses were my delight, with low thatched roofs, ivy up to the eaves, flowers all about the latticed windows, and buxom women or rosy children at the doors. Long low barns with hay ricks near by, trim hedges, fat cattle, green and yellow fields all about. Such perfect shades of color, delighted one's eyes, for grass was never so green, wheat so deeply golden, woods so dark, or rivers bluer."

She compared the European and American way of life. "Everything was so unyankee, so quiet and well kept," she marveled. "Nothing was abrupt, nobody in a hurry, and nowhere did you see the desperately go ahead style of life that we have." She joked, "The very cows in America look fast, and the hens seem to cackle fiercely over their rights like strong minded old ladies."

One more boat ride from Dover, England, to Ostend, Belgium, left Louisa prostrate with seasickness again. No sooner had she recovered than the trio made their way into France and sailed up the Rhine. She must have gotten her sea legs by then, for she published an account of that river journey in a magazine, *The Independent*. In it, she praised the beautiful riverside views and poked fun at everyone aboard—from the British tourists who "sat bolt upright, as if they had made up their minds to be surprised at nothing," to her American countrymen who "stared and asked questions."

They traveled to a health spa in Schwalbach, Germany, where Anna consulted doctors and took the waters, and George disappeared again in search of amusements. Louisa did her best to outwit boredom. This "quiet life" was beginning to grate. Anna Weld suffered chiefly from nerves and hypochondria; Louisa was suffering from the very real effects of mercury poisoning. After her water cure, Anna felt much better. Louisa never would.

She confided to her journal, "I tried my best to suit & serve her but dont think I did so very well." Still, Louisa reasoned, "many would have done . . . worse I fancy, for hers is a very hard case to manage & needs the patience & wisdom of an angel." She took her rambles alone by day, for she could not ever leave Anna alone at night. In short, wrote Louisa, "We walked a little, talked a little, bathed & rode a little, worried a good deal."

In Germany, the very different tastes of the travelers revealed themselves starkly. Louisa longed to see Goethe's house, for the writer-philosopher was her treasured childhood hero, but the Weld siblings scoffed. "Who was Goethe to fuss about?" they asked. Louisa was in no position to insist. She allowed herself to be swept into Heidelberg, "a charming place," and other famous cities, trying to be grateful for her opportunities. "A pleasant old city on the river," she called Frankfurt, "& I'm glad to have been there." The Welds chose fashionable spots to visit, such as Baden-Baden and Basel. Journeying through the gay whirl of the marketplace, the music and crowds, they gradually approached the mountains between Germany and

Switzerland. She was immediately touched by the grand, unfamiliar landscape, as if she could sense in advance that something new was about to happen.

They approached the Alps on October 8, "mother's birthday," Louisa noted. "I caught my first glimpse of the Alps," she wrote. They rose up like monuments, even at a distance. "Tall, white, spectral shapes they were, towering above the green hills & valleys that lay between. Clouds half hid them & the sun glittered on the everlasting snow that lay upon their tops." There was something fateful and eerie in this new setting. "Sharp, strange outlines against the sky they became as night came on." In her descriptions of the Alps the word *romantic* appears repeatedly. Freiberg, she wrote, "was the most romantic place we have been in." She described a "valley between two steep hills . . . watch towers stand all about the hills, & give a very romantic air to the place." The view down the valley was charming, and the lake waters "the loveliest blue."

They arrived "at last!" exclaimed Louisa, at Vevey, Switzerland, "a pleasant hour's sail to a very pleasant place." Vevey was a city in bloom, perfumed by autumn roses and herb gardens, with flowers spilling from decorative pots. Once they'd settled into their rooms, George took off for Paris again, looking for a livelier nightlife.

At the Swiss Pension Victoria—a sort of glorified boardinghouse—the two women came into close daily contact with fellow travelers. It was a motley, ever-changing cast of characters, many of whom Louisa described in her memoir, "Life in a Pension," including a former enslaver from the American South who insulted Louisa upon first meeting. For the first month, Louisa was alternately amused and irritated by her fellow boarders, most of whom she viewed in a comical light. Yet without a kindred spirit near, she found society more burdensome than rewarding. She grumbled in her journal, "I did not enjoy the life nor the society after the first novelty wore off, for I missed my freedom & grew very tired of the daily worry."

But in November, a fascinating new young guest arrived. He stood out from the pleasure-loving company in many ways. Poor and in ill health, he had been a Polish freedom fighter, and when he made his appearance at the Pension Victoria, he was still recovering from the war. Here was someone Louisa could befriend. In her journal she lists his arrival among two or three other guests,' but only his name earns emphasis: *Ladislas Wisniewski.*

Louisa's journal entries about Ladislas were brief and almost certainly edited with a heavy hand. She insisted that all her letters home from Vevey be later destroyed. We can turn to two fictionalized essays for what might have taken place. According to the essays, "My Boys" and "My Polish Boy," Louisa was at breakfast one chilly morning when the new guest came in to dine. Ladislas caught Louisa's attention with his "thin, intelligent face and the charmingly polite manners of a foreigner." The young Pole was shivering from the November cold, had a bad cough, and "cast wistful glances toward the warm corner by the stove" where Louisa happened to be sitting. It is possible that he was looking at her rather than at the fire, but Louisa, ever solicitous of others, instantly gave up her place for him, insisting that "the heat often oppressed" her.

Later that same day, she spied Ladislas passing through the salon, dashing in his military-style blue-and-white suit. He reminded her of her Union soldiers, those "brave boys in blue" for whom she already had a weakness. That night at dinner, the young stranger gallantly raised his glass to Louisa, as if to thank her for having given up her warm seat by the fire. Louisa quickly saw that Ladislas was bright and musical, and upon hearing that he had fought in the recent Polish battle for independence, her fervent heart "warmed to him at once." He was far from home, needing care and affection. Louisa was far away as well, craving some like-minded soul to care for.

Louisa and Anna Weld joined forces in coddling Ladislas Wisniewski. They must have made an odd threesome: Ladislas was barely out of his teens, accompanied by Anna, age twenty-nine, and Louisa, in her early thirties. Ladislas and Louisa had interests in common, but Anna made a helpful chaperone. As long as she was part of the trio, the friendship appeared innocent to outsiders, intimacy felt safer, and Louisa could go on playing a motherly role toward this handsome boy whom she quickly nicknamed Laddie.

Ladislas was not the first young man she'd ever called Laddie, but he was, she later confessed, the "best and dearest of all." She could justify the time and attention spent on him as long as she shared it with Anna. As she insisted, "being ill & much younger we petted him." The use of *us* and *we* turns the narrative from a love story into a story of love.

Because Louisa was such a fine storyteller, it is hard to say, 150 years after the fact, whether she exaggerated the degree of the intimacy between herself and Laddie—or downplayed it. One might make an argument for either, though trying to make it sound less momentous seems the likelier choice.

Louisa and Laddie sat together each evening in a quiet corner chatting while those around them played cards. They tutored each other in their native tongues. Laddie stumbled over English words, and Louisa knew only a few French phrases and no Polish. Still, she wrote, "the barrier of an unknown language did not long stand between us." The young handsome Pole had left behind the long hours and demanding conditions of university life. He spoke four or five languages, amazing Louisa with his swift progress in her native tongue, though he struck his forehead in exasperation, declaring, "I never can will shall to have learn this beast of English!"

They did not devote all of their shared time to study. They also joined in evening dances, outings, and games. Laddie was lively company, full of interesting and funny stories—the kind of company Louisa loved best. She daringly smoked a cigarette in his presence. They went on long walks through the Swiss landscape, where they dreamed aloud, sharing "splendid plans for the future." They even talked of running off to Paris together. Each night at dinner, Laddie presented Louisa with a single rose.

None of this sounds like the behavior of just a simple friend. Years later Louisa held on to the cache of notes she found tucked under her door. "He called them chapters of a great history we were to write together," she remembered. Though she described them as "merry little notes," she ultimately destroyed every last one before posterity could lay hands on them.

Laddie called her "little mamma," and he asked Louisa to call him "*varjo*," which means "shadow" or "umbrella." Was he trailing or protecting her? Or both? He obviously and openly adored her. He had a sly sense of humor, which she loved. He tricked Louisa into calling him "*ma drogha*" by telling her that *drogha* meant "friend" in Polish. Later on she learned that she had been calling him "my darling" out in public and "in the tenderest manner."

On her birthday that autumn, "a wild and windy day," Louisa recorded, "Usually I am sad on my birthday, but not this time." She felt "happy and hopeful," and the changeable weather matched her own excitable mood, "in its fitful changes of sunshine & shade." Even the fussy Anna Weld presented Louisa with a painting of Chillon, a red-roofed castle overlooking Lake Geneva.

Louisa wrote in her journal, "I feel rather old with my 33 years, but have much to keep me young." Laddie played a part in her rejuvenation, and she added hopefully, "I shall not grow older in heart as the time goes on."

The musically gifted Laddie serenaded her with "his sweetest airs" as a birthday present. He wished her, in words she recorded exactly, "All good & happiness on earth & a high place in Heaven as my reward." She seldom made a record of things people said to her—but for Laddie she did.

But by December, Anna had had enough of quiet Vevey and insisted that she and Louisa move on to Nice, France. As the paid companion, Louisa had no choice but to follow.

"A little romance with L.W.," Louisa scribbled in her journal, adding something undecipherable that she crossed out so vehemently she tore through the paper. It is the only instance in all of her journal writing when she erased her own words that violently. Later she added above the torn place only two stark words: "Couldn't be."

Louisa and Laddie put off their parting as long as possible, with Anna fretting to be on her way. The trip was put off for a few more precious days, due to widespread cholera in Nice. But here in her notes Louisa muddies the tracks for us. Suddenly she writes as if all along the romance with Laddie had been equally shared between herself and Anna—though there is no evidence that Laddie ever gave Anna a rose, spent cozy evenings at her side, or left notes under her door. Laddie and Anna did not sit together in corners tutoring one another or go on long walks dreaming of their future. It had been Anna's idea, and Anna's alone, to leave Vevey as soon as possible.

Louisa wrote, "Laddie went with us to Lausanne kissed our hands at parting & went back to V. disconsolate." Lausanne was a journey of about twelve miles—not far, but since Laddie undoubtedly made the trip back on foot, it was no small matter, either. Louisa's journal entries, with their new insistence on a trifold friendship, may have been written for Anna's eyes, in hopes of persuading her to prolong her stay in Switzerland. If so, the ruse did not work. Louisa goes on telling her story in the first-person plural. "Sad times for A. & I but we journeyed away to Nice & tried to forget our troubles."

Anna's emotions may have truly been involved, for from then on Louisa placed herself in the background in her own journal entries. "Anna troubled about Laddie who was in a despairing state of mind." Notes and letters from

Ladislas followed them all the way into Nice, but no trace of a single one survived.

The narrative gets more puzzling. It may be that Louisa used Anna's name and feelings as a decoy, a substitute for her own. Louisa later edited "I could not advise them to be happy," by changing "them" to "him," and finally crossed out the whole sentence entirely. If she was inventing truths to conceal the Louisa/Ladislas romance, it proved hard to keep her story straight. She is clear only about her own sad state of mind: "Dull days here, often homesick & very tired of doing nothing pleasant or interesting." She was already missing Laddie. Louisa tried to keep up with her study of French, but to little avail. It foreshadows the fictional Jo's growing friendship with her future husband, Professor Bhaer, who found his way into her affections by tutoring her in his native German—"but," wrote Louisa in real life, "with little time, less talent & no teacher I did not get on very fast."

Once settled into Nice for the winter, Louisa's restlessness only increased. She reported glumly that she received no gifts and no letters for the new year—which meant she'd gotten nothing from Laddie, either. "A quiet dull time generally," Louisa reported, for Anna was ill again and not responding to treatments. The only relief Louisa could find was now and then a walk alone, "driving sometimes, walking a little, writing letters & tending Anna." Clearly, something was troubling her. She reported that she felt stirred up, had trouble sleeping "& felt very poorly for my life didn't suit me."

By February Louisa determined to cut short her year abroad—three months earlier than promised—"though A. wants me to stay. I'm tired of it & as she is not going to travel my time is too valuable to be spent in fussing over cushions & carrying shawls." The resentful tone and indifference are very far from Louisa's usual behavior. Later, she admitted that she did not properly see things from her patient's point of view till she had become an invalid herself. But in that winter of 1866, following a rosy Vevey autumn, she felt trapped, discontented. All she wanted was her freedom back.

She told herself that Anna Weld's condition had improved, that "she will be as cosy as she can be any where." In short, she convinced herself that was not really abandoning her frail charge. Anna Weld might have been calm and cosy, but Louisa was not. She called that March "a tedious month which might have been quite the reverse had I been free to enjoy it."

She was immersed in writing again—her most reliable escape—perhaps working on a "potboiler" novel *A Fatal Love Chase*. She composed three new stories during these sleepless nights and restless days abroad. She was, after all, still the young woman who cried out for "a crust in a garret with freedom and a pen."

She and Anna were no longer getting along as they had during their last days in Vevey and even in their early sad days in Nice. "I'm rather fond of her," Louisa wrote bluntly, "but she wears upon me & we are best apart." She tried to coax Anna out of doors, arranging "pleasant hours" for her patient, for a rustic picnic lunch in a wheeled chair, along with other diversions, "but nothing lasted long," Louisa sighed. She continued to study her French without her favorite young teacher, escape for walks whenever she could, and write long letters home when she could spare the time. A new fellow traveler came along, likely another of Louisa's unlucky suitors, "full of German philosophy & poetry. Conceited but better than no one." Later she commented, "Queer times with him," suggesting a bungled courtship. After her "little romance with L.W.," the poor German philosopher had no chance. Nothing pleased Louisa that winter and early spring. She and her charge grated on each other's nerves. "Anna poorly & fidgety, nothing right in heaven or on earth," Louisa groused.

By April her mood had lifted considerably, with the prospect of her upcoming departure to buoy her. The whole Alcott family scrambled to send Louisa money for some European travel independent of the Welds. Her ailing but generous uncle Sam came through once more with the needed funds.

Louisa had her own itinerary in mind, which she

confided to no one at home. It was audacious, even reckless—had they known the details, her proper Boston relations would have fainted dead away.

It is unlikely Louisa ever told her family about the plan. She had more travel to do in London, yes—but her real goal was to meet up with Laddie in Paris and spend several days alone with him. It was a thing that genteel, well-behaved, young, single women simply did not, would not—ever—do.

On April 15, Louisa asked a friend for help finding lodgings in London, where she would visit before her boat journey home. She had already finalized plans to stop in Paris—the destination of her and Ladislas's dreams. She wrote to the friend, "I shall not be in England till the first week in May as I want a few days in Paris." She had no idea where she would be in London, but already had a Parisian address. As it turned out, she spent a good deal more than "a few days" in Paris—and they were the most unorthodox and mysterious in Louisa's very mysterious, unorthodox life.

Though she'd planned to leave Nice by late April, Anna Weld held on tight to her companion, tearfully refusing to let her go. Louisa did not make her escape till May 1, leaving behind "Anna & Nice . . . feeling as happy as a freed bird."

What followed was a true adventure—and the biographer's tantalizing mystery. Louisa had "a pleasant journey" by train and then found "Laddie waiting for me in Paris to take me to my room at Madame Dyne's." And that is the last she has to say about *that* in her journal. What follows are seventeen days of unrecorded activity. A gap in her life and history. Then she picks up where she left off—as if nothing had ever happened and Paris never existed.

For any clues of these missing Parisian days, we must look to Louisa's later accounts, tidied up and carefully framed for publication. In "My Boys" and "My Polish Boy," Louisa's version of this Paris rendezvous takes on corkscrew twists and turns. It's hard to see how anyone ever believed a word of it. First, Ladislas Wisniewski shows up at the Paris train station the way a genie pops out of a bottle. On her train ride from Nice, Louisa writes, she had been wishing she could see Laddie again—and lo and behold, there he is standing at the Gare de Lyon madly waving his familiar blue-and-white cap. He is right on time to meet her train. Yet she claims to be surprised. There is a "Fancy meeting you here!" quality to this scene that would be comical if it weren't also touching.

Louisa maintained that she and Laddie had been out of touch for months. In that case, how on earth did he know she was on her way to Paris, much less the exact time and date of her arrival? How would he know she'd left Nice? She doesn't bother to explain. Instead she suggests that Laddie figured it out on his own. Somehow he guessed where Louisa would be staying in Paris—a city home to hundreds of hotels and pensions. After that bit of detective work he apparently badgered Louisa's Parisian landlady, calling her at the pension every day till he magically deduced the precise day and time of Louisa's arrival.

We know that Louisa arrived alone in Paris on May 1, and that Laddie was at the station to greet her. He escorted her to her room at Madame Dyne's on the Rue de Rivoli. Once he had helped her settle her things, they wandered— scandalously—arm in arm through the Parisian streets and across the Seine to the bohemian Left Bank.

All of this was appallingly unacceptable in 1866. An unmarried American woman would never wander around a foreign city with a young man she barely knew without creating a scandal—not even in Paris. The liberal Alcotts would surely have wondered at it. But they too were apparently kept in the dark.

Louisa reported that once she had left Anna Weld behind, she quite independently managed to see "considerable for a lone woman, without funds, in a short space of time." None of those things were true. She was not alone in Paris, not without funds, and she had seventeen full days to sightsee.

For Louisa it was an enchanted fortnight, if we read her later accounts. She was free, and with someone she loved who adored her. For more than two weeks she and Laddie stayed wrapped in each other's company day and night. She was not laboring for anyone else; she was not even writing. For once, she gave herself over entirely to living. She enjoyed the luxury of a slower, leisurely pace in a grand, romantic city—her impatience for once suspended in "the days spent in seeing sights with Laddie, the evenings in reading, writing, hearing 'my boy' play, or resting."

In "My Boys" and "My Polish Boy" she remains vague about Laddie's own boarding arrangements. She mentions something about his staying "with friends," but those friends never again appear in either essay. It would have looked suspect had Ladislas stayed in the same lodgings— so if it is true, she left that fact out. We may never know what really happened during those seventeen days they spent together—and in the end it is not our business. Julian Hawthorne found it impossible to believe Louisa never had a love affair. "We never knew; yet how could a nature so imaginative, romantic and passionate escape it?"

We do know that Louisa and Laddie were devoted to each other. The morning after her arrival, while she was greeting the sun rising over Paris, Laddie was already at Madame Dyne's, waiting to escort her around the waking city. They went most often to the free attractions: parks and foot bridges, fountains, public gardens, and monuments.

Louisa had little money to spend; Ladislas even less. In one of the most touching scenes of their Paris sojourn, she tells how he took her shopping one day. They stopped inside a Paris millinery, and Laddie insisted that Louisa buy herself an elegant hat. The one they decided on at last was a simple, pretty pearl-colored hat with a single crepe rose adornment. Laddie gave his approval and conducted all the negotiations in French. The fact that he could not pay for the hat has its own stinging pathos—but Louisa was used to loving people without funds. Encouragement and affection he could give, and that he gave in abundance.

Her boy Laddie was only one in a series of eager, poor, and proud young lovers she re-created in stories, essays, and novels. With his comic antics and playfulness, his dark-eyed good looks, his fiery temperament, and his passion for music, he certainly recalls her most famous literary "boy," *Little Women*'s Laurie.

Both Ladislas and Laurie were doomed to love their independent heroines unrequitedly. Both went on to marry other women and to father children of their own. Though Louisa later suggested she had modeled Laurie on various young male friends—including Julian Hawthorne and Alf Whitman—Laddie, she confessed, was the "best and dearest of all."

In the wide, lovely city of Paris, Louisa "fearlessly went anywhere on the arm of my big son." She kept up the public fiction of a young mother sightseeing with her devoted son. That role kept her safe in many ways. But their parting was anything but maternal. Laddie had spent his meager resources and bought Louisa a going-away gift of

French cologne. She told him, "You have been so kind to me, I wish I had something beautiful to give you, Laddie."

It turned out that the "something beautiful" Ladislas wanted at the train station was a farewell kiss. Any questions about their future must by now have been settled. "This time it is for always," he reminded her sadly, "so, as a parting souvenir, give to me the sweet English good-bye." He said this, she recalls, "with a despairing sort of look," and so, despite the disapproving British ladies glaring, Louisa "drew down his tall head and kissed him tenderly, feeling that in this world there were no more meetings for us." It is very like Louisa that she bestowed rather than received the kiss. And it's revealing that her fictional Jo March takes the first kiss as well: "Stooping down, [she] kissed her Friedrich under the umbrella. It was dreadful, but she would have done it if the flock of draggle-tailed sparrows on the hedge had been human beings, for she was very far gone indeed, and quite regardless of everything but her own happiness."

The author may have been "very far gone indeed" as well, but she did not pursue "her own happiness" in romance. With her heart "rent within," Louisa rushed off to the first empty train carriage, clutching her little bottle of French cologne.

Paris itself was a second chance that extended their relationship beyond its natural course. There must have been tears and hard decisions before she arrived at her scrawled "Couldn't be" in her Vevey journal.

As it turned out, Laddie was wrong that their parting in Paris was "for always." He and Louisa wrote letters to each other even after he married and had children. She loaned him money at least once when he fell on hard times. He did settle in Paris, their city of dreams. He visited New York City at least once, and she saw him there, her favorite "boy." But the precious Parisian interlude between them was over "for always."

"On the 17th reluctantly went to London," Louisa wrote tersely in her journal. No keepsake or photo of Laddie has survived. We do not know what became of the little cologne bottle, though we may guess it was kept inviolate for a very long time.

We can also guess that he shared physical traits with the "Laurence boy" as Jo March describes him: "Curly black hair; brown skin; big, black eyes; handsome nose; fine teeth; small hands and feet; taller than I am; very polite, for a boy, and altogether jolly." Biographer Harriet Reisen notes, "Louisa had no photograph of Ladislas. None is known to exist." Instead she would fix his image forever in the pages of her most famous book.

CHAPTER FIFTEEN

Said I'd Try

On her return to America in mid-July, Louisa flew into her mother's arms. But she was stricken to see Abby "looking old, sick, & tired." Anna too had been ill that year, suffering from hearing loss that would worsen with age. Time had taken its toll on all of them—including Louisa, whose symptoms from the mercury poisoning had started to unmistakably show themselves. Bronson, stooped and gray, maintained his "placid" air of calm. But when he turned his observant gaze at Louisa, he saw that something was wrong. She needed to regain "strength and spirits for future works," he worried. Bronson even went so far as to say that Louisa, the sturdiest member of the golden band, seemed "disabled." That word appears again in a letter between Abby and her brother Samuel Joseph: "all the family disabled."

Sadness had darkened Louisa's outlook. By November—that "most disagreeable month"—Louisa mourned that while she didn't expect to find "the strong, energetic 'Marmee' of old," nothing had prepared her for her mother's steep decline. Abby, ill and weak now, was losing her lovely thick brown hair, so much like Louisa's own. The daughter again became her mother's nurse—again at the cost of her own writing. Louisa did not mind the sacrifice, declaring, "Thank the Lord, she is still here though, pale & weak, quiet & sad . . . fine hair gone & face full of wrinkles, bowed back & every sign of age."

Louisa's mercury poisoning, which would vex her till her death, had begun its deadly work, though she tried not to let on. "I am pretty well," she insisted, "& keep so busy I haven't time to be sick." She literally could not afford it. Too much depended on "the money-maker," as she called herself. She had sailed home to a mountain of new debts, as well as the personal loan her family had made to extend her trip abroad. "Bills accumulate and worry me," she wrote. Unlike Bronson—and probably *because* of him—Louisa had a dread of debt that drove her that fall and winter to take on more jobs. Most of it was easy-to-sell writing: potboilers and thrillers. Though she had grown sick of churning out such stories years earlier, she excused herself by saying, "I can't afford to starve on praise."

Critics today do praise her once-scorned potboilers, books like *A Long Fatal Love Chase*, but these show only glimpses of her genius. She did what she could with stock characters and cheap-thrills effects—much as she had done with her earliest theatrical productions made of cardboard and tinsel. She wrote a dozen such stories in the last six months of 1866 alone—roughly two a month. Production at that rate is not a recipe for great art—or good health. She was running on empty.

Louisa called these stories "rubbishy tales," but "they pay best," she noted matter-of-factly, and there were always bills to be paid. She turned out dozens of "necessity stories" for money, just as Jo does in *Little Women*. "'The Duke's Daughter' paid the butcher's bill," the narrator declares, and Jo's creator paid almost all the bills with similar "rubbish."

She kept up the mask of good health and good cheer as long she could, despite fatigue and relentless headaches. In a letter to her mother she wrote reassuringly, "Things look promising for the new year." She added, with her usual way of making light of difficulty, "It's clear that Minerva Moody [a nickname for herself] is getting on in spite of many downfalls." Despite her joking, she suffered a complete collapse later that same month.

Louisa spent the next several months in bed, too sick even to stand. It may have been partly emotional, of course—she had just experienced the freest weeks of her life, loving and being loved, and had landed back home in Concord with a thud. But much of it was sheer physical depletion. Louisa hated having to lie still. She had never been forced to remain so inactive for so long—not even after her nursing experience during the war.

Her friend Frank Sanborn wrote, "She is now forbidden to either read or to write—which is to her a great deprivation." He worried aloud about her condition. "Louisa Alcott has been alarmingly ill," he confided in a letter to a friend, "her head being overworked and taking revenge by neuralgia." Sometimes she thought she had re-activated her typhoid pneumonia. At other times she believed that sister Anna's neuralgia had mysteriously made its way into her system. She and those around her came up with a dozen different causes for her illness—too little sleep, too much travel, worry over debt—but the aftereffects of calomel never crossed their minds. Mercury poisoning was far too little known or understood.

In April she staggered back to her feet, only to relapse the very next month. Her journal details the sad situation at home: "Still gaining, but all feeble. Mother half blind, Father lame & I weak, nervous & used up generally. Cold, wet weather & dull times for every one." Earlier in the year she had joked with Abby about becoming "a used up old lady of 70 or so." At thirty-five, half that projected age, she was feeling "used up generally." What she had once written about her mother was now doubly true about herself: "Life has been so hard for her & she so brave, so glad to spend herself for others."

Louisa turned a corner in June, and as soon as she was able, she rushed back to her desk. "Better & began to write," she noted in June. In July: "Wrote Fairy tales for a Christmas book." That attempt came to nothing, though decades later, publishers fought for the rights to those tales. Her journal entries were short, clipped, mostly about money earned, given, or spent. She had no energy to spare for her journal writing. The "money-maker" had fallen behind and must make up for lost time.

In September, relief came in the form of two offers of lucrative work. She had no way of knowing that one would mark the turning point of her life. Louisa dismissively recorded both of them in her journal, using identical language for each. "Niles, partner of Roberts, asked me to write a girls book. Said I'd try. Fuller asked me to be the Editor of 'Merry's Museum.' Said I'd try." She showed little enthusiasm for either paying assignment. "Began at once on both new jobs, but didn't like either."

The job editing for *Merry's Museum*, a children's magazine, paid $500 a year and appealed to Louisa more than writing the girls' book. She described her new editorial role in her October journal. Her workload for *Merry's Museum* required reading manuscript submissions, as well as writing one story and one editorial for the magazine every month. She found the work almost as uncongenial as teaching. "I worked away at my editorials but didn't enjoy it."

But the work had one enormous advantage. The magazine provided her with enough salary to justify her leaving Concord and setting up an independent room for herself in Boston. After her collapse and long recovery, she could finally admit that she could not "keep well in C[oncord], so must try Boston, & not work too hard."

She allowed herself a rare moment of truth, describing her escape to Boston atop her load of furniture with Frederick Llewellyn Willis, one of her perennially favorite "boys." She knew it was impossible to stay healthy while caring for her aging mother and father; now she admitted to a feeling of liberation. The journey to Boston felt as if she "was going to camp out in a new country." Then, reining herself in, she added, "Hoped it would prove a hospitable & healthy land."

In Concord she would always be the household drudge. It didn't matter how much she loved her mother and father, or how willingly she sacrificed health and energy to their well-being. The artist in her needed to survive. She paid for her escape with her pen. Boston was the only place where she could freely "rest" and "scribble"—the promised land of her childhood dreams. And it was in Boston that she finally began to work on the second offer that had come her way. The unwelcome girls' book she'd dismissed with her curt "said I'd try" was none other than *Little Women*.

Thomas Niles had been that young assistant who had sat in the office at the *Atlantic Monthly* and watched his boss, James Fields, dismiss Louisa May Alcott with his brusque "You can't write." Niles had later offered to publish *Hospital Sketches*, but Louisa had chosen instead to publish with Redpath. Niles was determined this time to see if she would try her hand at an entirely new form, a children's novel written specifically for girls. He seems to have understood what Emerson had known all along: that Louisa was to be "the poet of children . . . she knew their angels."

Niles was an odd character, a dark, thin, intense, and quiet man. He worked at Roberts Brothers, an independent publishing house that had grown in size and scope since Louisa turned it down for *Hospital Sketches*. He was a "confirmed bachelor," conservative in tastes and habits. When the telephone came into popular use, he would never talk on it, but had others carry and deliver his messages in person. His literary taste was extraordinary by any measure. Not only did he court Louisa May Alcott; he also published Emily Dickinson's "unpublishable" poetry. As staid as he looked, he was willing to take risks. And as imposing as he must have seemed behind his sturdy wooden desk at 143 Washington Street—located halfway between the Old State

273

House and the Old South Meeting House—he proved a true and loving friend to Louisa.

Niles had seen the booming popularity of boys' books by Oliver Optic, the pen name of a minister who produced more than a hundred best-selling books and a thousand stories for the young. The Oliver Optic books sold at the fantastic rate of a hundred thousand copies a year. Niles, working a few doors down from Optic's publisher, decided that there must be a similar market for books written for girls. And he decided that Louisa Alcott was the right woman to write them.

When he'd first laid eyes on her, she'd been a twenty-one-year-old unknown. Her vulnerability and eagerness must have fixed her in his mind as someone who could understand and sympathize with young people. Louisa did indeed have something about her—some wholehearted-ness that made her a natural friend to the young. He had already seen her gift for the tragicomic in her popular *Hospital Sketches*. Niles wanted to forge an entry into this new reading market for young people, choosing girls as his target audience, and Louisa as his designated author. And he was not above using bribery to get her to do it.

In February 1868, Bronson traveled to Boston in hopes of publishing his book *Tablets*, a summation of personal philosophy that he had been working on for six years. It was hardly bestseller material. But Thomas Niles suggested that if Louisa would write her book for girls, he would arrange for father and daughter to be published together by Roberts Brothers.

Bronson immediately wrote a letter to Louisa that mixed bravado and pathetic appeal. "They want a book of 200 pages or more," he told Louisa. "He [Niles] obviously wishes to become *your* publisher and *mine*." He begged her to "come home." It was a summons Louisa seldom refused. "Come home soon and write your story," he pleaded.

She managed to avoid as long as possible both her return to Concord and Niles's offer. Though she'd said she'd try, she privately admitted to herself, "I could not write a girls' story, knowing little about any but my own sisters & always preferring boys." She must have felt the irony of being asked to write a book about girls, when she had spent her whole life longing to be a boy. But Bronson's hungry request—and his dependence on her for his own publishing future—left her no choice but to try. She tried to balance between the demands of Concord and the relative ease of Boston, working all the while.

The sweet interlude with Laddie in Switzerland and Paris was far behind her now. But her time alone in Boston brought its own sweetness. "I am in my little room, spending busy, happy days," she wrote in her journal that January of 1868, "because I have quiet, freedom, work enough, and strength to do it." Even May was earning a little money now from giving art lessons, and "the old people," as Louisa called her parents, were safely ensconced "in a cosey home," as she had planned so many years before. "After last winter's hard experience," she wrote in her journal, "we cannot be too grateful."

Just as she was preparing to commence her girls' book, Louisa spied a flower coming into bloom, a hyacinth "white and sweet,—a good omen," she hoped. She'd had a similar harbinger just before the publication of *Hospital Sketches*. She did not think of it as a good omen for herself alone, but also for her family as well as her country, which had been torn apart in the recent Civil War. "Perhaps we are to win after all, and conquer poverty, neglect, pain, and debt, and march on with flags flying into the new world with the new year." There were more good omens as well. One night she dreamed that she was an opera dancer and "waked up prancing."

Still, she continued to push off actually writing the dreaded girls' book. Her editorial work at *Merry's Museum* kept her busy enough—and it was laying some of the groundwork for her great novel, whether she knew it or not. She was writing tales again and had a good long talk with a younger friend "about the fast ways of young people nowadays, and gave the child much older-sisterly advice, as no one seems to see how much she needs help at this time of her young life." Louisa would write a book for girls only if she believed it would be a help in her readers' lives. Children and childhood were on her mind. She retained her own childlike quality. The illustrious writer and thinker Oliver Wendell Holmes had recently asked Louisa, "How many of you children are there?" Though she towered over him, she answered, "Four, sir."

A few weeks later her "second hyacinth bloomed pale blue, like a timid hope." She wrote, "I took the omen for a good one, as I am getting on, and have more than I can do of the work that I once went begging for." The magazine job consumed more time than she had bargained for. The publisher, she sighed, seemed to expect her to "write the whole magazine." When she wasn't grinding away at editorial work, she was kept busy with household chores at home, sewing May a new bonnet, and a flannel wrapper for Marmee, "who feels the cold in the Concord snowbanks."

Louisa was sometimes lonely, but she kept busy— acting in theatricals for charitable causes, sewing for others, writing to keep the bill collectors away. "Four tales this month," she noted in February. "Received $70, sent $30 home. No debts." She spent time with her young nephews, Freddy and Johnny, relishing their time together. One afternoon she watched the baby, Johnny, brooding over him "as if he were a heavenly sort of fire to warm and comfort us." A third hyacinth bloomed—this one pink.

At the end of February she packed up her independent

little Boston "sky parlor" and headed to Concord. "I am needed there," she wrote in her journal, admitting, "I am sorry to leave my quiet room, for I've enjoyed it very much."

At Orchard House she had to contend with the constant distractions of home and family. But, as an author for the young, she also had her most cherished family memories close by. She worked at her little half-moon desk by a small window overlooking the Lexington Road, which led in one direction toward her past at Hillside House, and the other forward into town. Her modest bedroom doubled as her study, while Bronson had a large, handsome study downstairs, lined with his books. Out the window beside her bed, Louisa could gaze into the woods surrounding Orchard House and the old Hillside property where she had spent some of the happiest years of her childhood. One minute's walk would take her backward into the territory of her youth.

Louisa spent March, April, and May caring for her increasingly frail mother, "providing Marmee with many comforts, and keeping the hounds of care and debt from worrying her." Louisa was busy hatching a plan for her new girls' book, thinking that it might be unpleasant work but at least would keep those she loved safe from "care and debt." Her youthful goal of becoming the family protector was coming true, even if she hadn't achieved fame or glory, the "something splendid" of her dreams. At least Abby no longer had to work herself to the bone. "She sits at rest in her sunny room," Louisa noted, half sadly, half proudly, "and that is better than any amount of fame to me."

Soon after the publication of her first book, *Flower Fables*, Louisa had promised her mother better books in the future, more true-to-life stories. "I hope to pass in time from flowers and fables to men and realities," she vowed.

Little Women from its beginning was meant to be a book of realities. Louisa could write it so clearly and vividly because, as she later explained, "We lived it." When Bronson traveled again to Boston to further solidify his book projects with Thomas Niles, Louisa took the hint and dutifully began writing. In her journal that May of 1868, she wrote, "Mr. N wants a girls story, and I begin 'Little Women.'"

She had no choice but to draw on her own childhood. The only girls she knew about, she insisted, were her sisters and herself. She set the story there on the spot at Orchard House, which was convenient since she could study its nooks and crannies every day. But she drew the events of the plot chiefly from the happy years next door at Hillside, where she and her golden band of sisters had spent their sweetest times. Her memories sat close by: the barn where they'd performed their elaborate theatricals, the fireplace where they'd gathered to chatter and sew. Visits to sick and poverty-stricken neighbors; "sleigh rides and skating frolics, such pleasant evenings in the old parlor"; and her father's favorite book, *The Pilgrim's Progress*, would all come into play in her novel.

So, too, would the occasional squabbles between sisters, their struggles with poverty, grueling work, and envy of others. In this she was absolutely radical as an author. No one had ever reported the real lives of teenagers before. Louisa May Alcott set out to do a simple and daring thing: to tell the truth. She asked each member of her family for their permission to write the book drawing from life experiences, hoping, she said, that one of them would turn her down and give her an excuse to stop. None did.

She noted with resignation, "Marmee, Anna, and May all approve my plan. So I plod away, though I don't enjoy this sort of thing." She added, "Never liked girls or knew many, except my sisters; but our queer plays and experiences may prove interesting, though I doubt it." Many years later, looking back over her journals, the famous author paused here and wryly noted, "[Good joke. –L.M.A]."

Louisa drew not only upon memory but also her powers of embroidery and invention to create the absorbing world of *Little Women*. G. K. Chesterton wrote, "It anticipated realism by twenty or thirty years; just as Jane Austen anticipated it by at least a hundred years." He added, perhaps thinking of Bronson, "For women are the only realists;

their whole object in life is to pit their realism against the extravagant, excessive, and occasionally drunken idealism of men."

Louisa began by exiling the father who had been at the center of her family's life. Writing is a way of revising reality; it is daydreaming out loud. Here, in Louisa's fictional world, four sisters and their wise Marmee live in their own female sphere, unaided for the most part by men. Each of the four little women works out her own fate, develops her own character, and finds—or loses—her own life. The first rule of order in any book for young readers is to get the parents out of the way; this may explain the incredibly high number of exiles, orphans, and semiorphans in children's literature.

For Louisa, sending the fictional Mr. March off to war provided freedom of movement for the little women. Even when he finally makes his (late) appearance in the book, he is an invalid who must be cared for—not the centrifugal early force that was her real-life father. Some might argue that it would have been well to exile Marmee, too. Many readers would welcome more of the little women, less of the all-wise, all-knowing grown one.

Of course the fictional March family—note the play the name *March* presents instead of the family name *May*—a highly idealized version of the Alcotts. Bronson, her idea-obsessed, complex father, is sent offstage to serve in the Civil War. Marmee is Abby with a golden halo on top. Nearly every bit of wisdom in the book, every aphorism—and all its preaching—comes from Marmee's lips.

At the heart of the book, however, dwells the tightly knit group of four sisters, mirroring their real golden band. Anna Alcott turns into the reliable eldest sister, Meg. Quiet, domestic Lizzie becomes the household angel, Beth, while elegant May transforms into the "snow maiden," Amy. (Swap the letters around and you arrive at the same name: May/Amy.)

Of course Jo is a mirror image of her creator at the center of the action, with her wild "boyish ways," her moods, her scribbling, her theatricals and stubborn independence. Though much altered, she is a barely disguised Louisa. The two are so closely aligned that it's sometimes hard to tell where Louisa leaves off and Jo begins.

No fictional young women like the March girls had ever been seen before. They struggle, squabble, tell lies, preen, and triumph. These were unmistakably real girls, with weakness as well as strength. Meg could be vain, Jo rude, Amy self-centered, and even the saintly Beth too shy for her own good. Their adventures and misadventures are made of the ordinary daily human experiences that any girl might understand—even today. It is one reason *Little Women* endures 150 years after its creation. The book has no thrilling cliff-hanger adventures, no gothic melodrama.

(Unless you count Jo's theatrical productions, for which she borrows her creator's actual russet leather boots.) The sisters are not ravishing beauties; they do not find treasure; they are not courted by nobility.

Even the book's most heart-crushing scenes take place within a domestic circle. The battles fought are largely internal, and the battlefield is daily life. Perhaps because the story was Louisa's own, it flowed easily once she had put pen to paper. As biographer Madeleine Stern rightly notes, "The great facts were the near ones."

Louisa had no lofty aspiration for this book, so this time ambition didn't get in her way. She recorded no writing vortex, no image of herself as the burning literary genius. She simply wrote what was in her to write.

Louisa turned "the brains that earn the money" into a writing machine that spring. In less than six weeks, she had finished twelve chapters of *Little Women*, as well as three more tales for two other publishers. She sent the first twelve chapters to Thomas Niles and waited. The response was disheartening, especially after his eager courtship of her work. She noted simply, "He thought it *dull*; so do I." Nevertheless she persisted. Once she had begun a task, she was not one to give up.

She also had her material well in hand. Before she'd ever thought of writing a book called *Little Women*, she had created stories featuring four sisters, and had also at times incorporated other family members into her fiction. She reused elements of those stories now. And she understood her young audience better than ever, thanks partly to her work editing children's material for *Merry's Museum*. The stars had aligned for this one inevitable work of genius. She had learned firsthand what worked for a young readership and what didn't. If ever she understood "their angels," it was now.

Louisa sat at the epicenter of American thought and ideas—scribbling at her small, wooden half-moon desk, with Emerson about a mile away by the Lexington Road. Her father, the great thinker, sat just downstairs. Any one of them might have been expected to create the great work of 1868, but it was Louisa May Alcott who did it.

As always, she consulted her "home folk" as she wrote. Her family warmly approved the manuscript. Anna praised it because it was so unlike the novels they had disliked as young women where "the heroine cries too much and is too perfect." Jo March neither wept copiously, nor was she saintly. Her imperfections would endear her to generations of readers.

After Louisa had shipped off the first twelve chapters to Thomas Niles—her only copy of the work—she had to complete the rest without checking what she had already written. Her original plan was to write a total of twenty chapters. Niles urged her to lengthen the book and stretch it out over more than four hundred pages. She told Niles bluntly, "I don't see how it can be spun out to make twenty four chapters & give you your 400 pages. I will do my best however."

By July 15, four weeks later, she had finished her book. In the end she made it twenty-three chapters long, and the manuscript ran to 402 pages. She hoped against hope that Niles might possibly be interested in a sequel, which she proposed to call *Young Women*. She asked May to create some artwork for it, as if her talented sister's illustrations might make the book more palatable.

"Hope it will go," she wrote anxiously in her journal. Having produced the novel, she suffered from a writer's version of postpartum depression. "Very tired, head full of pain from overwork, and heart heavy about Marmee, who is growing feeble." The older and wiser Louisa again commented on her own journal entry: "[Too much work for one young woman. No wonder she broke down.]"

In August she recorded gratefully that "Roberts Bros. made an offer for the story." She traveled to Boston to finalize the details with the cool, precise Thomas Niles. Roberts Brothers sat at the publishing epicenter of Boston, a few doors down from the successful publisher of Oliver Optic, and a few doors farther from the office where she had been brusquely turned out and told to stick to her teaching. There was no hint here of a future windfall.

Roberts Brothers' office was cramped, the signboard dingy, and Thomas Niles sat behind a green cloth curtain that separated his desk from the front door.

Niles was thorough when it came down to business. He laid out Louisa's alternatives. She could accept an advance of $300 and give up all other rights to the book, or she could forgo the meager advance, retain her copyright, and earn 6.66 percent royalties on each copy sold. It was a question of whether to put some much-needed cash into her pocket or risk gambling on herself. Left to her own devices, she might not have taken the chance. Louisa was feeling tired and discouraged. She had written a new story, "Morning-Glories," that same spring and feared she would "get nothing" for it. Sensing her hesitation, Thomas Niles advised her to keep the copyright for herself and earn the royalties. "So I shall," she noted. In the end it made her a fortune.

Roberts Brothers moved quickly to publish *Little Women*, which is to say, the first half of the two-part book as we know and love it. On August 26, 1868, Louisa received the first proofs. She was surprised and pleased to find that she liked her own work. "It reads better than I expected," she remarked. She gazed at her newborn brainchild with a cool clarity that resembled her father's journals about his flesh-and-blood offspring. Hardcover published copies soon followed. So did copies of Bronson's book, *Tablets*.

By September, Louisa wrote in her journal, "Father's book came out. Very simple outside, wise and beautiful within." She invested more in his publication than in her own. "Hope it will bring him praise and profit, for he has waited long."

Louisa compared her new book with her old blood-and-thunder stories and was content with her latest effort. "Not a bit sensational," she commented, "but simple and true, for we really lived most of it; and if it succeeds that will be the reason of it." The hard-to-please Thomas Niles "likes it better now," she noted with some relief—Niles's niece had laughed and cried over the book. Niles reported hopefully: "Some girls who have read the manuscripts say it is 'splendid!'" As always, Louisa kept her expectations low, and her hopes focused on others—including young readers. If they liked her book, she had succeeded. "As it is for them, they are the best critics, so I should be satisfied."

Eight hundred copies of Bronson Alcott's *Tablets* were published that September, as well as two hundred elegant "deluxe" copies. *Little Women* had no such special edition, but Louisa believed her small red clothbound novel handsome enough. The book's title and the author's name— L. M. Alcott—were inscribed in gold letters inside a simple oval. May Alcott contributed three illustrations and a frontispiece—all of which the young artist thought to be failures. (Critics agreed with May's assessment.) *Little Women* was scheduled to sell for $1.25, but its publication was delayed a few weeks, and the price of the little red volume rose to $1.50. Louisa fretted over the new price. Would anyone think her book worth $1.50? A first edition of *Little Women* now sells for more than $20,000.

By September all the residents of Apple Slump were in a slump. No news reached Concord about *Little Women*'s success or failure in the world. It seemed to have sunk without a trace. "No girl, Mother poorly," Louisa fretted in her journal. Again the burden of family life fell on her heavily. "May busy with pupils, Nan with her boys, and much work to be done." Having had a taste of full-time writing life, she returned dutifully to the kitchen, but she'd learned that her "tastes and gifts lie in other directions," so it was harder to "pull the plan steadily."

October saw Marmee's sixty-eighth birthday come and go. Bronson led Abby to her comfortable red chair, where copies of Bronson's book and Louisa's lay in waiting, while Anna's two boys paraded around the room, blowing horns. More presents sat piled on the table in Bronson's study— fur slippers from Anna, handkerchiefs from May. Abby "laughed and cried over our gifts and verses."

Louisa's chief anxiety that fall was not about books but about her increasingly frail Marmee: "I feel as if the decline had begun for her, and each year will add to the change which is going on, as time alters the eager, enthusiastic home-mother into a gentle, feeble old woman, to be cherished and helped tenderly." It is hard to imagine the fiery Abby as a "gentle, feeble old woman." It must have been harder still for Louisa to see the change.

It is said that good news is slow to arrive, while bad news rushes at us. Louisa waited in silence for any word of *Little Women*'s reception. No word came. She concluded that her book must have foundered miserably. Finally, on October 30 Louisa visited Niles in person to ask about her latest "offspring."

A cheery Thomas Niles informed Louisa that *Little Women*'s first edition had already sold out, with more copies on order and a London edition forthcoming. He expected to "sell three or four thousand" copies before the year was up. Louisa was gratified to learn that Niles wanted "a second volume for spring."

That second volume was what readers now read as part two of *Little Women*. The first volume earned the author "pleasant notices and letters" and, as a surprised and pleased Louisa wrote in her journal, "much interest in my little women, who seem to find friends by their truth to life, as I hoped."

CHAPTER SIXTEEN

Hard Times Over Forever

Within a few days of the reassuring report from Niles and his promise of a second volume's publication, Louisa leaped back to writing. "Began the second part of 'Little Women,'" she noted on November 1. For *Little Women*, part two, Louisa set herself a Herculean task: to write the entire book in one month.

Page after page of blue-lined paper piled up on the desk in her rented room in Boston. She wrote in black ink on ordinary lined paper, her handwriting spiky and surprisingly upright. (She once advised an aspiring writer to never "write with steel pens or you will . . . lose the use of your thumb, as I have.")

In the ample journals and letters that survive, the author tells very little about writing of *Little Women*. She instructed Roberts Brothers to destroy the printer's copies, and she herself destroyed nearly all working copies of her manuscripts. She wrote to a friend that part one was "very hastily written to order" and that she'd had "many doubts" about its success. But she admitted, "The characters were drawn from life, which gives them whatever merit they possess, for I find it impossible to invent anything half so true or touching as the simple facts with which every day life supplies me."

Her work ethic was positively brain-spinning. She declared, "I can do a chapter a day, and in a month I mean to be done." This schedule meant writing fifteen to twenty publishable pages every day—and keeping up that pace for a month steady. "Can't work slowly," she wrote. "The thing possesses me and I must obey till it's done." Troubling physical symptoms may have alerted her to another level of urgency. She was determined to provide for her family as long as her health allowed. It was not clear how long that might be. Louisa had moved to a quiet room in Boston where she could sequester herself "to spin, like a spider."

By now she'd read the warm reviews of *Little Women*, part one. She'd had a taste of success once before, with the popular *Hospital Sketches*. Now she dared to hope that *Little Women* might be nearly as well-received. Reviews were positive, if mixed. *The Nation* called the novel an "agreeable little story," and then went on to brutally criticize May Alcott's "indifferently executed illustrations." The *Boston Daily Evening Transcript* identified Louisa chiefly as the famed Bronson Alcott's daughter but added that she was "one of the best writers for the young that New England has produced for many years." "Capital," exclaimed the *Ladies' Repository*, "Our Sabbath Schools will all want it." Not everyone agreed. "Don't put in the Sunday school library," warned *Zion's Herald*. Others rushed to the author's defense: "Miss Allcott [sic] . . . is too appreciative of the truly beautiful in childhood to attempt to preach them into stiff-backed, spiritless propriety."

Louisa celebrated each bit of success with delight. "A little success is so inspiring," she confessed, "and as I can launch into the future, my fancy has more play." She had made her meager living every way she could—as servant, seamstress, teacher, nurse, and traveling companion. Now at last she had permission to earn as a full-time writer.

The only blot on her joy, she fumed, was the inevitable question from readers, asking "who the little women will marry, as if that was the only end and aim of a woman's life."

Louisa had just published an essay titled "Happy Women," defending a woman's right to remain single. She makes a fierce defense of unmarried life, urging young women "to remember that the loss of liberty, happiness, and self-respect is poorly repaid by the barren honor of being called 'Mrs.' instead of 'Miss.'" At age thirty-five Louisa considered herself a spinster for life. The term "spinster" was originally intended to describe an industrious woman, one who knew how to spin and make her own living—remember Louisa's image of her writing self as a "spinning" spider. She declared herself to be part of an honorable "sisterhood" composed of "superior women who, from various causes, remain single, and devote themselves to some earnest work . . . remaining as faithful to and as happy in their choice as married women."

Most readers of *Little Women* expected to see Jo married off to her devoted, wealthy, charming next-door neighbor, Laurie. Louisa had other plans for her freedom-loving heroine. She declared, "I won't marry Jo to Laurie to please any one." She had intended to keep her central character Jo permanently single—but she was a realist when it came to her readers. She observed tartly, "Publishers . . . insist on having people married off in a wholesale manner which much afflicts me. Jo," she explained, "should have remained a literary spinster but so many enthusiastic ladies wrote to me clamorously demanding that she should marry Laurie, or somebody, that I didn't dare refuse." In the end she half bowed to popular demand and selected for Jo's possible mate the least romantic character possible: bumbling German Professor Bhaer, whom a furious Laurie calls "that old man!" Louisa had given in to public pressure, but as usual, she had done so in her own inimitable way. And even so, she never entirely reconciled herself to Jo's marriage.

In *Jo's Boys*, the final book about the March family,

Louisa would sneak in one last defense of a single life: "'We do need just such helpful women in the world. I sometimes feel as if I'd missed my vocation and ought to have remained single; but my duty seemed to point this way, and I don't regret it,' said Mrs. Jo"—rather cool words from a wife and mother!

While working through part two of *Little Women*, Louisa vowed to take an occasional day off—attend a lecture with Bronson or have lunch with friends—but she soon gave it up. She was back to her manic method of composing. "I am so full of my work I can't stop to eat or sleep, or for anything but a daily run." She worked in a single room on Boston's Brookline Street without distractions.

Her birthday in late November differed from her mother's autumn celebration. There was no joyful gathering, no family party—no pile of gifts. "My birthday; thirty-six. Spent alone, writing hard. No presents but Father's 'Tablets.'" She turned her sense of deprivation into a new one of appreciation. "I never seem to have many presents, as some do, though I give a good many. That is best perhaps, and makes a gift very precious when it does come."

Another reason for the lack of birthday festivities was that Abby had left Orchard House and headed north of Boston to stay awhile with Anna and her boys. With Louisa so focused on her writing, the house had grown too isolated. Bronson still traveled, away on lectures of various kinds. That winter Abby cried out to her journal, "All alone!

Alone! Alone! Alone!" She felt more at home living close to Anna, her kind son-in-law John Pratt, and two lively grandsons.

Anna enjoyed housekeeping and excelled at it, while John kept things comfortable and steady. "Am enjoying the warmth and comfort of a neat house," Abby wrote contentedly. She even considered spending her remaining years "in this sweet home of peace and comfort," which would have meant leaving Bronson, May, and Louisa to fend for themselves. Louisa would have been horrified to know that the "sunny, cosy corner" she had labored so hard to make had not kept Marmee happy.

Readers now consider part one and part two as a single novel called *Little Women*, but there are notable differences between the two halves. Part one of *Little Women* begins with teasing and bickering among the young sisters. Part two starts with a wedding. Part one's opening chapter is "Playing Pilgrims"—a title that suggests both the childlike and serious tone of the novel. Part two begins with a chapter called "Gossip," a more teen-friendly topic, geared toward Alcott's new audience. Louisa skipped three years ahead from part one to two, hurrying Meg along to a marriageable age.

The beginning of the second volume is not as strong as part one's opening salvo: "Christmas won't be Christmas without any presents." The author promises adult readers that there won't be "too much lovering" in her sequel, while reassuring her avid young readers that there will. She gives Mrs. March an arch, coy speech to make about her "four gay girls" and the "dashing young neighbor over the way." It sounds nothing like the dignified Mrs. March of part one, and as far from Abby's real-life conversations as one can imagine.

By part two, the Civil War has ended, and Mr. March comes home to take up his rather small corner of the novel. Louisa works hard to make him loveable, "a minister by nature as by grace,—a quiet, studious man, rich in the wisdom that is better than learning, the charity which calls all mankind 'brother,' the piety that blossoms into character, making it august and lovely." Had the author gone on much longer in this sickly vein, we might never have heard of her, or of *Little Women*. Even Louisa had her doubts, worrying that part two of her book would never achieve the popularity of part one.

Luckily for her—and for us—she quickly set her characters in motion. Jo and neighbor Laurie begin sparring—and the novel is off and running. Jo scolds "boy" for his airs and extravagance:

"'I don't see the use of your having seventeen waistcoats, endless neckties, and a new hat every time you come home. I thought you'd got over your dandy period; but every now and then it breaks out in a new spot. Just now it's the fashion to be hideous,—to make your head look like a scrubbing-brush, wear a strait-jacket, orange gloves, and clumping, square-toed boots. If it was cheap ugliness, I'd say nothing; but it costs as much as the other, and I don't get any satisfaction out of it." Laurie takes his revenge by teasing Jo about her sister's forthcoming wedding, with "a long low whistle, and the fearful prediction, as they parted at the gate, 'Mark my words, Jo, you'll go next.'"

Gossip had already spread among local readers about the possible real-life model for Laurie. Was he a suitor, a family friend? Louisa said nothing about Ladislas, but she did joke later that "every lad I ever knew claims the character" of Laurie. She wrote more sternly to an acquaintance, "None of the characters in my books are drawn from life but the Marches." She cast doubt even regarding the resemblance between the Marches and the Alcotts, telling a Dutch admirer, "I am 'Jo' in the principal characteristics, not the good ones." None of that stopped the endless speculation about the models for her fictional characters—not then or now.

Bronson always insisted that Laurie was based on the intellectual Llewellyn Willis, while Anna once confided that she thought he was really Julian Hawthorne. Alf Whitman is another contender for the "tender, sweet side" of Laurie, as Alcott's Orchard House director Jan Turnquist points out. Louisa wrote in an 1869 letter to Alf that "'Laurie' is you & my Polish boy 'jintly.' You are the sober half & my Ladislas . . . the gay whirligig half; he was a perfect dear." But she also hinted at other possibilities over time. Just as she amused and protected herself by keeping her potboiler authorship under wraps, she seemed to relish this guessing game as well.

We don't have the details we crave about how Louisa wrote her famous book. Did she prefer to write in the morning, the afternoon, or late at night? Did she dress for the part? In *Jo's Boys*, Jo "rumpled up her hair, took off her cuffs, and hurried to finish her chapter; for thirty pages a day was her task, and she liked to have it well done before evening."

To learn about her sentence-by-sentence writing process, there is no better source than the original manuscript pages, which are open to the public at the Concord Free Public Library—nor could they have come to rest at a better home. The library houses five hundred manuscript pages in Louisa's own hand, including two original chapters from *Little Women*.

By some miraculous bit of luck, one of those two surviving chapters is "Heartache," the chapter where Jo turns down a heartbroken Laurie's proposal a final time. Nowhere is Louisa's process and genius more evident. The handwritten pages are full of cross-outs and scribbled revisions. "Poor Laurie" is turned into the "poor young lover." A hat is "dashed" down instead of flung. Louisa must have already decided to pair him to the elegant, lively youngest sister, Amy. In the "Heartache" chapter Jo turns down Laurie's proposal half a dozen times in as many pages. But how would she finally reject him, and on what terms?

Louisa's handwritten manuscript shows that she considered a radically different turn of events. Jo has already tried to let Laurie down as gently as possible. He resists every effort. At last, in exasperation she cries, "I'll never marry you, and the sooner you believe it the better for both of us—so now!" In this first draft, the enraged and heartstricken Laurie responds like "gunpowder" touched by fire. "Laurie looked at her a minute as if he did not quite know what to do with himself, then he caught her in his arms and *kissed her violently*" [emphasis mine].

He kissed her violently! The whole Jo/Laurie love story twists in the wind that instant. That kiss would have shocked Louisa's reading public, I'm sure. It also would have damaged every plot point that follows. How could Laurie marry Amy after passionately embracing and kissing her sister? How would Jo marry another man?

Louisa snatched back the mistake. One inked line slashes through the words, followed by another cross-out below it, striking out the word *violently* and substituting *turned sharply away*. Here is the revised scene as all readers know it: "Laurie looked at her a minute as if he did not quite know what to do with himself, then turned sharply away."

He *turned sharply away*. Those three words are written with more force than any others, as if Alcott wished to emphasize them to herself. It is a revision comparable only to the despairing *couldn't be* in her Swiss journal entry, scrawled over a deleted and torn cry from the heart.

Laurie's passionate kiss might have served in one of Louisa's sensational stories, but it would have spoiled *Little Women*—and Louisa knew it. By now she understood her material, her audience, her characters. Tempted though she was to head toward something more "sensational," she stayed true, as she'd once promised Abby, to the "realities of men." If anyone wants proof of Louisa May Alcott's writing genius, it shines out from this single revised page.

Louisa did not meet her one-month deadline for the composition of part two—despite all her valiant efforts. She delivered the finished manuscript on New Year's Day 1869. Even then, she couldn't think of the right title. (Niles had come up with *Little Women* for part one.) She offered a few lackluster ideas: *Little Women Act Second* or *Leaving the Nest. Sequel to Little Women*. She jokingly suggested *Wedding Marches* because, as she remarked, "there is so much pairing off," but Niles eventually arrived at the title *Good Wives*. She only grumbled to herself, "I don't approve."

Sequels fall flat more often than not, as Louisa well knew. "Hope it will do as well as the first," she fretted in her journal. She dared not raise her hopes too high. She kept on working at a frantic pace, editing *Merry's Museum* and writing two further stories a month for the *Youth's Companion*. But she needed to slow down. Her illness was getting the best of her.

She felt the pressure from all sides to keep up the pace.

"I shall do so if I am able; but my headaches, cough, and weariness keep me from working as I once could, fourteen hours a day." The headaches, coughs, and fatigue were all recurring symptoms of her mercury poisoning, but Louisa viewed her illness as a moral failing. If she had been stronger, braver, more selfless, she thought, all would have sailed smoothly forward.

Family responsibilities placed the greatest burden on her time and health. "Louisa is not so much sick as worn out," Bronson confided to a friend. She had been suffering for six months with a cough that robbed her "of temper and time, coveted for thought and creation." Though Bronson saw her weary load, he did little to help. Louisa closed up Orchard House for the winter while Bronson was traveling for his Conversations and her mother was still staying with Anna. In March it fell upon Louisa to reopen and clean the whole house for spring. Abby had begun to feel homesick for Orchard House, and Bronson missed his books and study. Louisa had experienced a brief lift in health and spirits while away in Boston, but now she found Concord "cold and dull; not able to write; so took care of Marmee and tried to rest."

She took on all the housework, at the same time keeping creditors at bay. Her sister Anna shrewdly saw in Louisa's face "that drawn tired look." Louisa grew increasingly gloomy that early spring, but comforted herself that she was keeping the family's head above water.

Money had been a worry all her life. She could breathe a little easier at the moment. "Paid up all the debts, thank the Lord!—every penny that money can pay—and now I feel as if I could die in peace." Louisa's hopes for part two remained modest, but she had fewer worries about going through the rest of her life unpublished and penniless. "My dream is beginning to come true; and if my head holds out I'll do all I once hoped to do."

April found her nearly broken down. "Very poorly. Feel quite used up," she wrote in her journal. "Don't care much for myself, as rest is heavenly even with pain, but the family seems so panic-stricken and helpless when I break down, that I try to keep the mill going."

Part two of *Little Women* was published on April 14. Louisa had given up whatever small spark of hope she'd had for it. She told a friend a few weeks earlier, "A sequel will be out early in April & like all sequels will probably disappoint or disgust most readers." As usual, the silent Thomas Niles gave Louisa no further news. Hoping for some word of encouragement, Louisa visited his office on Washington Street and found it even more busy than usual, with trucks, crates, and clerks all outside the building, snaking in a line down the street. Everything was in a state of chaos and confusion. Dressed in her worn clothing, feeling lost, she managed to squeeze through the crowd, thinking something tremendous must be going on.

As Louisa later told Julian Hawthorne, she found her

usually calm editor Thomas Niles crouched over his desk like the letter *G*. He leaped up when he saw Louisa. Had she gotten his letter? he roared at her. No, she answered. Had she heard the news? No again.

Her book, he announced to the astonished author, was "the triumph of the century!" *Little Women* had pushed all other bestsellers to the back shelves. There had never been anything like it. Roberts Brothers company was overrun. Even with all hands on deck, the publisher could not keep up with the demand. Three thousand advance copies had sold before the book had even appeared! They expected to sell twenty thousand by Christmas. Would she like an advance check? Niles asked. Any amount. Money was no object.

A dazed Louisa made her way back to Concord. Her mother was in the kitchen, as usual, paring apples for a pie. May perched on a piano stool while Louisa told them the astonishing news. "Hard times for the Alcotts are over forever," she announced giddily.

Over the next days and weeks, more sales kept rolling in. The numbers were staggering. Within two weeks, part two had sold thirteen thousand copies. By Christmastime, Niles's cheerful prediction had been left in the dust—the book had sold thirty-six thousand copies. Letters from fans poured in—some weeping over Beth, others disconsolate that Jo had turned down the appealing Laurie.

Critical reviews of part two offered universal praise.

One reviewer wished he "need never part company, with these earnest, delightful people" and expressed his "sincere wish that there were to be a third and fourth part." Roberts Brothers, who paid close attention to this sort of remark, pressed Louisa to produce another book as fast as possible.

She recorded none of these triumphs in her private journal. She may have been too stunned to take them in. Only the recollections of friends and family, and snippets from her letters give us a glimpse into her bewildered, joyous state of mind. She had always hesitated to count on any happy event, afraid she'd jinx it. Now she fell silent.

Abby recorded simply that Louisa's connection to Roberts Brothers had been "most appreciable and profitable," while an exuberant Julian Hawthorne celebrated "the first flowing of the liberating tide." Louisa sent a note thanking Thomas Niles for "an unusually merry" Christmas. She gave a partial vent to her relief. "After toiling so many years along the uphill road,—always a hard one for women writers," she wrote, "it is peculiarly grateful to me to find the way growing easier at last, with pleasant little surprises blossoming on either side, and the rough places made smooth."

Neighbors in Concord saw only the sudden, overwhelming success of their neighbor, Louisa May Alcott, daughter of the peculiar Bronson Alcott. They had not watched all her invisible hours of labor and disappointment. They witnessed only the flocks of reporters, books prominently displayed in stores, and glowing reviews. To them Louisa's success seemed an overnight fluke like a snowstorm in June, and bound to vanish as fast.

Louisa's success had not happened overnight, of course—far from it. She had been laboring for years, at great sacrifice of time and strength. She had teased out a small and agonizingly slow living, one story at a time. But glory, fame, and fortune came all in a flash.

So did notoriety—a less welcome guest. "People begin to come and stare at the Alcotts," she recorded in her journal. There was a touch of glee in the observation at first. She tried to handle her fame graciously. But the novelty wore quickly off. Unlike the outgoing Bronson or May, Louisa had always been uncomfortable at the center of attention, except among her closest friends and family. Of all the sisters—even timid Lizzie—Louisa may have been the most awkward of the four. "May makes a lovely hostess," Louisa wrote, "and I fly round behind the scenes or skip out of the back window when ordered out for inspection by the inquisitive public."

The quiet life of the Alcotts was changed forever. "It is called 'fame,' and considered a blessing," Louisa observed wryly. "Let 'em try it." Bronson flourished in the attention, commencing a new flirtation with a young woman named Ellen Channing. He suggested to Louisa that she write her next book about *him*.

Letters flooded in from all over the country and, soon,

from all over the world—demanding sequels, threatening, cajoling, and "bullying" by turns, as Louisa joked— but fan letters at least could be ignored.

It was harder to ignore the demands of her publisher. Even with this great new financial windfall, Louisa could not bring herself to refuse lucrative work. The habit of feeling at the edge of ruin was too strong to give it up easily. She wrote to one editor, "I find that I must make hay while my sun shines, & so wish to earn all I can before Fortune's wheel takes a turn & carries me down again."

She was thrilled and confused—and a little irritated—when she was invited to teas and literary parties thrown by the same Boston literati who had once snubbed her. She was courted wherever she went. Of course, there were a few naysayers—as there always are. Her family "friend" the novelist Henry James, who had shredded her novel *Moods*, felt called upon to throw cold water on her again. At dinner, the young Henry James leaned toward the author. "Louisa—m-my dear girl—er—when you hear people—ah—telling you you're a genius you mustn't believe them; er—what I mean is, it isn't true!'" Years later, reminded of that dinner, James still insisted, "'But—well, you know, after all, dear Louisa isn't.'"

With or without Henry James's approval, Louisa's reputation continued to rise. Soon there were forty thousand copies of *Little Women* in print—more than any book by any male author in her day, including her late eminent neighbor, Nathaniel Hawthorne. Her satire in the *Springfield Republican* about her sudden fame shows her comical view of the madness.

She wrote under her old pen name Tribulation Periwinkle to report on the new "tribulations" of success. She joked that a new hotel was about to be erected in the center of Concord, "where pilgrims to this modern Mecca can be entertained." Not just the Alcotts but their closest friends came in for teasing. "The house will be filled with Alcott's rustic furniture," she promised, "the beds made of Thoreau's pine boughs, and the sacred fires fed from the Emersonian wood-pile." Visitors to modern-day Concord—especially those who travel to Orchard House, Walden Pond, and Emerson's house—may feel as if her bizarre predictions came true. She guaranteed that "guides will be in attendance," with telescopes provided for spying, and photos of the illustrious will "have conferred immortality upon one of the dullest little towns in Massachusetts."

The remark about the "dullest little town" was not kind to Concord, but she was even less kind when it came to outsiders. She wrote that "a flock of reporters . . . roost upon Concordian fences, chirp on Concordian door-steps." She was beginning to feel the loss of privacy and liberty that accompanied fame. The constraint grew tighter over time. The "female inhabitants" of Orchard House, she wrote—by which she meant herself, her mother, and visiting sisters—were chased no matter where they went; "the words 'private life,' 'sanctity of home,' 'domestic seclusion,' are a hollow mockery."

Louisa began some of the strangest legends about the extremes to which went in order to escape her adoring public. Some details are based in fact; others are flights of fancy. She cast herself as an "irascible spinster, driven to frenzy by twenty-eight visitors in a week," who would rush out back and vigorously water the garden, splashing it whenever visitors came near.

In her journal she grumbled, "Reporters haunt the place to look at the authoress, who dodges into the woods à la Hawthorne, and won't be even a very small lion." She ran away through the very trees where she'd once spied her elusive neighbor. For the time being, the chase was still merry. And she could still escape. But early in her life of fame, she wrote in the *Springfield Republican*, "No spot is safe, no hour is sacred, and fame is beginning to be considered an expensive luxury by the Concordians."

When she tallied her earnings that year, it was the highest sum she had ever imagined—a number that would have dazzled her any year of her life. She could afford to put $1,200 into savings, "pay all the debts and make every one as comfortable as I can." The only one's comfort she had not yet considered was her own.

CHAPTER SEVENTEEN

Traveling About,
Doing Just as They Like

Louisa followed the success of *Little Women* with a more satirical novel, *An Old-Fashioned Girl*. It became her habit to follow a serious book with a lighter work, and *An Old-Fashioned Girl* fit the bill. First published in *Merry's Museum* the summer of 1869, *An Old-Fashioned Girl* consisted of only six serialized chapters. Since Louisa worked under salary for *Merry's Museum*, she could kill two birds with one stone—satisfy the magazine and buy herself time to complete the new novel for her publisher.

She added to the six published chapters, jumping forward several years, much as she had done in the gap between part one and part two of *Little Women*. In this way she was able to stretch the new novel to nineteen chapters. *An Old-Fashioned Girl* is a classic country mouse / city mouse tale, with the heroine, Polly Milton, visiting and ultimately transforming the sophisticated city lives of her relations. The book allowed Louisa plenty of scope for mocking extravagance and pretension—the very things she'd had to tolerate among the Mays. The novel is not as original or fresh as *Little Women*, but Alcott's lively playfulness and character creation shimmers through, along with what she herself would call her "moral pap," and her readers were eagerly waiting for this next book.

Even as she worked, Louisa's health was crumbling. There is still debate about the exact cause and nature of Louisa's illness, and scholars have proposed everything from lupus to rheumatism to mercury poisoning to some form of Lyme disease. It's possible that her army-days pneumonia triggered ill health that gathered momentum as it went—or that she suffered from numerous poorly diagnosed conditions all together. It's challenging to accurately judge a person's health from a distance—much less with 150 years between you. We know that her headaches worsened. She lost her voice for a month. Her joints ached like an old woman's. She was in so much pain that she finished writing *An Old-Fashioned Girl* with her left hand in a sling and her right foot propped up on a chair. When a few readers chided her for grammatical errors, Louisa responded, "If people knew how O.F.G. was written, in what hurry and pain and woe, they would wonder that there was any grammar at all."

Roberts Brothers rushed the new novel into print, and, capitalizing on the author's success, they also issued a brand-new edition of *Hospital Sketches* with the addition of a few of her old wartime tales. The same stories that had once been rejected found fame in this new form. Everything she touched seemed turned to gold.

In hope that *An Old-Fashioned Girl* might generate the same high sales as *Little Women*, Louisa asked for a raise in royalties, up from 6.66 percent to 10 or 12. The cautious Thomas Niles refused. He wasn't counting on a second miracle. But when *An Old-Fashioned Girl* appeared in spring of 1870, it was a huge success. Twelve thousand copies sold in advance of publication, and the first bookstore orders called for twenty-four thousand books.

The author wrote in *An Old-Fashioned Girl*, "I deeply regret being obliged to shock the eyes and ears" of purists and critics, but in writing about the young, for the young, she declared, "I feel bound to depict my honored patrons as faithfully as my limited powers permit." For the first time in her life Louisa could defend her use of slang—and get away with it.

Mysterious physical ailments vexed her. She suffered from stomach problems, boils, aching joints, and swollen hands and feet. She shuttled from Boston to Concord and back, endlessly consulting doctors who ordered painful and useless procedures. Her shifting pains were attributed to rheumatism and neuralgia, to flu and hypochondria, but none of the cures helped.

That summer, her sister May was set to sail to Europe as the traveling companion of a wealthy female friend. May would at last see the famous artworks she had studied from afar for so long. Perhaps remembering her own difficulties under similar circumstances with Anna Weld, Louisa offered to come along as buffer and guide, happy to pay her own way. She no longer had to scrimp or serve others in order to go abroad. Instead she traveled as a celebrity guest, adding luster to the group.

John Pratt accompanied Louisa and May by train to New York City. It was John who had greeted Louisa at the dock when she'd returned from her first voyage to Europe. Then she'd been alone and unknown, grateful for a glimpse of one of her "home faces." Now people recognized her wherever she went, from autograph hounds to the most elegant guests on board the ship.

A train boy tried to sell Louisa a copy of her own book, *An Old-Fashioned Girl*, pitching its charms; John Pratt gently pointed out the boy's mistake. The parting from home and family was bittersweet. Louisa joked that they were departing on April Fool's Day—but her sharp eye detected that as soon as Abby gaily waved farewell with her white handkerchief, she quickly raised the same handkerchief to dry her eyes. It pained Louisa to leave behind her aging mother. She was sailing off into an unknown future, and how could she know, she fretted, who she might be leaving forever?

Louisa was supposed to take notes for a book of travel sketches she would call *Shawl-Straps*. But she suffered miserably on the long sea journey out and spent most of her time lying below deck, wondering if they could rename the steamer *Nausea*. Even in her cabin sickbed, fans managed to find her: "Little girls . . . came in a party to call on me, very seasick in my berth, done up like a mummy."

Her traveling companions were the opposite of the culture-spurning, petulant Anna Weld. May quickly made friends with her fellow travelers. Louisa crowed that her sister "was liked by all." Alice Bartlett, May's traveling companion, was nothing like Anna Weld. Unlike Miss Weld, Alice Bartlett had good cause for her sadness and low spirits. In the course of three years she had lost mother, father, and her only brother. Louisa liked and pitied Alice—and she loved the gay company of her own sister May.

A natural world traveler, Louisa relished "the queer sights and sounds" of Breton and the French provinces. She wrote lively, detailed letters home—no doubt hoping to generate more material for *Shawl-Straps* as well as to soothe "the old folks"—taking care to emphasize how thrifty she

315

was being, and urging the home folk to treat themselves well.

She wrote in France, "The climate must cure me, for they say throat and lung invalids always get well here." In a private note for Abby's eyes only, Louisa also added, "I think this is to be one of our lucky years, and this trip a success if things go on as well as they have begun." It was rare for Louisa to sound an optimistic note.

The three travelers toured Italy, where May dashed around to art galleries and museums while Louisa gratefully stayed "warm and cosey" in their apartment, "as it rained for two months" and then froze into ice. Despite her plans to start her travel book, she hadn't "written a thing as yet and don't feel as if I ever should." For once she was truly on vacation. She wrote to Abby, "The girls are ever so good to me." Louisa was recognized and treated like traveling royalty wherever they went. The three young women were given the best rooms, the loveliest views. They ate whenever and whatever they pleased, sometimes skipping dinner altogether, devouring chocolates instead and drinking coffee in bed.

"Can this be the poor Alcotts," Louisa marveled to May, "traveling about and doing just as they like?" Usually thrifty when it came to her own expenses, Louisa relaxed her guard and ordered a handmade Parisian walking suit of silvery-gray silk. Even in her extravagance she pointed out that the silk cost only ninety cents per yard.

Because her leg pained her— "the curse of my life," she called it—she consulted a former British army surgeon in Dinan, France: the "rich bachelor" Dr. William Kane. Though May and Alice teasingly called him Louisa's beau, Louisa was interested only in the doctor's friendship—and his diagnosis. Dr. Kane assured Louisa that she probably suffered from rheumatism next to the bone—a painful but not dangerous condition. He ordered potassium dissolved in alcohol and opium to help her sleep. Unsurprisingly, she slept soundly under his orders. He also advised her, rather confusingly, to stay off her feet, go for walks, keep warm, and get plenty of fresh air.

He did offer one important insight. As Louisa explained in a letter home, Dr. Kane had guessed that "my leg trouble and many of my other woes come from the calomel they gave me in Washington. He has been through the same tribulations with an Indian jungle fever, and has never got the calomel out of him." It was the first likely diagnosis of the root of her miseries—and the first suggestion that her condition might prove incurable. If the good doctor "never got the calomel out," what chance did Louisa have for a complete recovery? She'd announced long ago after her pneumonia, "I was never ill before this time, and never well afterward." She did not allow herself to dwell on the darkest possibilities—then, or ever, not even in her last moments. After all, she assured her family, the doctor had found relief for his symptoms—she might well do the same.

317

Louisa followed Dr. Kane's orders as closely as possible and convinced herself she was getting better. It was a pattern of raised hope, effort, and disappointment that would play out repeatedly in the difficult years ahead. She told herself and others that sickness was a helpful teacher: "Perhaps pain has a good effect upon my works." If so, she had plenty of its "good effect," and we should not wonder at the abundance of her genius.

Louisa, May, and Alice decided to stay abroad for a full year—a very long time to be away from Concord. In her journal she insisted, "I was very poorly & enjoyed little." Yet she wrote gay letters home, which were seldom rewarded by return correspondence. Each place they visited, she checked first for a letter from Orchard House, but each note seemed to be lost or delayed en route. Every day abroad brought new adventures—a twisting train ride "under, over and through the mountains," boat rides, rambles, and sails. One day they were chased away from a farm by angry pigs. Louisa "flew over a hedge" while May lay on her back howling with laughter, with the pigs, two cows, a dog, and a boy looking on. The sisters scrambled to safety, roaring and tumbling "like a routed garrison."

After France, they arrived in Vevey, Switzerland, the place where Louisa had once had her "little romance" with Laddie. At the time she did not say much about this visit to the past, but later, in "My Boys," she confessed, "Lake Leman will never seem as lovely again as when Laddie and

I roamed about its shores, floated on its bosom, or laid splendid plans for the future in the sunny garden of the old chateau. I tried it again last year, but the charm was gone."

Gone as well was Louisa's youth. Catching sight of herself in a window, Louisa observed that she looked old and fat. While in Vevey, she dreamed she'd come home to an unrecognizable Concord. A neighbor in the dream informed her that Orchard House had been sold and Bronson had built a grand school in its place, with "'the great fortune his daughter left him, the one that died some ten years ago.' 'So, I am dead, am I?' says I to myself, feeling so queerly."

Louisa blamed the dream on some "cowcumbers" eaten the day before. In typical Louisa style, even in her upside-down dream world she chose to stay dead and not trouble the family: "I better go away," her dream self decided, "and not disturb anyone."

The dream may have also been an eerie forewarning of another death. In Rome at Christmastime, Louisa was glancing through an American weekly when she came across heart-stopping news. Her brother-in-law, John Pratt, that gentle, reliable soul, had died suddenly the month before, after being ill for only a week. Louisa wrote home to her grieving sister Anna, "You need not be told what he was to me, or how I mourn for him, for no born brother was ever dearer & each year I loved & respected & admired him more & more."

But in the midst of this sudden family tragedy, Louisa

made the most inexplicable decision of her life. Instead of sailing home to comfort the mourners, as any Alcott would be expected to do, she extended her stay in Europe. There is no way to explain it. Her beloved sister was in America, a young impoverished widow now with two small sons in her care. Abby and Bronson grieved as well, broken in body and spirit by the loss. John Pratt had not earned enough to keep his family secure, as Louisa must have been aware. For the first time, Louisa, the great comforter and supporter, did not come home to comfort or support.

On January 9, 1871, while still in Rome, Louisa penned a letter to her cousin Lizzie Wells excusing herself. She asked cousin Lizzie to "fill my place a little till I come," offering the most threadbare excuse for staying away. "Annie bears her loss so beautifully," she wrote, "that it makes it possible to stay away now in order that I may be more useful by and by." She even called on John's memory to defend her absence: "John leaves so sweet & precious a memory of his simple upright life & lovely character that Annie has much to sustain & comfort her."

The family must have been stunned by Louisa's declining to sustain and comfort Anna herself. Louisa offered one excuse after another. "My heart is very anxious about mother," she wrote to Lizzie Wells, "& I ache to go to her, but winter, distance, health & my duty to Alice hold me till April." Winter would be winter in Rome or New England. And it's hard to fathom why Louisa felt more "duty to Alice" than to her sister Anna, whom she had adored all her life. If Alice required a chaperone, why not let May stay behind? May was Alice's traveling companion. None of Louisa's explanations made sense. For once, "Duty's faithful child" refused to do her faithful duty.

Louisa stayed on in Italy, buying furs for the winter, strolling through the Carnival crowds in February, attending parties with May and Alice, and enjoying the comforts of their apartment on the Piazza Barberini. Her life was not all frivolity. She picked up her pen in earnest now, in honor of John Pratt, and "for the good of the two dear little men now left to my care, for long ago I promised to try and fill John's place if they were left fatherless." Her nephews, Fred and Johnny, were the "dear little men" who inspired her next novel, as well as its title: *Little Men*. She would devote her time and all of her book's profits to those nephews.

In her decision not to return till April—nearly five months after the death of John Pratt—perhaps the reality of Louisa's poor health remains the only good excuse. She often was afraid to let the family see her true deterioration. She feared "neuralgia would claim me for its own if I went," as she wrote in letters to America. Gossip circulated back home that Louisa was not merely sick but dying. Thomas Niles himself had to dispel the rumors in order to reassure Alcott's fans—but the idea must have come from somewhere. Louisa encountered friends from home while traveling abroad. Did she look ghastly enough to start those rumors? Even Bronson, seeing a portrait of Louisa painted in Rome, was stricken by "the flesh . . . haggard and the features too elongated."

In Europe she was at least free, and went on avoiding the cage that awaited her in Concord. For the first time she was not beholden to personal or financial burdens. At home, her aging parents awaited her care—and now a grieving sister and two young nephews had been added as well. She may have feared that she would break under the strain—and then be of no use to anyone. Some biographers skip over these months entirely and focus instead on Louisa's selfless work on *Little Men*, from which she never took any profit. Tour guides and biographers have passed over this period in silence, emphasizing how Louisa generously took her sister May traveling all over Europe.

In fact, Louisa nearly sent May home to Concord to serve in her place. She wrote to her family in an unusually light tone, given the grave situation: "In the spring, one of us will come home to run the machine." Further, she hinted, "I fancy it may be May if I can make up my mind to stay, for Alice can't remain without duenna [chaperone] and I can be one and also *pay my own way*." Alice was hardly in need of free assistance. She was a wealthy young woman who'd happily traded her antique diamond-and-emerald ring and a solid gold chain for Louisa's inexpensive new watch.

On the prospect of cutting short May's time abroad,

Louisa grumbled, "A year of pleasure . . . is all May should expect or accept *I* think." As for herself, "I dont want to stay," she repeated, "but if I'm not tip top by spring, I should feel as if I ought, for fifteen years' mischief cant be mended in twelve months." A year abroad—which had once seemed such an unthinkable luxury—now felt too short.

Alice Bartlett decided to return to America that April, removing Louisa's last remaining excuse to stay away. Alice sailed home alone on May 11, and two weeks later Louisa followed, writing in her journal, "A very pleasant year in spite of constant pain, John's death, and home anxieties." Without apparent irony she added, "Very glad I came, for May's sake."

May, that golden "child of fortune," was free to stay on in London another six months, studying the works of the great artists. She too might have volunteered to come home to help. Instead she stayed on. No one demanded more of her.

Louisa survived another rough crossing on the journey home, but she was greeted at the other end by Bronson and editor Thomas Niles displaying "a great red placard of 'Little Men.'" They brought glorious news as well: *Little Men* had sold fifty thousand copies—before the book was even published.

In *Little Men*, Louisa returned to her natural voice. She wrote it quickly, driven by grief and guilt, and the desire to

323

provide for the two "little men" in her life. *Little Men* leaps ten years forward from the end of *Little Women*. Jo has married Professor Fritz Bhaer. They have opened a pastoral Temple-style progressive school for boys at Plumfield—which Aunt March (rather inexplicably) has left to her least-favorite niece. Fritz Bhaer uses the same teaching methods that Bronson had employed—asking questions of his students instead of lecturing, inviting confidences, employing reverse psychology, and mixing play with lessons. In this roundabout way, Louisa had done just as her father asked—she'd written a book about him.

Little Men also allowed Louisa to express her ideas about education, and society at large. With her newfound popularity, Louisa discovered a platform for speaking out. The little men sent to learn and board at Plumfield are a motley crew. Some are poor and neglected, others rich and overzealously attended by relations. Louisa understood that deprivation comes in many forms. In *Little Men*, as in *Little Women*, she found a place to express her outrage and theories, as well as practical advice and ideals—and of course, tales of adventure and mischief. Writing about boys came easily. As she'd once told Alf Whitman, "I'm fond of boys, as you may have discovered." In *Little Men* she enjoyed a whole bookful of them. She understood and felt at ease with them, she declared, as she hadn't when attempting a book for girls.

She was hoping to earn a new male readership, too.

It can't have escaped her notice that nearly all of her fans were young women—"those so cracked girls," as she described them to her mother, dismissing their fan letters from abroad with an airy "The rampant infants must wait."

Though *Little Men* proved a success, it never won Louisa the devoted male readers for which she'd hoped. In Philadelphia, she was besieged by an army of girls who wanted her autograph and asked countless questions. Afterward she was requested to go downstairs a second time, to speak separately to the boys. As it turned out, there were only two of them, who wanted to know if her fictional pillow fights were based on real life. On learning they were (Saturday nights, before the linen was washed), they quickly disappeared.

When Louisa arrived home from her second trip to Europe, she barely noticed the fanfare over the newly published *Little Men*. Life within the family claimed all her time and attention. Anna had aged from grief, her lovely hair gone gray. She appeared "well and calm," noted Louisa, "but under her sweet serenity is a very sad soul." Admired by the world for her "calm acceptance," Anna confessed in her diary, "I do not feel resigned . . . I feel so disconsolate at times, so pitiful and wretched, that I cannot bear to think about it, and it makes me feel ashamed to have people praise my resignation."

Bronson, on the other hand, appeared untouched by age or sorrow. His long hair was silver, his blue eyes as clear and tranquil as ever. Abby had suffered a terrible change in Louisa's absence. Louisa wrote in her journal, "Mother feeble and much aged by this year of trouble." She vowed, as she'd done before, "I shall never go far away from her again." Abby was laid lower still by the summertime death of her beloved brother Samuel Joseph, her financial and emotional mainstay and, Louisa noted, "our best friend for years." Abby was now the only survivor among ten siblings.

Anna's two boys, Fred and John, were "tall bright lads, devoted to Marmee, and the life of the house." Orchard House needed their high spirits. As Louisa wrote, "Boys are always jolly,—even princes." Louisa brought her own "touch of the old cheerfulness" to Orchard House, where any happiness was much needed. Freddy and Johnny slept in a small add-on room that Bronson had built especially for them, beside the largest bedroom.

Louisa tried to keep things "jolly" for her loved ones. But it did not take long for ill health to torment her again. She began taking morphine in order to sleep. She confessed to her journal, "Too much company and care and change of climate upset the poor nerves again."

As soon as she could decently make her escape, she fled to Boston "to rest and try to get well" so that she could work. "Anything is better than the invalidism I hate worse than death." She needed a quiet corner in which to write— and hopefully, a place where she could hide.

In Concord Louisa was now a very large fish in a small pond. She was besieged by prying fans at Orchard House. "O dear, what a bother fame is," she complained. "I can't entertain a dozen a day, and write the tales they demand also." Visitors came to gape at her; never-before-known "friends" left stacks of calling cards. One eager child came to Orchard House, and upon meeting the flesh-and-blood author, exclaimed in a stricken voice, "I thought you were beautiful."

Anna Pratt, a sharper observer than she is given credit for, remarked on her sister Louisa's altered appearance. She wrote, "The . . . change is the inevitable one which age & sickness always bring & a certain elegance & stately grace which we never thought to see in our topsy turvy boyish Louie." In Boston, Louisa could manage anonymity and escape the worried sympathetic glances of those who knew her best. Her long black silk dress and black velvet hair ribbon helped her fit in with the other city folk. When she craved company and culture, she had as much as she desired. But soon she could no longer escape notice even in busy Boston. She was recognized in the street, on the streetcars. "Saw people, pictures, plays, and read all I could, but did not enjoy much, for the dreadful weariness of nerves makes even pleasure hard." Her teeth had begun to crumble—another side effect of mercury poisoning, though Louisa took it as a sign of age.

In November, May sailed home from Europe and took on some of the demands of daily life. Bronson was often far from Orchard House, offering lectures that drew crowds to see "Louisa May Alcott's father." Everyone in the family was suffering one way or another—Abby feeble, Anna overwhelmed, Louisa exhausted and ill, so "one strong head and hand is wanted at home." May could help where the indomitable Louisa could not, and Louisa's big-sisterly resentment and pride went hand in hand. Of her sister's long stay abroad, Louisa wrote, "A year and a half of holiday is a good deal, and duty comes first always." Yet she sympathetically mourned the loss of May's freedom, "Sorry to call her back. . . . I don't want her to be thwarted in her work more than just enough to make her want it very much."

Louisa knew what it meant to "want it very much." Now that she had achieved the fame and accomplishment she'd craved, she had new burdens to shoulder. Roberts Brothers hounded her for more books. Exhausted, she suggested they reissue her old collection *Morning-Glories and Other Stories* and she pulled together some new pieces, which she aptly titled *Aunt Jo's Scrap-Bag*. She had turned her boyish, eternally youthful heroine into a spinner of tales, like her creator. She had not minded being compared to the young, tomboyish Jo. It troubled her a bit to be confused with the more staid character of Aunt Jo.

May stayed on in Concord for less than six months.

The cheerful and charming baby of the family entertained the neighbors and kept Louisa's fans at bay. May made "a lovely hostess" while Louisa skipped out "the back window when ordered out for inspection by the inquisitive public. Hard work to keep things running smoothly, for this sightseeing fiend is a new torment to us." Abby bathed in the glow of May's sunny personality. Three daughters now surrounded her. Her youngest, May, was a special delight. She celebrated that fact in her journal in June: "Our home is full of joy sunshine and roses."

Unlike Louisa, "duty's obedient child," May had never quite mastered the trick of self-sacrifice. By spring, she returned to England, taking with her the "cheerful element she always brings into the house." As long as May had stayed on in Concord, Louisa enjoyed her "quiet, sunny room" in Boston, for she could trust her sister to "run the machine in her cheery, energetic style, and amuse Marmee and Nan with gay histories."

Louisa gave May $1,000 for her return to an artist's life in England, and her blessing, though it forced her home to Concord in harness. May created so many pieces of art, she joked, if her ship wrecked at sea, she would "build a raft of [her] pictures and paddle gaily to shore." Louisa, too, longed to paddle her own canoe. She could only stand on shore and watch others.

She comforted herself with improvements she could afford to make at Orchard House. She hired two girls to help with the housekeeping and installed a large new central furnace. "Mother is to be cosy if money can do it," she vowed, "and my long-cherished dream has come true, for she sits in a pleasant room with no work, no care, no poverty."

Abby, meanwhile, was watching her declining daughter closely. She wrote of Louisa in her journal, "What more could I have hoped for? One thing, good health. Here," she wrote astutely, "may prove the bitter drop in this cup overflowing with success."

CHAPTER EIGHTEEN

Marmee

In the summer of 1873, Louisa returned once more to *Work*, the literary novel she had been unable to publish at any price. Now the *Christian Union* offered $3,000 to serialize *Work*, and Roberts Brothers paid $2,000 in royalties in addition, which she donated to the working poor: "that large class of women who . . . are driven by necessity, temperament, or principle out into the world to find support, happiness, and homes for themselves." Louisa had recently learned that Laddie Wisniewski had lost his fortune and was living in France—so she sent money to him as well. At long last she could afford to be financially as well as personally generous.

The reviews of *Work* were nearly as harsh as those of *Moods* years before. *Harper's* magazine commented snidely that *Work* would never have made the author's reputation—but her reputation might possibly make the book. Her reputation as "the Children's Friend" was more secure than ever. In the 1870s, she published two more sparkling novels, *Eight Cousins* and *Rose in Bloom*, both immensely popular with her "young set."

In Europe, she'd had a break from the hounding of fans and autograph seekers. Her mother held her fan letters while she was away, and she even evaded the badgering of her editor, Thomas Niles by reminding him of the goose that laid the golden egg. Killing the goose would do no one any good—including Roberts Brothers.

In Europe, courteous admirers had given her room to breathe. Not in America, where fans surrounded her at home so that she barely dared to step outside. "Reporters sit on the wall and take notes; artists sketch me as I pick pears in the garden; and strange women interview [nephew] Johnny as he plays in the orchard," Louisa wrote, dismayed. Anna watched "strangers swarming around" Orchard House—alarming, surely, to the mother of two young boys. Louisa generally hid inside while Anna answered the door. One day, with Anna out elsewhere, Louisa in desperation pretended to be her own housekeeper, telling her callers in a strong fake country accent that the writer herself was "nowhere about."

Self-appointed friends materialized out of the barest acquaintance—or no acquaintance at all. Concordians who had never spoken to the Alcotts now pursued them. Strangers hunted Louisa down, demanding autographs and photos. In *Jo's Boys*, Alcott wrote about one man who came calling because he wanted to collect grasshoppers from her lawn! Young women felt as if they knew Louisa from her books and pressed her for help and advice, "upon every subject, from 'Who shall I marry?' to 'Ought I to wear a bustle?'" (The answer was no. All Alcott women were opposed to the constricting fashions of the times.) Dozens of callers dropped by unannounced. Over time, there would be hundreds.

Her old childhood friend Lydia Maria Child noted Louisa's "hatred of lionizing." Louisa insisted she would not be "even a little lion"—but the choice wasn't always hers. Her growing fame fell upon her like a smothering blanket. All told, her books had sold a hundred thousand copies—she could not become unfamous.

One breathless fan promised Louisa that if she ever came to visit Oshkosh, Wisconsin, "Your feet will not be allowed to touch the ground: you will be borne in the arms of the people! Will you come?" "Never!" exclaimed a horrified Louisa, adding in her journal, "This, this is fame!"

She did travel sometimes, of course—to Philadelphia, New York City, and Seneca Falls. She was admired and enveloped by adoring fans wherever she went. Even at the theater, she complained, she was "kissed to death by gushing damsels." The writer who for so long had been overlooked could barely see over the heads of her crowds.

At Vassar College, she spoke with four hundred girls and agreed to autograph "stacks of albums and schoolbooks, and kiss every one who asks." Even that wasn't enough for her young fans. They demanded a speech from the author. She declined. The students asked her to place herself in a prominent position and turn around in a circle so that everyone could see her from all angles. This she "consented to do," rotating slowly, she remarked drolly, like a figure atop a music box.

Bronson could not understand his daughter's aversion to acclaim. He relished being known as "Louisa May Alcott's father," or "the father of little women." He basked in all the attention. As the famous author's father, Bronson Alcott no longer spoke to scant audiences. Now when he lectured out west, he added Louisa to his pantheon of "New England Authors," alongside Emerson, Thoreau, Margaret Fuller, and Nathaniel Hawthorne. He signed autographs on Louisa's behalf. As Julian Hawthorne pointed out, "Some malign wit said that she was her father's best contribution to literature." Louisa had to warn him, half jokingly and half seriously, not to spread the details of her private life far and wide. "Pa, if you talk about Jo in public," she cautioned, she never *would* write *his* biography, as he still pressed her to do.

Louisa begged one journalist to remind her readers that "L.M.A. doesn't . . . send autographs, photographs &

autobiographical sketches to the hundreds of boys and girls who ask them." She also asked Thomas Niles to "nail up" her old papers. "I squirm to think of my very old scribbles being trotted out." She began destroying her private papers and urged those around her to do the same.

In the midst of all this notoriety, she seized one last chance to try her hand at anonymity again. For years she had secretly scribbled away at her "blood and thunder stories," ecstatic for a payment of ten dollars. She'd published these under a variety of pen names—some so well hidden that they would only be unearthed a century later by a brilliant researcher/detective named Madeleine B. Stern, one of Alcott's finest biographers.

Louisa found a way to have her privacy again. During the same productive years in which she published *Work*, *Aunt Jo's Scrap-Bag*, *Eight Cousins*, *Under the Lilacs*, and other children's classics, she added a new gothic thriller—*A Modern Mephistopheles*—to Thomas Niles's anonymously published No Name series.

Only Louisa's mother knew the author's true identity. Abby gave her seal of approval—the new novel, she exclaimed, "surpasses its predecessors in power and brilliancy," and she assured her daughter that she "will not be easily recognized by its readers." *A Modern Mephistopheles* became that season's mystery among the Boston literati. Everyone tried to guess the author's identity. Famous names were bandied about—but never Louisa May Alcott's.

This well-kept secret ensured that Louisa protected her pristine reputation as "the Children's Friend" while at the same time allowing her to work in an old favorite genre. She wrote *A Modern Mephistopheles* quickly, taking just a few weeks to finish. "Enjoyed doing it," she wrote, "being tired of providing moral pap for the young."

The book allowed Louisa to return to darker, moodier themes; to invent scenes of jealousy, revenge, lust, and self-destruction. There was no danger of her taking herself too seriously. She mocked herself as a renewed writer of "rubbish." After she read the first perplexed reviews of *A Modern Mephistopheles*, she wrote, "I enjoy the fun," adding mischievously, "especially when friends say, 'I know you didn't write it, for you can't hide your peculiar style.'"

She had of course been "hiding her peculiar style" for decades, veering back and forth between the lurid and the sanctimonious, wild melodrama and domestic comedy. Both styles were her own, and while she is most famous for her works for and about young people, her anonymously published "gorgeous fancies" also sustained and absorbed her. It is fair to say that neither half of her writing self could have survived without the other. She fed the world with her realistic fiction and nourished herself with the fantastic.

According to Anna, success had "not spoiled her one bit. She is the same old jolly generous simple Louie." She could do household chores one moment and write her stories the next. Before the word *multitasking* was invented,

Louisa was a master at it. All her self-portraits are comical sketches. If she saw the foolish side of those she had worshipped, she loved and admired them all the same.

She described her now-elderly friend and benefactor Ralph Waldo Emerson after a house fire "wandering about in his night gown, pants, old coat & no hose. His dear bald head lightly covered with his best hat, & an old pair of rubbers wobbling on his Platonic feet." She was not always so kind to strangers. Sometimes her hidden prejudices revealed themselves: "W. bowed his Jewish head, and rolled his fine eye at me. Several dreadful women purred about me, and I fled."

In the mid-1870s, Louisa traveled to Syracuse, New York, to attend a women's congress. Louisa remained a fervent voice for women's suffrage and women's rights. She attended the conference with her cousin Charlotte, taking a hidden seat among the others onstage. The instant the meeting ended, however, the stage was swamped with "beaming girls all armed with Albums and cards and begging to speak to Miss A." One girl asked Louisa to lift her veil "so we can see how you really look." Another demanded a kiss, and Louisa finally "had to run for my life with more girls all along the way, and Mas clawing at me as I went."

Not every admirer was impressed by Louisa in the flesh. Louisa joked to one young correspondent, "I sympathize with the disappointment of your friends on seeing my picture, for I remember I was so upset when I saw Fredrika Bremer, whose books I loved, that my sister, Nan & I went into the closet & cried though we were great girls of sixteen and eighteen."

She tried to keep a sense of humor about it all, but her distress at being continuously interrupted was very real. After all, she was the girl who fled to the woods when she needed solitude, who ran like a horse till she reached a place of peace and exhaustion. Now she threw herself into housekeeping with the same furious energy. As she wrote to one admirer, "I'm glad there is ironing & preserving to rest the busy brains with good wholesome work. I believe in it so heartily that I sweep my eight rooms twice a week, iron & scrub round for health sake, as I have found it better medicine than any doctor ever gave me." But scrub as she might, she could not erase her fans—she couldn't even keep them from barging in.

She wrote, "I don't believe any one knows how bored we are by company, over a hundred a month, most of them strangers. A whole school came without warning last week & Concord people bring all their company to see us. This may *seem* pleasant, but when kept up a whole season is a great affliction." More sadly, she added, "Mother says we have no home now." Their cozy house was fast becoming a public thoroughfare.

Louisa had always been ill at ease in a crowd; now she was afraid of behaving like a crank to visitors who came hoping to meet a friend. As a young woman, she herself had been snubbed too many times. It troubled her to "shut the door upon them and seem rude." Young fans came eager to see the fifteen-year-old boyish Jo and were disappointed to find the middle-aged author in her place. "You can't make a Venus out of a tired old lady," Louisa apologized.

She was less patient with "strangers who come out of mere curiosity." As a species, she wrote, she hated the "modern lion hunter and autograph fiend." Bronson, on the other hand, was more than happy to entertain strangers— he had been doing it for years in his public Conversations. May, when around, was a perfect hostess, and Anna in her gentle, quiet way made herself agreeable. Even Louisa was willing to twirl herself in circles if it would make others happy. But "I have resolved," she wrote, "to defend Marmee's health & home at the point of the bayonet, & be called a cross patch for my pains."

Louisa traveled away from Concord in the summer of 1873 just long enough to take her nephew John on a short seaside vacation. No sooner had they unpacked than they were urgently called home again—Abby had suffered something called "dropsy of the brain" (probably a stroke). "For several weeks she did not know us, or seem like mother," wrote a mournful Louisa. She nursed Abby back to health, Anna wrote, lavishing "every comfort & luxury. She pours out her money like water, and scarcely leaves her night or day."

Abby believed she was nearing the end of her life and had recently written in her journal, "I fear little, I hope much . . . I love long, love much and hope to be forgiven." It was new for Abby to acknowledge she might have done anything to need forgiveness. She had lost none of her passion for the world, nor her high idealism. While her mother was still recovering from the stroke, Louisa received a letter from the head of a suffragist organization, asking for the author's support.

"What shall I say?" Louisa asked her mother.

"Tell her I am seventy-three," Abby exclaimed. "I mean to go to the polls before I die, even if my three daughters have to carry me!"

Abby never cast a vote, but she never stopped trying either. In 1875, still alive and active, she composed a fiery petition for suffrage, objecting to women being "taxed without representation." She argued that the women of Concord—including Emerson's well-to-do wife and her own daughter Louisa—paid one-tenth of the total taxes collected in town. Yet they could not vote. "This is . . . extortion," she wrote. The Massachusetts legislature dismissed Abby's petition, Louisa fumed, "with as little regard as the stump of a well-worn cigar."

Five years later, Louisa would become the very first woman in Concord to cast her vote—for a school board election. She had to pay an extra tax for the honor. Proudly she noted, "Paid my first poll tax. As my head is my most valuable piece of property I thought $2.00 a cheap tax on it."

Louisa continued to juggle work and home, art and duty. Boston gave her the solitude and freedom she needed to write. Concord brought the affections and burdens of family life. Sacrificing either was out of the question. She put on her brightest face but now and again allowed herself to admit the difficulties in her journal: "Concord is so hard for me, with its dampness and worry."

Between her chronic ill health and her mother's, she wrote, she was "tied to my sofa for some weeks"—not as she'd been as an overactive toddler, but held by family loyalty and sickness. She could not make plans for the future. "The state of my mother's health forbids my making any very binding engagements this year, so I can only say I will if I can." *I will if I can* became her stock reply to any invitation.

To help stop the tug-of-war, Louisa rented an apartment large enough to hold her parents, Anna's family, and herself in Boston. They lived on Franklin Square opposite an elegant hotel, just a few steps from her parents' original honeymoon boardinghouse. Abby liked being back in her home city, especially when Bronson was staying away farther and longer every winter. Each spring, the family returned to Orchard House.

Within a few years, Abby had neither the strength

or desire to bounce back and forth between two places. Bronson, vigorous as ever, boasted, "I may possibly reach my hundredth birthday." He spent hours with his old friend Emerson and carried on a few last flirtations—for instance, with a vibrant young woman named Mary Baker Eddy, the founder of Christian Science.

With May off in Europe, Bronson—that "dear man"—away, Anna busy with her growing boys, and Louisa busily writing in Boston, Abby wrote in her journal, "I find myself inevitably alone much of the time."

Her thoughts turned inward. Abby gained weight and moved heavily; she lost much of her former strength. Louisa wrote with sorrow, "The poor old body, now such a burden to her. The slow decline has begun, and she knows it, having nursed her mother to the same end." Anna, too, observed, "Mother is somewhat of an invalid owing to her extreme size, and inability to exercise, but . . . writes her diary as in old times, sews, and reads a great deal."

Louisa and Anna each took turns taking care of their mother. One mild day Louisa brought Abby to visit King's Chapel, where a tablet to Grandfather May had been erected. Louisa wrote, "Mother sat alone in the old pew a little while and sung softly the old hymns." Later Abby told Louisa, "This isn't my Boston; all my friends are gone; I never want to see it any more."

"She never did," added Louisa.

Abby had struggled for survival most of her life; now,

at last, the ferocious woman had given way to a more peaceful one. In one of her last journal entries she wrote, "Why should we not be content; Life is much the thing we make it, by cheerful endurance of its evils and acceptance of joys."

Louisa often took her mother out for morning drives, going by wagon and stopping to pick flowers in the nearby woods. "It keeps her young," wrote Louisa, "and rests her weary nerves."

May was now a serious artist and a grown woman in her midthirties. She wanted to live and paint full-time in Europe. Abby spoke and thought constantly of her youngest daughter and often wrote about her in her journal. She urged May to return to Europe, and partly to please her mother, partly out of her usual openhandedness, Louisa offered to fund the journey. Bronson accompanied May as far as Boston and watched as May waved her white handkerchief goodbye, just as "Marmee" had always done for her little women. It gave Louisa a pang. The lively May, Louisa wrote, seemed "sober & sad, not as gay as before; seemed to feel it might be a longer voyage than we knew."

In America's centennial year of 1876, Louisa thought a good deal about the future of her country. She had spent much of the previous year in New York City, which felt to the born-and-bred New Englander like a foreign land— complete with its own customs, friends, institutions, and ideas. The sheer size of New York City with its dense and diverse population, introduced her to species of child suffering she had never seen before. She witnessed how the newsboys lived—in dire hardship, children as young as five or six selling newspapers for pennies. She toured the downtown New York City jail known as the Tombs, the city's crowded public schools, and a home for former female prisoners. All were grist for her reformer's mill and charity.

Louisa also took up the banner of woman's suffrage that her mother had laid down only in extreme illness. Women everywhere, she saw, were overworked, underpaid, and abused. Louisa found a glimmer of hope for the future in her young female readers. She admired their "nerve and courage," and as she wrote to one aspiring female author, "Many ways are open now, & woman can learn, be & do much if they have the will & opportunity."

She was pleased to hear herself called "a New Yorker" rather than "a prim, prejudiced Bostonian," but New York was not home. Of friends who asked if she intended to stay, she wrote, "I tell em I dont belong anywhere & shall stay as long as I like." Except she couldn't ever "stay as long" as she liked. Instead she left New York in mid-January "as mother was feeble & I tired of a gay life . . . so home to nurse mother who seemed to need more care."

In 1876, she gratefully accepted $3,000 for producing still more work for her publisher, declaring that her "mill must keep grinding, even chaff."

Back in Concord, ill health dogged her, as it would continue to do again and again. She dared not stop "the writing machine." She published the newly completed *Rose in Bloom*, a sequel to her novel *Eight Cousins*. Her writing was nearly as fluid and energetic as ever. One would never know from her sparkling prose how badly she suffered from chronic pain and weariness.

Louisa had made a poor investment in the railroads, and, with May across the ocean still to support, she wrote to her publisher, "I have to help her till she can sell her pictures & pay her own way." No matter the evidence, Louisa dared not trust her own good fortune. She always felt financially strapped. Nor was May the only burden Louisa carried. "My dear old people," she wrote, "need many small comforts & my boys a lift with their education." But her chief reason for staying close to home was her promise never to "travel far" from her mother's side. "I could not let anyone else care for the dear invalid while I could lift a hand."

That winter Louisa began to plan seriously for the future for Anna's boys, now aged fourteen and twelve. They had outgrown the little nursery room that Bronson had created for them at Orchard House. It was time to consider a more permanent and substantial home.

Thoreau's house came on the market unexpectedly, after the death of his last surviving sibling, Henry's beloved sister Sophia. The Thoreau home held special meaning for the Alcotts, of course. It sat just under a mile from Orchard House on Main Street. The Thoreau home was—and still is—a fine-looking house, a solidly built square colonial. Anna could never have afforded the house on her own, but Louisa pitched in generously, and the Thoreau house was purchased for the handsome sum of $4,500.

Louisa couldn't help an occasional twinge of discontent. May was joyfully pursuing her art and dreams in Europe. Home-loving Anna had her heart's desire now as well. "She has *her* wish, and is happy," wrote Louisa wistfully. "When shall I have mine? Ought to be contented. . . . But I'm selfish, and want to go away and rest in Europe. Never shall."

Louisa felt stronger that June of 1877, hoping against hope that she had finally conquered her last bout of illness. She helped Anna with the move to the Thoreau house, performed the housekeeping chores at Orchard House, and nursed her mother diligently. Louisa offered to pay for May's passage home, but her mother waved it away. May was not to be disturbed in her pursuit of art; Louisa could manage alone. Louisa made a poignant statement, unconscious of its deeper truth: "I had always been her nurse, and knew her little ways."

Bronson wrote that he too believed she was well enough to serve as "our housekeeper during the summer." By July, however, having pushed herself again to the limits of her strength, Louisa suffered another relapse. While Abby slept, as she now did most of the time, Louisa lay in her own room across the hall, too worn out to write or keep up with chores. Louisa may have believed that she was dying, too, across the hall, for she wrote that she lay "happily at rest, wondering what was to come next." Her mother's nearness comforted her.

By August Louisa had recovered well enough to resume her new children's novel, *Under the Lilacs*. She had nearly finished it by the start of September. It is one of Alcott's loveliest books, an escape from the worries and busyness within the household. Abby's heart was failing. Louisa's health was precarious, Anna in the midst of the move to Thoreau's former home. Bronson chose this peculiar moment to begin a speaking tour of New England. He was in Connecticut when Abby began to experience difficulty breathing. The doctor gravely informed Louisa that her mother's end was near. He predicted she had only a handful of days to live. But Abby, stronger than anyone predicted, lived on and celebrated her seventy-seventh birthday that October.

It was a true Alcott-style celebration. Anna and Louisa built a pyramid of birthday flowers at their mother's bedside. Close friends and relatives stopped by. Louisa read aloud a letter from May announcing that her art work had been chosen for display in the Paris Salon—a rare honor, and especially rare for a female artist. Louisa and Anna again offered to bring May home. Again, Abigail refused.

Louisa's symptoms came and went and surged again. Each exertion sapped her of strength. By mid-October, she was again bedridden. "In danger of my life for a week," she wrote. In desperation she hired a nurse, fretting that she might not be physically able to "stay by . . . and help" when her mother's time came.

Anna and the boys finally settled at the Thoreau house nearby. By early November, Louisa felt well enough at least to resume her round-the-clock vigil by Abby's side. Her mother presented her with the leather-bound family Bible. Louisa discovered a earmarked passage in the book of Isaiah. It read, "He will be very gracious unto thee at the voice of thy cry; when he shall hear it, he shall answer thee."

In mid-November Anna and Louisa moved their mother to the Thoreau house for better, more convenient care. Louisa arranged to install a central furnace to keep Marmee warm for the winter. The girls saw to her "ascension," carrying her upstairs to the promised "sunny room" looking south. A peaceful Abby told Louisa, "The power that brought me here will take the kindest care of me wherever I may be hereafter." She wrote in the last pages of her journal, "The twilight is closing gently about me, & I am going to my rest in the arms of my children." A lifelong reader, she closed the pages of a favorite book soon after, remarking, "I shall read no more."

A few days before her forty-fifth November birthday,

Louisa woke by her mother's bedside to find a cold rain falling outside the window and her mother's room dank and chilly. She hurried to make a fire. The winds of late autumn had already stripped the leaves from the trees. Abby lay in "a semi-conscious state, whispering to herself," Bronson noted. She stayed in a half-dreaming state all that day, murmuring about the past and smiling. At nightfall, she looked up at Louisa and said one word, "Marmee." She died a few hours later, in her daughter's arms.

Louisa performed all the last rites for her Marmee and would let no one relieve her of these duties. She closed her mother's eyes. Later she wrote, "She died in the arms of the child who owed her most, who loved her best."

Abigail May Alcott was buried beside her third daughter, Lizzie, in the Sleepy Hollow Cemetery. Abby had often visited Lizzie's grave, winding her way between the sunshine and shadow of the graveyard's many shade trees. She had written in her journal, "Here I wish to be laid." The Alcotts honored Abby's wishes. She had also written, "Although I often say it is of little consequence where we are finally laid in the flesh . . . yet, I must own a preference . . . to rest among our kindred. . . . The birds of the air, the dews from heaven, the Stars above us, even the snows of winter, are beautiful to contemplate as our companions in their seasons. The daisies will not forget to smile above me."

The day after the funeral, the Alcotts arranged a private

service at Anna's new house. They sat grieving with the Emersons, who had lost so many of their own "nearest and dearest." Sitting in his friend Thoreau's old house must have increased Emerson's sorrow.

Elizabeth Peabody sent Louisa a kind and unexpectedly revelatory letter. "I lived with your mother," she wrote, "in perhaps the most intense period of her suffering experience of life, and feel as if I knew the heights & depths of her great heart as perhaps only you & Anna can do." She paid tribute to the woman with whom she had quarreled so bitterly that Abby renamed her daughter to shatter the connection. "I have never known a greater, more tender, more self-sacrificing human being," Elizabeth wrote. She concluded by paying tribute to the great bond between Louisa and her mother. "You *understood* her—the first person perhaps who ever did sufficiently to do justice to her—Let me congratulate you. —'Many daughters have done virtuously—but thou excellest them all.'"

Louisa and Bronson stayed with Anna and the boys at the Thoreau house that winter. Louisa was as lonely as her mother had often been, a woman without a mother, without a clear place in the world. "A great warmth seems gone out of life," a broken-hearted Louisa wrote that December. "There is no motive to go on now. . . . I think I shall soon follow her, and am quite ready to go now she no longer needs me."

Louisa had never forgiven Orchard House for being

the locus of her beloved sister Lizzie's sickness and death. Now she associated it with her mother's dying as well. Louisa "dismantled" the house, stripping it bare of all but a few sticks of furniture and the parlor carpeting, and she found it cold, almost unrecognizable in its stripped-down state—"for summer, pictures, books & 'Marmee' made it lovely."

There was another reason Orchard House could never regain its past charm. That spring of 1878, the thirty-seven-year-old May got married abroad, suddenly and unexpectedly, after only a brief engagement. Her husband, Ernest Nieriker, was a Swiss businessman, younger than May. May lied about her age, claiming to be twenty-eight, but Ernest was only twenty-two. They held the wedding in London and settled in Paris—creating a new and permanent rift from the Alcott family in Concord.

By spring, Louisa was ready to rent the vacant Orchard House to any likely tenant. They had abandoned it for winter, and Louisa hoped to avoid any major repairs. Bronson still clung to the old homestead or Louisa would have sold it at once. She wrote to a neighbor who inquired about the property, "If your friends want quiet, sunshine & strawberries they can be had at Apple Slump, but there is little else to offer."

CHAPTER NINETEEN

Illness and Charity

"When I had the youth I had no money; now I have the money I have no time; and when I get the time, if I ever do, I shall have no health to enjoy life," Louisa mourned three years earlier. By 1878, her words were truer than ever.

She compared her narrow, lonely life with her sister May's happy existence—painting and sketching by day, attending concerts at night, accompanied by a loving young husband. Louisa allowed herself a rare moment of self-pity. "How different our lives are just now!—I so lonely, sad, and sick; she so happy, well, and blest."

The January after Marmee's death, Louisa confessed she had spent "An idle month at Nan's, for I can only suffer." By spring she began to venture out and even felt well enough to consider a visit abroad to see May and meet her new brother-in-law. The new couple urged Louisa to come as soon as possible. They had settled into a sunny Paris apartment with a balcony and garden. "I plan and hope to go to them if I am ever well enough," Louisa wrote in her journal, but added pitifully, "I long to go, but cannot risk the voyage yet. I doubt if I ever find time to lead my own life, or health to try it."

She arranged for a trip in September, looking forward hopefully to it all spring and summer, but in the end she realized she couldn't manage the long sea journey, "fearing to undo all the good this weary year of ease" had done and worst of all, to arrive at the newlyweds' apartment only to "be a burden." A few days after her decision to stay home, Anna broke her leg, and Louisa turned to nursing again. She wrote, "It is well I stayed, as there was no one to take her place but me."

The weather that year was as stormy and changeable as Louisa's mood. She observed that it was "a queer wild season with eclipses, tornadoes, great heat, rain & tempest." Between 1869 and 1880 she would produce six more volumes around the ever-popular *Little Women* characters, as well as other novels, essays, and dozens of stories. She worked at top speed, like someone who feared she was running out of time. Soon she found herself running out of ideas.

She turned to friends and acquaintances for fresh plot ideas—"any good experiences, funny adventures or interesting incidents in girl-life"—to keep up with the endless demand of her hungry readers. To one friend she suggested that the writing now was "easy." By *easy*, she meant easy to publish, for the work came at great cost to her health and liberty. She doubted she would ever possess either again. "My vacation time has not come yet & I begin to think it wont come till I am too old to enjoy it," she admitted.

She had donated all the proceeds of *Little Men* to her nephews, helped fund a new home for Anna, paid for May's trips abroad, and provided money to "her Laddie" after he was a grown man with a wife and two children. Louisa had always been generous to her loved ones, but now her thoughts and concerns ranged further afield. Her donation of proceeds from her novel *Work* to the working poor had marked a strong beginning of her charity toward the wider world.

Her first lesson had come at age three, sacrificing her own "plummy cake" to a birthday guest. According to Louisa's rueful account, she gave up the birthday treat reluctantly. In her forties she had learned to give gladly, without hesitation. What she'd once done out of duty became a pleasure, and giving *up* turned to giving *gladly*.

Louisa spent a Christmas in New York bringing comfort to the needy. Accompanied by friends, she visited children on Randall's Island, near Manhattan. On a damp

December morning they set out to a hospital for poor children, next to what was then called an "idiot house," passing around dolls, toys, and candy to all the inmates, children and young adults alike. Louisa wrote in a letter to her family, "I've had a pretty good variety of Christmases in my day, but never one like this before."

She attended a morning chapel service for orphans, the littlest ones dressed in neatly starched holiday pinafores. Next came the children's ward, "and there the heart-ache began," wrote Louisa. The ward was overflowing with the diseased, the blind and half-blind, the crippled and the dying. One burn victim eagerly took a "gay red dolly" and a pink candy from Louisa's outstretched hand.

Last was their visit to "the idiot house"—a mix of every mental disability thrown together—"and there I had a chance to see faces and figures that will haunt me a long time," Louisa wrote home. These were not the semicomical lunatics of "Transcendental Wild Oats," but a hundred or more disabled boys and girls. Many were no longer children. Boys of nineteen reached out for dolls, and "young women of eighteen cuddled their babies and were happy," wrote Louisa. "The boys chose from the toy-table, and it was pathetic to see great fellows pick out a squeaking dog without even the wit to pinch it when it was theirs." A few of the inmates had beards; one thirty-five-year-old sat hunched over a little toy Noah's ark.

Many of the nurses they saw that day were paupers

themselves, while others were well-to-do volunteers working with needy and suffering children. "Such a life!" exclaimed Louisa. "Oh, me! Who *can* lead it, and not go mad?" Despite this, she reported "cheers of rapture," choral singing, and "cries of delight." Everywhere they were greeted with joy. She arrived back at her hotel exhausted that night, only to realize belatedly that she had missed both lunch and Christmas dinner. "Thus my Christmas day was without dinner or presents, for the first time since I can remember," she wrote home. "Yet it has been a very memorable day," she concluded, "and I feel as if I'd had a splendid feast seeing the poor babies wallow in turkey soup, and that every gift I put into their hands had come back to me in . . . their unchild-like faces trying to smile."

She came to the rescue for three adult female friends as well. These were the Joy sisters; one of them became the married "Mrs. Dr. Lawrence," who was to be Louisa's closest companion for the last years of her life. The women needed to borrow $3,000 for a down payment on a house that would become a convalescent home for Dr. Lawrence's patients. Louisa may or may not have had an inkling that she would one day become a resident. She insisted on giving the loan against all financial counsel, and wrote to her lawyer uncle, "The house is just the place many of us used up people need to go to for repairs."

A semi-invalid herself, she remembered her trip abroad with Anna Weld and was sorry now that she hadn't shown the young woman more sympathy. She tried to make up for the past by kindness to those who struggled. She sat for hours by the bedside of a dying friend. "Go often to see her & feel great sympathy with her," she wrote in her journal. She even hired a professional nurse to care for her friend during her last days.

In all charitable acts she claimed that she simply took her mother's life as her model. On the first anniversary of Abby's death, Louisa carried flowers to the graveside at Sleepy Hollow. "Her grave is green," wrote Louisa. "Blackberry vines with red leaves trail over it. A little white stone with her initials is at the head, & among the tall grass over her breast a little bird had made a nest."

Louisa gave help of other kinds. She offered solace, encouragement, and practical advice to young writers reaching out for help. She subscribed to a magazine begun by a new golden band of young sisters and wrote them encouraging letters. To another young writer she made suggestions about the kinds of stories that editors were looking for and the best places to send them, sharing whatever information she had, including editors' names and addresses. She wrote self-deprecatingly about the low fees she had received early on and reported about the current going rates. She advised her young correspondent to be practical. "Beginners must take what they can get," she declared.

She never forgot how it felt to be a struggling young

writer. She advised patience and determination: "There is no *easy* road to successful authorship, it has to be earned by long & patient labor, many disappointments, uncertainties & trials. Success is often a lucky accident, coming to those who may not deserve it, while others who do have to wait & hope till they have *earned* it. That is the best sort & the most enduring."

To an aspiring nineteen-year-old, Louisa offered very practical advice: "Mind grammar, spelling, and punctuation, use short words, and express as briefly as you can your meaning." She urged avoiding adjectives and foreign words to gussy things up—"The strongest, simplest words are best." But she kept the important goals in sight. "Write, and print if you can; if not, still write, and improve as you go on. . . . Work for twenty years, and then you may some day find that you have a style and place of your own." She closed with a favorite Michelangelo quote she'd also used in *Little Women*: "Genius is infinite patience."

Through poverty, struggle, failure, and ill health, Louisa never lost awareness of the large world around her. She saw suffering and injustice and fought fervently against it. Her methods were more practical than abstract—she'd heard plenty of theorizing in her youth. "The town swarms with budding philosophers, & they roost on our step like hens waiting for corn," she once complained. "Speculation seems a waste of time when there is so much real work crying to be done. Why discuss the Unknowable till our poor are fed?" She always wanted the solutions *now*. "So hard to move people out of the old ruts. I haven't patience enough."

Louisa was keen to win rights for women—meaningful work, self-expression, freedom, and the vote. She had proudly been the first woman in Concord to register for elections—long before they won the Constitutional right to vote. She'd urged her Concord friends and neighbors to join her in the crusade. It was, she insisted, the "most vital question of the age." She met with resistance, as she complained to her father's long-ago love interest, Ednah Dow Cheney, now a sister suffragist. "Our meeting last eve. was a small one," Louisa fumed, "& nobody had registered because of 'jelly-making, sewing, sickness or company.'" Louisa took charge, as she'd done in childhood: "I gave them a good scolding & offered to drive the timid sheep in a van to the fatal spot where they seem to expect some awful doom."

Like her mother before her, Louisa was impatient with inaction. Her neighbors seemed to like socializing more than they cared for the cause. "They will go & say afterward 'How well *our* meeting went off.' So slow!" Even Ellen Emerson, her once favorite pupil, dragged her feet and finally "decided not to register." Louisa signed her "grumbling" letter to Cheney, "Yours disgustedly, L.M.A."

By October 1879, she had failed to stir up a good crowd of women voters for even a local "vote for school committee." Only seven out of one hundred eligible, tax-paying women registered for the vote, she reported grimly. Still Louisa refused to surrender. She urged her editor, Thomas Niles, to help the cause, alternating praise and lecturing: "For we are going to win in time, and the friend of literary ladies ought to be also the friend of women generally."

She used her voice to pen an open letter to the *Woman's Journal* in October 1879. She praised "the few brave and sensible women who have done their duty," but she could not resist a dig at her town's complacency. "A very poor record for a town which ought to lead if it really possesses all the intelligence claimed for it." She reported on how simple and easy it had been for her to vote—one need only bring last year's property tax bill, she insisted, then report to the registrar and answer a few questions.

According to an eyewitness, however, the encounter between Louisa and the town selectman had been a bit more troublesome than that. When she was asked for the previous year's tax receipt, Louisa realized she hadn't brought it. "Won't this year's tax receipt do just as well?" she asked. "Oh, yes, but you have not paid it," the man responded. "A little comical look came on her face," reported her neighbor. Louisa said, laughingly, "I never did hanker to pay my taxes, but now I am in a hurry to pay them."

By March, the great day for the school election arrived. Only twenty women showed up to vote. The *Concord Freeman* reported that the women looked like "a person who is about to have a tooth extracted," but Louisa gave her own comical version in her letter to the *Woman's Journal.*

The female voters were informed that in order to vote they "could take their chance with the men or come later." Bronson, who had shown up on purpose to smooth the way, asked if the women might vote first as an act of courtesy. Embarrassed, the male moderator agreed. All the men sat in silence while the women stepped forward and dropped in their ballots. "No bolt fell on our audacious heads, no earthquake shook the town," reported Louisa. But a moment later laughter and applause broke out when, in protest, the polls were immediately closed "without a man's voting, a perfectly fair proceeding, we thought, since we were allowed no voice on any other question."

But at least the women had made a beginning. "*We* elected a good school committee," Louisa announced. Even the men agreed that the women had voted just as they would have done. "The ice is broken," Louisa declared, "and I predict that next year our ranks will be fuller, for it is the first step that counts." She was both right and wrong. The Nineteenth Amendment constitutionally guaranteeing women's right to vote wasn't ratified for more than forty years. It became the law of the land in a whole new century.

But Louisa had also been right: that first step in Concord mattered.

Louisa's social and political activities revolved mostly around Concord, as did she. The life of the town took up a central role in her existence. Boston had provided an escape from small-town living and the demands of family and home. Closeted away in a small room inside a large city, she found rest and space to work. Now Boston and Concord switched places. More often than not, she fled from Boston to the calmer world of Concord.

She was too sick and sometimes too sad to enjoy the hectic city life. She wrote in her journal, "Go to B[oston] for a week but dont enjoy seeing people." She quoted *The Pilgrim's Progress*, the book she had loved as a child and referred to all through *Little Women*. "Souls are such slaves to bodies it is hard to keep out of the slough of despond when nerves jangle & flesh aches." In her journal of 1879 she confided, "Home to Concord rather used up. Find a very quiet life is best, for in B[oston], people beset me to do things & I try & get so tired I cannot work."

She found solace in the calm company of her sister Anna, "the best woman I know, always reasonable, just, kind & forgiving." The lives of her family and neighbors provided her with a fund of stories. She had found her own "style and place," and stayed with what worked best. Her nephews, Fred and Jack (John), were growing into teenagers, providing more grist for her "mill." She wrote to one of her editors, Mary Mapes Dodge, "We have many little romances going on among the Concord boys & girls & all sorts of queer things which will work into 'Jack & Jill' [her novel] nicely."

Though she yearned to visit her youngest sister in Paris, she reassured herself, "May is no longer lonely & Anna would be if I left her." In Concord, they waited and hoped for news of a pregnancy, for May had reported that she and her husband Ernest were ready to start a family. When at last the joyful news arrived, Louisa and Anna got busy preparing "dainty things" and necessary items for the coming birth. Louisa confided in her journal, "Even lonely old spinsters take an interest in babies."

CHAPTER TWENTY

The Coming of Lulu

Louisa was determined to travel to her youngest sister in time for the birth. She had written in her journal earlier, in February 1879, "Her hopes of a little son or daughter in the autumn give us new plans to talk over. I *must* be well enough to go to her then." But when autumn arrived, family members and doctors insisted that Louisa was too weak and ill to undertake the journey. Louisa reluctantly agreed, crushed by the disappointing news. She wrote, "I mourn much because all say I must not go to May; not safe; & I cannot add to . . . cares at this time by another invalid." She added, "Give up my hope & long-cherished plan with grief. May sadly disappointed." And, she put in dolefully, "I know I shall wish I had gone." She was filled with foreboding about May's coming childbirth. Try as she might, she could not calm or silence her worry. "Anxious about May," she wrote in her journal.

But soon a jubilant Louisa and her family learned that her newborn niece had safely "arrived in Paris at 9 p.m., after a short journey. All doing well. Much rejoicing." There was another delightful bit of news to celebrate—the baby was named *Louisa May*, in honor of her aunt. "Ah, if only I had been there!" Louisa cried. "Too much happiness for me."

Her happiness was soon cut short. "May not doing well," she recorded tersely. Her forebodings seemed to be coming true. "The weight on my heart is not all imagination," she noted apprehensively. A friend's letter from abroad brought the news that May had not yet fully recovered from childbirth. The letter sent Louisa into a tailspin. She feared the worst.

On May's honeymoon the year before, she had written home to declare that she and her husband possessed a little "Eden" of their own. Newlywed Abby had once said exactly the same of her marriage to Bronson. Now Louisa fretted over that as well: "She was too happy to have it last, & I fear the end is coming. Hope it is my nerves; but this peculiar feeling has never misled me before." It was an agonizing Christmas, and Louisa could not shake off her dread.

They learned the desperate truth just before the new year. Louisa wrote on December 29, "May died at 8 a.m., after three weeks of fever & stupor." She added, "I *felt* the truth before the news came." It was Emerson's job to deliver the terrible news. May's husband, Ernest, had sent word to the Alcotts' great friend, hoping his presence might soften the blow.

Louisa was alone in Orchard House when Emerson came by. She found him standing in the drawing room "looking at May's portrait, pale & tearful, with the paper in his hand." The old man turned to her. "My child," he began. He wished he could prepare her, he said wretchedly—then his voice broke and he could not go on.

Louisa took the telegram from him with frozen calm. "I was not surprised, & read the hard words as if I knew it all before. 'I *am* prepared,' I said, & thanked him."

It fell upon Louisa to break the tragic news to Bronson and to her sister Anna. "A very bitter sorrow for all," she reported bleakly. She blamed herself for not having braved the visit to May and Ernest that fall. Now her words—*I know I shall wish I had gone*—came back to haunt her with sickening force. It was her job—it had *always* been her job—to nurse each member of the family back to health. As a thirteen-year-old girl, she had vowed to protect them and keep them safe. She had failed to uphold her promise. "I shall never forgive myself for not going even if it put me back," she mourned. "If I had lived to see her & help her die," then she added pitifully, "or save her, I should have been content."

It was a given that the father, Ernest Nieriker, would raise Lulu abroad. She was only one month old when May died. "The dear baby may comfort E[rnest]," Louisa wrote, "but what can comfort us?" Louisa entered the darkest period of her life. In her journal she confessed, "Of all the trials in my life I never felt any so keenly as this." She wrote that she wished she had died in May's stead.

But there was one final strange and extraordinary twist in Louisa's life—perhaps the most stunning turn of all. The family learned to their amazement that a dying May had bequeathed to Louisa her two most precious possessions: her artwork—and her newborn child. The spinster was suddenly to become a mother, in her middle age.

Louisa must have been astonished when she heard the news from Ernest Nieriker. She was, after all, ill, exhausted, overworked, and nearly fifty years old. But she never expressed anything but instant acceptance and gratitude. "All she had to leave. Rich payment for the little I could do for her." At last she forgave herself for having survived. "I see now why I lived. To care for May's child & not leave Annie all alone." It gave her a sense of purpose and a renewed commitment to life.

The dying May kept asking when Louy would come. She already knew she wanted Louisa to be her newborn daughter's guardian and had clearly made her wishes known before she'd fallen dangerously ill. Louisa wrote, "May felt a foreboding, & left all ready in case she died. . . . Her diary written up, all in order." Some might have expected Ernest Nieriker to fight for custody of his daughter, but, as Louisa noted gratefully, "E. obeys all her wishes sacredly." He was also an aspiring young businessman who had no choice but to go out into the world and make a living. He was unprepared to raise a baby alone.

All this came clear to the Alcotts in the dead of winter. Lulu would not arrive in America till the next fall. Ernest's sister Sophie offered to accompany the baby to America, but one delay after another kept pushing back the date. In the meantime, Louisa tried to distract herself with her new novel, *Jack and Jill*—unsurprisingly, one of her most scattered works. She was too preoccupied to do her best. To steady herself, she threw herself into working for the rights of women and children, the condition of local prisons, and a host of other causes. She signed one letter, "Yours for reforms of all kinds." From racial integration to fair wages to protections for the poor, she opened her wallet and her heart and picked up her pen to help.

She also prepared for the coming of Lulu in her usual down-to-earth way, readying a room for the baby and buying the needed clothing, toys, furniture, and supplies. "A funny, fat, little thing in her carriage," Louisa commented, looking at a photograph of her niece. This photo was the only scrap of her niece that she had to go on. For now, she was still kept at a distance from the little stranger, geographically and emotionally. She would not quite bring herself to admit "that it is May's child, & that she is far away in a French cemetery, never to come home again." To accept Lulu's coming was to accept May's going.

But Louisa could tidy the house, buy warm baby clothing, put her own papers in order, and "make a cosy nursery for the darling." She could chant "prayers over the little white crib that waits for her if she ever comes"—but she would not make herself believe the new reality till Lulu was there safe in her arms.

On September 19, 1880, the tiny newcomer sailed into Boston Harbor. She was carried off the boat by the ship's captain, a second "snow maiden," with her mother's yellow hair, snub nose, and "lively blue eyes." Louisa, rendered speechless for once, held out her arms and could barely stammer out the baby's name. Lulu stared at her a moment, sizing her up, then tottered toward the strange woman's embrace. "Marmar?" she asked wistfully. For Louisa, it was a lightning-bolt moment. She saw her sister mirrored in this "happy thing, laughing & waving her hands, confiding & bold, with a keen look in the eyes so like May, who hated shams & saw through them at once."

Lulu had a well-defined personality early on. Strangers peered into Lulu's baby carriage, Louisa wrote drily, "but she does not allow herself to be kissed." The toddler also took after her namesake, Louisa, at the same age—she was stubborn, active, stormy, and hard to manage. But Louisa was too in love with Lulu to care. At night, Louisa would tiptoe into Lulu's nursery to reassure herself that this new life was real, "to see if she is really *here*, & the sight of the little yellow head is like sunshine."

Nearing fifty, Louisa's health was as fragile as that of a much older woman. Friends remarked that she looked thin and drawn, her shoulders stooped. Her headaches and weakness returned. Though she played the part of the breezy "Aunt Weedy," she was still mourning her sister. Her buoyant spirit did not bounce back quickly from that blow. A year after May's death, Louisa confessed, "My grief meets me when I come home, & the house is full of ghosts."

To keep depression at bay, Louisa threw herself into caring for her new charge. She admired everything about the baby: Lulu's "broad shoulders, fine chest & lovely arms"; the touch of her small hands that took "away the bitterness of grief." Louisa confided to her friend Maria Porter, "As I don't live for myself, I hold on for others, and shall find time to die some day, I hope."

Motherhood, it turned out, was a full-time job. Louisa was too busy to write on assignment, too busy to travel. Her world had been turned upside down and shaken like a snow globe. "Too busy to keep much of a journal. My life is absorbed in my baby." She joyfully recorded the day when Lulu took her first step. Like her father, Louisa kept detailed child-rearing notes, but unlike Bronson's cool observations, hers were love notes. The house was filled with "boys and baby," she wrote happily to a friend. She put off Mary Mapes Dodge's request for a new story serial, explaining she would be "too busy singing lullabies to one child to write tales for others or go anywhere even to see my kind friends."

Lulu's one-year birthday was an extravaganza, as Louisa could not help bragging to her father. Bronson must have understood the contrast between Louisa's birthday celebrations and Lulu's. Lulu was also born in November, "that dismal month," but her first birthday was anything but dismal.

Louisa gleefully recounted the festivities: "Her first birthday was very pretty, for after dinner, when she was fresh from her nap & airing, we took her to the parlor in her new white boots, blue sash & green crown, & there was a table full of gifts." To the man who had steadfastly chosen ideas over possessions, deprivation over comfort, she detailed: "picture books, flowers, a doll, silver mug, rattle with bells, & some gay cards from her friends." She could not have provided a clearer contrast to her own childhood birthdays.

Louisa indulged Lulu in all the ways she had been deprived as a child. They had hired help, beautiful, spacious places to live, vacations, and an endless supply of games and treats. Lulu recalled being doted on by both Louisa and her aunt Anna, wearing "little hats . . . and a pom-pom all around." She owned twenty-five dresses, and once when she admired a canary, Louisa bought it for her on the spot.

Though Louisa wanted her niece to blossom "in an atmosphere of adoration," she was often at sea about how to raise her little charge. Nothing had prepared her for motherhood. Like many new mothers, Louisa's state was one of exhilaration alternating with exhaustion. Lulu was not an easy baby. She combined the stubbornness of her aunt "Weedy," as she called her, with May's smooth knack for getting her own way.

Louisa had been laboring independently all her life, reliant on herself. Though she took on other people's burdens, she had remained separate and apart in the essentials. Sometimes even now she behaved like a single person. She spoke of setting up her "own establishment in Boston," citing a number of other "artistic and literary spinsters" who maintained their own space. She struggled over her writing schedule, filled with "doubts as to the leisure & quiet needed for such tasks being possible with a year-old baby." She shortened stories out of necessity and tersely turned down an offer to write her father's biography. "His philosophy I have never understood, & biography is not in my line."

Lulu grew like a weed, turning into "a fine, tall girl full of energy intelligence & health," bragged Louisa. Lulu scorned crawling, waiting till she was sure she had the knack of standing upright—then began at once to run. The growing toddler displayed a potent mix of "a strong will & quick temper" with "tender, generous & noble instincts."

She gave her caregivers a run for their money. Lulu eavesdropped on the grown-ups, threw temper tantrums, came down with croup, and tumbled headfirst down the stairs, frightening Louisa "but not hurting herself a bit." Louisa tried to fool herself into believing Lulu needed her "less & less each month, being an independent, sturdy young woman"—at age *two*.

Now and then a worn-out Louisa would briefly escape to the peaceful Bellevue Hotel in Boston—but never without a pang of guilt. "Missed my dear baby, but need quiet," she confessed. She confided to a friend, "Freedom was always my longing, but I have never had it, so I am still trying to feel that this is the discipline I need & when I am ready the liberty will come."

For a year she had written little besides suffrage tracts—and a few bedtime stories for Lulu, to soothe her while she was teething. Louisa's return to Boston meant she was ready to settle down to writing again. She had not given up on herself or her art, if only, she prayed, "our faith hope and charity are only strong, bright, and broad enough." She was beginning work on her last great novel, *Jo's Boys*, believing that her life might yet return to normal, when Bronson suffered a paralyzing stroke.

Six months earlier, the mighty Ralph Waldo Emerson had passed away, "the nearest & dearest friend father has ever had." Louisa felt the loss almost as keenly as her father.

"I can never tell all he has been to me," she mourned. Emerson had grown frail, his famous mind faltering. At the funeral of the poet Henry Wadsworth Longfellow, Emerson stood confused by the casket, murmuring, "Whose house is this? And who is the sleeper?"

Emerson's last words to Bronson were, "*You* are very well. Keep so, keep so." The tranquil Bronson had kept well longer than anyone could have predicted, visiting friends, giving fifty lectures in one year, composing dozens of sonnets. The most famous of these was his grateful poem to Louisa, with its prophetic last lines: "Sounding in this and the farther hemisphere,— / I press thee to my heart as Duty's faithful child."

Louisa blamed herself for her father's stroke. In her brief absence, the man who had been the keystone of her childhood suddenly collapsed. He went at one blow from a "tall, rosy old man" to a bedridden paralytic "like a felled tree."

She raced home to where Bronson lay, a "pathetic wreck," unable to speak or move. The doctor's predictions were dire, and Louisa expected the end to come quickly. "I think if spring finds him here, it will only be a shadow of his former self. I hope that he will be gone to the eternal summer." While she prepared herself for the worst, Bronson surprised family and medical experts by recovering strength within a month.

His first spoken word after the stroke was *up*. That word, Louisa noted, summarized her father's essence, "& seems very characteristic of this beautiful, aspiring soul." He regained his power of speech, and his long-forgotten Connecticut accent from childhood unexpectedly returned. Soon he was able to sit up and his appetite returned. But his traveling and even his writing days were over.

Bronson lived his last years ensconced in a modest, comfortable house on Louisburg Square in Boston, the city he loved best. After his stroke he continued to improve slowly and steadily, but with limitations. He could eat, but only from a spoon. He was often confused, with brief moments of clarity. In December when he saw Louisa hanging a green wreath, he touched it, saying, "Christmas, I remember."

Louisa was caught between family members again—sandwiched between the demands of a helpless little child and a helpless old man. She "vibrated back and forth" between the two, as she'd done at the Union Hospital, lacking capable nurses for her father and childcare for Lulu. A friend remarked that Louisa seemed fated "to fill vacant niches, being a wife to her father, a husband to her widowed sister, and a mother to her little niece."

Lulu and Bronson were jealous of each other, each one clamoring for Louisa's undivided attention." She joked to her cousin Lizzie Wells that, between her "two babies looking for me at once, I feel like a nursin ma with twins."

Bronson suffered lingering effects from his stroke—his right side remained weak, his arm was swollen, his speech slurred, and he became uncharacteristically irritable, which made it harder to find—and keep—good nurses. "Much trouble with nurses," grumbled Louisa. "Incapable, lazy or nervous with too much tea. . . . Could do better myself." That November birthday, when Louisa turned fifty, Bronson insisted he was twenty-three instead of eighty-three. He could hold a pen and out of long habit would reach for his pencils and paper only to realize that he could no longer use them. He said garbled things that made no sense, arguing heatedly with one nurse because she would not bring him the Trinity.

Young Lulu was growing and changing day by day, with a fierce will of her own. As a woman in her nineties, Lulu ruefully recalled, "I don't think I was afraid of the devil. I was a little devil myself." On one memorable New Year's Day, she threw such a long, howling tantrum that her exasperated aunt Weedy finally spanked her. "Do it, do it!" the little girl urged. But Louisa wrote, "Her bewilderment was pathetic, & the effect, as I expected, a failure." She was appalled at herself. "Love is better," she acknowledged, "but also endless patience." Lulu tested her aunt Weedy's patience each day. And as she grew, she became harder to control. Despite her many failures, Louisa insisted, "I can always manage her." Lulu, on the other hand, grew up believing "I could do anything I liked."

If finding help for Bronson was hard, meeting Louisa's standards for childcare turned out to be nearly impossible. Louisa tried six different workers but noted, "I . . . found none fit to be a helper to me in the training of my young immortal." One nursemaid was too lofty; another drank— and Louisa was part of the New England temperance movement. The best tempered candidate proved too sickly. Another one quit. A Miss C. was hired as governess, but after six months she was let go. Louisa wrote in her journal, "No love in her. Cold & tired & careless."

Louisa could find no help with even the simplest tasks: to walk, dress, or just play for a few hours with her young charge. "The ladies are incapable or proud, the girls vulgar or rough, so my poor baby has a bad time with her little tempers & active mind & body. Could do it myself if I had the nerves and strength but am needed else where & must leave the child to some one."

Between attempted hires, Louisa tried to manage by herself. Some days all the care for both her niece and father fell on her at once—as when one of Bronson's nurses showed up drunk. It was difficult to find replacements, since her father was growing "hard to take care of being unreasonable, fretful & weak."

That summer, Louisa took Lulu on a holiday to seaside Nonquitt, where she could run and play freely. They brought along a new nanny, "a nice little person for Lulu." Anna's boys, Fred and Jack, now "fine young men," joined them in their games and outings, and Louisa cast an approving eye over her growing family.

As a parent she hovered constantly between confidence and despair. Her journal sounds like it was written by two different people, each one contradicting the other. "A gay time for our baby" alternated with "a hard summer"; "Father improved" and "Father so much care." She thought of getting her own place in Boston with Lulu but could not bear to leave Bronson home alone. Though she tried to stay optimistic, she once cried out, "Long to go away . . . & do as I like. Shall never lead my own life."

In the early days after Bronson's stroke, he lay in bed, speechless and unmoving hour after hour. Louisa wrote to his old love interest, Ednah Dow Cheney, "We do not hope to see him ever his old self, nor to keep him long." But Bronson had at last forgotten even the lovely Ednah Dow Littlehale. He did not recognize her name when she wrote to him.

Louisa and Bronson laid aside their old arguments, their old differences. She found comfort in her father's calm acceptance. "It seems to be a beautiful & happy ending to a wise & blameless life," she wrote, and "very helpful to us who look after the ascending saint to catch a glimpse of Heaven as he enters in."

CHAPTER TWENTY-ONE

Glimpse of Heaven

Between caring for father and niece, Louisa's own health was unraveling. Overwork and strain led repeatedly to a state of collapse. She confessed in a letter, "I have no bright word to say. I 'trudge in harness' and find my burdens heavy & various." Lulu would later recall her other aunt, Anna, as "very serene," like her grandfather, Bronson Alcott. Louisa was "the one who was nervous."

To escape the strain of daily life, Louisa bought a cottage in secluded Nonquitt, on the southeastern shore of Massachusetts. It was a favorite seaside spot, where her nephew Jack would visit, and they'd put on dramatic performances as in the old days. The eager Lulu adored her cousin Jack, and Louisa enjoyed a carefree kitchenless house—no cooking, and less fuss or cleaning.

A restful vacation was not a complete cure, however, and by 1885 Louisa began to hunt in earnest for relief from her ailments—among them, throbbing headaches, loose teeth, dizziness, sore muscles, unsteadiness, and exhaustion. Some of her doctors were traditionally trained physicians. Others were far outside the mainstream. Louisa was skeptical but willing to give almost anything a try. She would get a few days' relief from some unorthodox treatment, only to have it fail within days.

In February 1886, she noted in her journal, "Try massage & feel better, thank God! It is tiresome to be always aching. Why can't people use their brains without breaking down?" A few days later, however, her vertigo returned. She tried the mind cure—similar to today's meditation—and reported to a friend, "I felt very still then very light. . . . Once or twice I seemed to have no body. . . . I felt as if I trod on air & was very happy & young for some hours." A few hours of relief were all she got—her arm and hand hurt so that she could not hold a pen long enough to write. After thirty treatments of the mind cure, she wrote, "[it] made no more impression on me than a moonbeam."

Ever the pioneer, she was open to new philosophical and spiritual ideas as well as physical treatments. She wrote, "The simple Buddha religion is very attractive to me, & I believe in it." In between hours of sickness, she took advantage of every bit of energy she possessed. She even managed a short visit to the White Mountains of New

Hampshire, and whenever she could, of course she wrote. She was still "the brains that earn the money" for the growing family. But the task was becoming more impossible with each passing month.

The "beautiful runner" who once believed she had been "a deer or a horse in some former state" stumbled along with a lurching gait. Weary, sick, and often depressed, Louisa struggled to finish *Jo's Boys*, her last great book—though she didn't think of it that way. She was tired of writing about the Marches. She wished, she wrote only half jokingly, that "an earthquake . . . should engulf Plumfield and its environs."

Doctors tried to stop her writing entirely, but Louisa fought back. She—the author who had once written for twelve or fourteen hours at a clip—gained grudging permission to write for thirty minutes a day. In 1885 she described her new work habits to a librarian: "I write in the morning. Any paper or pen suits me. Quiet is all I require. Winter is the best time. I enjoy solitude. . . . I do not enjoy society, and shirk its duties as much as possible." The rhythm of her writing had changed. She wrote in short, exhausted sentences. Aware of this, she added a postscript to the letter: "P.S. I am an invalid from too much head work, and my right hand is partially paralyzed with writer's cramp, so my writing is, as you see, not a copy for your young people to imitate." Every rebounding effort drew on her failing supply of energy. By now, it was likely that she also suffered from an autoimmune disorder. Her illness was nowhere and everywhere at once.

Louisa's last novel was published under the title *Jo's Boys, and How They Turned Out*. The book has the grace, humor, and wisdom of her first grand success, *Little Women*. It is tinged with a feeling of farewell. She told her friend Maria Porter, "I mean if possible to keep up till after Christmas, and then I am sure I shall break down." So much rested on her shoulders. Lulu was now an active seven-year-old. Her father grew weaker. Louisa tried to assure herself that she had everything well in hand. Lulu was "good & happy. Father comfortable, & plenty to make all safe & easy."

She was right about the coming breakdown. Right after the publication of *Jo's Boys*, Louisa took to her bed in the Roxbury rest home owned and run by her closest friend, Dr. Rhoda Lawrence. She found comfort in the doctor's company that she had found nowhere else. Some biographers have theorized that Dr. Lawrence was more than a friend and that theirs was a May-December love affair. Most of Louisa's close relationships in the latter part of her life were with women. She described another doctor, Dr. Laura Whiting Hosmer, as the "most beautiful woman" she'd ever known. Louisa enthused, "She is a great comfort to me with her healthy, common sense & tender patience, aside from skill as a doctor & beauty as a woman. I love her much & she does me good."

But were these love affairs? We don't know any more

than we know what happened in Paris between Laddie and Louisa. The customs of those times were different from ours. Both women and men wrote passionate "love" letters to their same-sex friends. Abraham Lincoln slept in the same bed with his housemate. Women held hands in public and called each other "darling" and "beloved." Some *were* lovers; others were not. What we do know is that these female friendships were intense, enduring, and all-sustaining.

Dr. Lawrence's home in Roxbury became Louisa's final haven. She called the place Saint's Rest. Shortly before resigning herself to full-time care, Louisa wrote a poem of acceptance: "Rest, weary brain, thy task is done, / The Burden of the day is past."

She understood that she was in the last stages of illness, but she never fully knew the cause. Though the doctor in Switzerland had named calomel as the source of her illness, Louisa rarely referred to his diagnosis again. Her father's poetry acknowledged the "poison dart," and Abby also wrote about her daughter's "sacrifice of health" at the Union Hospital. Louisa's everchanging but always-terrible symptoms made it harder to be sure of the sickness itself, much less its cause. Louisa named many causes of her illness—overwork, too much excitement, writer's cramp, poor diet, unhealthy climate. These things seemed curable; mercury poisoning was not.

She confided just once to her journal, "Voice gone,

389

head bad, & spirits low, being tired of the long fight for health. The hospital experience was a costly one for me. Never well since. Yet it turned the tide and brought success." Only Louisa could have found the apple around the bitter worm. She referred to her hospital experience once again in her last known letter. In it she supplied "a few facts" to an inquiring fan: "I narrowly escaped with my life after a fever which left me an invalid for the rest of my days." She compared herself in the pneumonia's aftermath to "the likeness of a shadow." The shadow had all but eclipsed the shining woman.

Her last jotted journal entries read like gasps of breath. They are the barest descriptions of her condition and treatments—and those in the fewest words possible. Her life at Saint's Rest had become a matter of day-to-day survival. Many pages were torn from these last journals. Louisa had already destroyed most of her private writings. Now she did away with more. "Sorted old letters & burned many. Not wise to keep for curious eyes to read, & gossip-lovers to print by and by."

She updated her will and legally adopted her nephew John Pratt so that he could become heir and executor of her copyrights. She arranged schooling for Lulu, who was an indifferent student at best. From her sickbed Louisa tried to orchestrate even the smallest daily affairs, advising Lulu on a theater visit: "Take a fan, & if you get hot & tired go out and walk between the acts. There is water & a W.C.

in the ladies room to the left as you leave the parquette."

Louisa could manage a rare outing, or a brief visit to her father in Louisburg Square in Boston, but inevitably she landed back in bed. "Excuse me if I appear to flop," she'd once joked to a crowd of friends. Now she collapsed where there were few friends and no clowning. The solitude she'd always craved became a hard burden to bear. She was lonely much of the time. Most days her journal reported only "No calls" and "do nothing."

She could rouse herself for the occasional welcome visitor, but her journal entries tracked the long, dull, cheerless days. She lost twenty-five pounds in less than six months. Her symptoms sound terrifying, even secondhand. "Queer feeling in head. Blue light, no breath, heart beat." "Head dizzy at times. Sore spot in throat better." "A little feeling in the bottom of lungs." "Legs queer & stiff & blue." "Very stiff. Lump under knee. . . . Back very bad. Lie down in p.m. Begin Nitre for kidneys." (Nitre was an inhalation treatment of a sodium carbonate.) She also tried warm water packs, oxygen, compresses, and the advice of a clairvoyant who provided a better diagnosis than most: "Enlarged spleen, torpid liver, tired brain, worn out stomach, bad legs." One by one, Louisa's organs were shutting down.

The words that appear most often in her final journal entries are *sleep*, *rub*, *bad*, *better*, and *bath*. Her world was shrinking down to a sick and dying body in a room. She described her mood most often as "worried" or "cross."

But she could make an effort to keep up not just her own spirits, but those of everyone in her orbit as well. She spent much of her time resting, reading, or sewing.

Dr. Lawrence read aloud to her, one of Louisa's few remaining entertainments and distractions. Once or twice, even within months of the end, Louisa climbed out of bed and—astonishingly—went out for a run. But her final journal entries record little or no activity. "Bad day. Head ache & sad. Weak & disappointed. Legs better. Stand up, walk a few steps."

Louisa was aware of her disease's deadly progress. In 1887 she wrote, "On this day Sept 1st I make a prophesy. The end is not far off. The Drs. see it, & I feel it. Amen." Yet she took time to reassure others. "Sorrow has no place at such times & death is never terrible when it comes as now in the likeness of a friend," she wrote to her old friend Maria Porter. In the face of death, her thoughts grew wider and deeper.

She committed herself to final acts of charity, sharing her resources with friends and favorite causes to the end. Giving to others was one of her earliest acts; it was also among her last. She asked Jack and Fred to "be generous" after her death, insofar as it "seem not unwise or impossible." She directed funds to the poor and needy. She consulted her aunt Louisa Bond on how to aid a broken and bereft family living nearby. "A poor little woman has just died, leaving four children to a drunken father. Two hard-working aunts do all they can, and one will take the oldest girl. We want to put the two small girls and boy into a home till we can see what comes next."

She directed the outstanding debt owed on Saint's Rest canceled after her death. If she got well again, she wrote, she would devote herself "to settling poor souls who need a gentle boost in hard times." Writing to editor Mary Mapes Dodge, she confided that the $250 from her last two stories had been used for "my charity fund." Her gifts were practical and specific. "The $250 has put coal, food & clothes into the home where a good woman . . . was trying to keep her little girls safe under her wing. . . . It has also given many comforts to a young girl dying of consumption."

She dismissed her own responsibility for these generous acts, pointing again to Marmee's influence, insisting that they were also her "best medicine & amusement during this long year of exile from home at Saint's Rest." Would-be contemporary biographers pestered her, but she put them off. "So much has already been written about L. M. Alcott that there is very little left to tell." She was self-effacing to the very end. Nothing in her history "could make it interesting, as it had been for the last ten years the life of an invalid." Even her "father's history," she admitted, "is so well known there is nothing left to tell but the end, which is approaching so slowly & beautifully the words 'rest & patience' tell it all."

To a young friend struggling with religious doubt, she

wrote, "Everyone has to come to the faith in his own way, some early, some late, some easily, some with much tribulation. Joy teaches this one, sorrow that, & some only catch a glimpse of the comfort near the end of life. But *it is there*, & to those who knock it shall surely be opened." She was conscious of drawing closer to the great mysteries. She wrote, "Life was always a puzzle to me, and gets more mysterious as I go on." She was not afraid to die. She asserted, "Death never seemed terrible to me."

Even at the end of her life, Louisa celebrated moments of joy. Her fifty-fifth birthday brought a happy day at Saint's Rest, one final birthday party. "The busy people here had a surprise table for me this a.m. when I came to my parlor," she wrote to Anna, who had helped arrange it. "A cake, a vase of flowers, a pot of blooming white chrysanthemums, a scent bottle & quaint pin cushion, paper poppies very pretty, & many kind messages." She added, "[Dr. Lawrence] brooded over me so tenderly I could only lay my head on her fat buzzom & cry. I shall *have* to get well to thank em for it all."

She could not recover, however—not even for the sake of those she loved best. She told one doctor, "Oh, I never expect to be well again, only patched up for a while." Her nephew Fred was married that February, to Louisa's delight, but she had no more hope of going to the wedding, she knew, "than of going to the moon."

On January 12, 1888, the doctor gave her an inhaler to

keep her going. She noted, "Can't have callers yet, nor eat. Must wait. No freedom yet."

Her thoughts returned to the past. "Lay quietly and lived in my mind," she wrote, "where I can generally find amusement for myself." As she sorted through old papers, she was thrown back into her childhood and youth. "Lived in the past for days, & felt very old recalling all I have been through. Experiences go deep with me."

During her last conversation with Julian Hawthorne, they spoke about their shared memories as next-door neighbors and comrades. Julian reported the exchange:

> "There has never been anything else like our nights at Apple Slump," I said.
>
> After her smile the corners of her mouth drooped. "Everything belonging to us, that can be seen and touched, drops away," she said, "till nothing is left. But maybe the things we wanted and never got are more real than the others and the rest is just padding."
>
> "And perhaps the things we never got are waiting for us somewhere?"
>
> "I'll ask father about that some day—he ought to know!"

For his part, Bronson too lay dying, at his home in Louisburg Square. Whenever Louisa could possibly drag herself there, she visited his bedside. On March 1, 1888, she noted briefly in her journal, "In to see Papa. Very sweet & feeble. Kissed me & said 'Come soon.'"

Her friend Maria Porter was present at this same visit. Maria was shaken by her vibrant childhood friend's haggard appearance. "The sight of her thin, wan face and sad look shocked me . . . I felt for the first time that she might be hopelessly ill."

Father and daughter had their last, tender encounter. Louisa had summoned all her strength to get there. Bronson lay in his parlor, still and weak. His right side was paralyzed. Over the previous few days he had said only a few words, but his blue eyes were serene as always.

Louisa lifted her father's hand to her lips and kissed it. They were silent together a moment. Then she said, "What are you thinking of, dear?" He looked upward and gestured. "Up there; you come too!"

Within a few days of this visit, Louisa complained of a crushing pain in her head, a sensation of a "weight like iron." She thought she might have come down with meningitis. In truth, she had suffered a massive stroke. Her last hopeful words were directed to Dr. Lawrence. "Then it's not meningitis?" she asked. A few hours later she fell into a coma from which she never awakened.

Father and daughter shared the same birthday. They died within two days of each other, Bronson on March 4, and Louisa on March 6. Neither knew that the other was passing or had passed. Louisa once wrote, "It takes three or four women to get each man into, through, and out of the world." She stepped back one last time to let her father out first. Bronson's funeral occurred on the morning of March 6. Even the vigilant Anna left Louisa's side just long enough to attend the funeral. While all her loved ones were listening to Bronson's eulogies, Louisa slipped away alone.

Word of her death came drifting to the mourners still at the funeral. Bronson's service was a publicized event attended by "notable men and women." His body lay in a handsome coffin wreathed with ivy, violets, and wild white roses just beneath a draped portrait of Louisa.

Louisa's funeral a few days later, at her request, was small and private. A friend laid white roses on her grave. The weather had held unseasonably warm and mild the first week in March, but within days of Louisa's death, snow began to fall. A few days later the whole eastern coast would be shaken by the Great Blizzard of 1888, known as the Great White Hurricane. Heavy snow fell for days, from down in Chesapeake Bay to northern Maine. Drifts piled thirty and forty feet high, drifting up over the roofs of second- and third-story houses. No one could visit Louisa's or Bronson's grave at Sleepy Hollow Cemetery. They had each other for company.

Louisa's obituary in the *New York Times*, published the day after her death, passed over her accomplishments as an author but described her father's recent funeral in detail.

They portrayed Louisa as the offspring of the "venerable" Bronson Alcott, New England's philosopher. "Miss Alcott" had been her father's "constant and loving nurse," the *Times* declared, "the daughter who had solaced his decline." Her most famous work, *Little Women*, was dismissed in a single line: "Its merit lay in its pretty pictures of the simple home life of the author and her little sisters."

Louisa's last novel, *Jo's Boys*, ends with a ringing farewell to her reader. She was done writing about the Marches, done with story writing, nearly done with life itself. The author of so many beautiful and enduring books for young readers at last laid down her busy pen for a well-earned rest. The novel opens with a scene between the two oldest March sisters, Meg and Jo, surveying the world around them "with mingled sad and happy thoughts." Louisa closed the book with a wryly sweet goodbye: "And now, having endeavored to suit everyone by many weddings, few deaths, and as much prosperity as the eternal fitness of things will permit, let the music stop, the lights die out, and the curtain fall forever on the March family."

EPILOGUE

Fifteen-year-old Louisa May Alcott made her famous vow to an empty autumn field near her house in Concord: "I *will* do something by-and-by. Don't care what, teach, sew, act, write, anything to help the family; and I'll be rich and famous and happy before I die, see if I won't!" She could never have guessed that she would make good on that promise beyond even her own wildest imaginings.

Louisa never married; she never gave birth to children. The only job she held longer than six months was as a writer, laboring on her own. Louisa lived a self-reliant life woven into an extensive web of family, friends, artists, radicals, and fellow thinkers.

The hopeful American transcendentalist movement was born in her front parlor. Her first natural science teacher was Henry David Thoreau, author of *Walden*, who led Louisa and her sisters on long tramps through the woods, playing his flute, skimming them along the Concord River. Her first teenage crush was on the famous Ralph Waldo Emerson; she serenaded him (quietly, so as not to disturb the great man) and left anonymous gifts of flowers on his doorstep. Shy Nathaniel Hawthorne and his family lived next door, in the house where the real-life events of *Little Women* had taken place. Dorothea Dix, the country's leading mental health reformer, hired Louisa to be a Civil War nurse. The catalogue of her friends and neighbors reads like a who's who of great American minds and activists.

A modern-day view of Louisa May Alcott's early life could provide ample material for a dysfunctional-family memoir. The Alcotts provided a bare-bones existence for themselves and their four daughters—controlling their diet, education, morals, and self-expression. They had moved twenty times before Louisa turned twenty-one. Bronson Alcott, her idealistic father, refused to work for wages, even when the family was starving. Her mother, Abby Alcott, defended his views unquestioningly for years. They borrowed money they could not repay; often they lived on bread and water. They sent their daughters out to work when they were only fourteen or fifteen.

Louisa's childhood and youth may look from this distance like a story of miserable poverty and neglect. But Louisa and her three sisters did not experience it that way. They cherished their family all their lives, and though they remembered the hard times, they recalled with love their "jolly" days and unusual freedoms: games, swimming, picnics, rambles, singing, and full-blown homemade theatrical productions.

Louisa was the most challenging child of her four sisters. As a toddler she ran away so often that her mother tied her to the living room sofa in despair.

Years later, observing her older sister Anna's domestic marriage, Louisa declared, "I would rather be a free spinster and paddle my own canoe." Crowded as she was, squashed and pulled and jostled between affectionate and needy family members, she proudly remained single—though often lonely—all her life.

Her self-reliance was tempered by the needs of others; her craving for solitude constantly interrupted. A fierce individualist, she spent a year of her childhood living in a commune. She was childless, yet she raised her sister's daughter and adopted her eldest nephew.

She both loved and admired her unconventional father, Bronson—if at times with a touch of exasperation. Abby she loved unconditionally. Her parents were her greatest influences. But Louisa's greatness is her own. She worked impossibly long and hard, taking on the roughest labors: scrubbing and sweeping, cooking and sewing, nursing, "going out to service," living in boarding rooms and falling-down houses. She taught herself to become a writer by endless trial and error. There was no genre she didn't try, from fairy tales to horror to medical reportage on the Civil

War. She found her voice and kept it to the end. Her last words were not a declaration but a question.

Louisa May Alcott was an artist to the core, though she mocked herself as merely "a spider,—spinning my brains out for money." In the midst of composing she'd drop headfirst into a writing "vortex," from which she'd emerge days later, sleep-deprived and hungry. She created dozens of lighthearted novels and stories for children, two "serious" literary novels, countless works of adventure, murder mysteries, gothic romances, stories, poems, and essays. Yet her life was perhaps her most radiantly beautiful creation. She was that rarest of creatures—a real-life heroine.

Her young neighbor Julian Hawthorne tells us: "Louisa was both deep and broad; her sympathies were worldwide." She fought for equal rights, for justice to the poor, and to protect the downtrodden. She was a passionate, lifelong abolitionist and suffragist, one who believed in equality and lived her beliefs. Her thinking raced so far ahead of her time that even now—almost two hundred years later—she is still light-years ahead of us.

Like *Little Women*'s heroine, Jo March, Louisa could be fierce—she used a system of signals with a pillow so that family would know when it was safe to approach— but she was also uncommonly tender, generous, and a loyal friend. She faced failure and loss repeatedly; she never surrendered, not even when a celebrated publisher told her, "Stick to your teaching—you can't write."

She was comical. She was heartbreaking. "One must have both the dark & the light side to paint life truly," she wrote to a friend.

While still in her mid-teens, she made that vow to become rich and famous and accomplish something splendid. But when success came, she didn't trust her own great fortune. Her fame dazzled and often irritated her. She was hopelessly clumsy and athletic, cutting and kind; her constitution was strong, yet she spent her last years too weak to hold a pen, suffering from a mysterious, ever-shifting disorder.

There are writers who put the best of themselves into their writing, leaving nothing over for those they should love. This was not true for Louisa. Her life was as gorgeous as her art. She was amazed by her success in the nearsighted world that had seen only peculiar Bronson Alcott's very peculiar girl. Her stories teach us about kindness, laughter, self-sacrifice, and goodness—even to the point of preachiness. Her brilliance makes the preaching palatable. The reader winces, accepts the sermon, and moves on to the next vivid tragicomic scene. Her life story demonstrates how to stay the course. "I am not afraid of storms," she announced, "for I am learning how to sail my ship."

BIBLIOGRAPHY

In researching this book, I read and drew from all of Louisa May Alcott's work.

Alcott, Louisa May. *Hospital Sketches*. Boston: James Redpath, 1863.

———. *The Journals of Louisa May Alcott*. Edited by Joel Myerson, Daniel Shealy, and Madeleine B. Stern. Boston: Little, Brown, 1989.

———. *Louisa May Alcott: An Intimate Anthology*. New York Public Library Collector's Edition. New York: Doubleday, 1997.

———. *Lulu's Library*, Vol. 3. Boston: Little, Brown, 1906.

———. "Poppy's Pranks." In *Morning-Glories and Other Stories*, 89. New York: G. W. Carleton, 1867.

———. *The Selected Letters of Louisa May Alcott*. Edited by Joel Myerson, Daniel Shealy, and Madeleine B. Stern. Boston: Little, Brown, 1987.

———. "Transcendental Wild Oats: A Chapter from an Unwritten Romance." *The Independent* (New York) 25, no. 1307 (December 18, 1873): 1569–1571.

Bailey, Susan. *Louisa May Alcott Is My Passion* (blog). https://louisamayalcottismypassion.com.

Bedell, Madelon. *The Alcotts: Biography of a Family*. New York: Clarkson N. Potter, 1980.

Cheever, Susan. *Louisa May Alcott: A Personal Biography.* New York: Simon & Schuster, 2010.

Cheney, Ednah D., ed. *Louisa May Alcott: Her Life, Letters, and Journals.* 1889. Reprint, Carlisle, MA: Applewood Books, 2010.

Dedmond, Francis B. "Sophia Hawthorne and Louisa May Alcott's 'Thoreau's Flute.'" *The Concord Saunterer* 16, no. 1 (Spring 1981): 24–26.

Emerson, Ralph Waldo. *Essays and Lectures.* New York: Library of America, 1983.

Emerson, Ralph Waldo, and Henry David Thoreau. *Nature/Walking (The Concord Library).* Boston: Beacon Press, 1994.

Hawthorne, Julian. "The Woman Who Wrote *Little Women.*" *Ladies' Home Journal,* vol. 39 (October 1922): 25, 120–122, 124.

The Hub of Literary America (walking tour). http://www.bostonbyfoot.org/tours/Literary_Landmarks.

Ives, Charles. "The Alcotts." In *Essays Before a Sonata, and Other Writings.* New York: W. W. Norton, 1962.

LaPlante, Eve. *Marmee & Louisa: The Untold Story of Louisa May Alcott and Her Mother.* New York: Simon & Schuster, 2012.

LaPlante, Eve, ed. *My Heart Is Boundless: Writings of Abigail May Alcott, Louisa's Mother.* New York: Free Press, 2012.

Marshall, Megan. *The Peabody Sisters: Three Women Who Ignited American Romanticism.* Boston: Mariner Books, 2006.

Matteson, John. *Eden's Outcasts: The Story of Louisa May Alcott and Her Father.* New York: W. W. Norton, 2007.

Meigs, Cornelia. *Invincible Louisa: The Story of the Author of Little Women.* New York: Little, Brown, 1995.

Mellow, James R. *Nathaniel Hawthorne in His Times*. Boston: Houghton Mifflin, 1980.

Myerson, Joel, and Daniel Shealy. "Three Contemporary Accounts of Louisa May Alcott, with Glimpses of Other Concord Notables." *The New England Quarterly* 59, no. 1 (March 1986): 109–122.

Peabody, Elizabeth Palmer. *Record of a School*. Boston: James Munroe, 1835.

Pratt, Anna Alcott. *Diary, 1859–1862*. Transcribed and annotated by Ray Angelo, 2018. http://www.ray-a.com/AnnaAlcottPrattDiary.pdf.

Reisen, Harriet. *Louisa May Alcott: The Woman Behind Little Women*. New York: Henry Holt, 2009.

Shealy, Daniel, ed. *Alcott in Her Own Time*. Iowa City: University of Iowa Press, 2005.

Shepard, Odell. *Pedlar's Progress: The Life of Bronson Alcott*. Boston: Little Brown, 1937.

Stern, Madeleine B. *Louisa May Alcott: A Biography*. Boston: Northeastern University Press, 1996.

Thoreau, Henry David. *Walden, or, Life in the Woods*. Boston: Ticknor & Fields, 1854.

Ticknor, Caroline. *May Alcott: A Memoir*. 1928. Reprint, Carlisle, MA: Applewood Books, 2012.

Wagoner, Jean Brown. *Louisa May Alcott: Girl of Old Boston*. Indianapolis: Bobbs-Merrill, 1943.

Willis, Frederick L. H. *Alcott Memoirs*. Boston: Richard G. Badger, 1915.

ACKNOWLEDGMENTS

I do not think of myself as a biographer-scholar, but rather as an author for young readers who tells, as best she can, the story of her subject's life. In the case of Louisa May Alcott, the source material is enormous, as is the scholarship, extending in all directions.

I am indebted, therefore, to the true Alcott scholars who came before me and, with their knowledge, hard work, and insight, helped pave the way. They gave the signposts; it is my own fault if I have gotten lost along the path. Every author listed in the bibliography guided these pages; the help was incalculable. Alcott scholars don't completely agree on the truth of Alcott's life. Some biographers paint Bronson Alcott as an egocentric demon, others as a saint. I have tried to allow the reader to draw their own conclusions about this whole cast of characters.

Readers may find inconsistencies in spelling, grammar, and chronology because the sources do not always agree, and Louisa herself made many changes and revisions.

Beyond all those listed in the bibliography, I also owe a special debt of gratitude to:

The staff at Orchard House, especially director Jan Turnquist, not only host and tour guide but a deep well of information and insight about all things Alcott.

Leslie Wilson, former curator of special collections at the Concord Free Public Library, who granted me a genuine *aha!* moment among the manuscript pages of *Little Women*.

Susan Bailey, whose website *Louisa May Alcott Is My Passion* is an ongoing labor of love and whose help was invaluable in catching and correcting several points of fact.

Staff and resources at the Fruitlands Museum, the Wayside House, the Houghton Library in Cambridge, the Berg Collection at the New York Public Library, the Walden Woods Project, and the Ralph Waldo Emerson House.

My gratitude to illustrator Diana Sudyka, who brightened each chapter, and to all at Candlewick Press who brought this book to light, the copyeditors who caught many blunders, the patient, kind Ainslie Campbell, and especially Liz Bicknell, editor-of-a-lifetime.

Thanks and love to family and friends who tolerated an author's distraction over the past four years. To the memory of David, the presence of John, the birth of Eli and Anna's Max, and above all to my favorite little woman, my daughter, Lily.